MOBILE AND WIRELESS COMMUNICATION NETWORKS

T0189399

IFIP – The International Federation for Information Processing

IFIP was founded in 1960 under the auspices of UNESCO, following the First World Computer Congress held in Paris the previous year. An umbrella organization for societies working in information processing, IFIP's aim is two-fold: to support information processing within its member countries and to encourage technology transfer to developing nations. As its mission statement clearly states,

> IFIP's mission is to be the leading, truly international, apolitical organization which encourages and assists in the development, exploitation and application of information technology for the benefit of all people.

IFIP is a non-profitmaking organization, run almost solely by 2500 volunteers. It operates through a number of technical committees, which organize events and publications. IFIP's events range from an international congress to local seminars, but the most important are:

• The IFIP World Computer Congress, held every second year;
• Open conferences;
• Working conferences.

The flagship event is the IFIP World Computer Congress, at which both invited and contributed papers are presented. Contributed papers are rigorously refereed and the rejection rate is high.

As with the Congress, participation in the open conferences is open to all and papers may be invited or submitted. Again, submitted papers are stringently refereed.

The working conferences are structured differently. They are usually run by a working group and attendance is small and by invitation only. Their purpose is to create an atmosphere conducive to innovation and development. Refereeing is less rigorous and papers are subjected to extensive group discussion.

Publications arising from IFIP events vary. The papers presented at the IFIP World Computer Congress and at open conferences are published as conference proceedings, while the results of the working conferences are often published as collections of selected and edited papers.

Any national society whose primary activity is in information may apply to become a full member of IFIP, although full membership is restricted to one society per country. Full members are entitled to vote at the annual General Assembly, National societies preferring a less committed involvement may apply for associate or corresponding membership. Associate members enjoy the same benefits as full members, but without voting rights. Corresponding members are not represented in IFIP bodies. Affiliated membership is open to non-national societies, and individual and honorary membership schemes are also offered.

MOBILE AND WIRELESS COMMUNICATION NETWORKS

IFIP 19th World Computer Congress, TC-6, 8th IFIP/IEEE Conference on Mobile and Wireless Communications Networks, August 20-25, 2006, Santiago, Chile

Edited by

Guy Pujolle
University Pierre and Marie Curie (Paris 6), France

 Springer

Mobile and Wireless Communication Networks

Edited by G. Pujolle

p. cm. (IFIP International Federation for Information Processing, a Springer Series in Computer Science)

ISSN: 1571-5736 / 1861-2288 (Internet)

ISBN: 13: 978-1-4419-4185-5   eISBN: 10: 0-387-34736-4
Printed on acid-free paper   eISBN: 13: 978-0-387-34736-3

9 8 7 6 5 4 3 2 1
springer.com

MWCN'06

A Survey on Wireless Ad Hoc Networks

Marcelo G. Rubinstein[1], Igor M. Moraes[2], Miguel Elias M. Campista[2], Luís Henrique M. K. Costa[2], and Otto Carlos M. B. Duarte[2]*

[1] PEL/DETEL/FEN – Universidade do Estado do Rio de Janeiro
R. São Fco. Xavier, 524 - 20550-013 - Rio de Janeiro - RJ - Brazil
[2] GTA/COPPE/Poli – Universidade Federal do Rio de Janeiro
P.O. Box 68504 - 21945-970 - Rio de Janeiro - RJ - Brazil

Abstract. A wireless ad hoc network is a collection of wireless nodes that can dynamically self-organize into an arbitrary and temporary topology to form a network without necessarily using any pre-existing infrastructure. These characteristics make ad hoc networks well suited for military activities, emergency operations, and disaster recoveries. Nevertheless, as electronic devices are getting smaller, cheaper, and more powerful, the mobile market is rapidly growing and, as a consequence, the need of seamlessly internetworking people and devices becomes mandatory. New wireless technologies enable easy deployment of commercial applications for ad hoc networks. The design of an ad hoc network has to take into account several interesting and difficult problems due to noisy, limited-range, and insecure wireless transmissions added to mobility and energy constraints. This paper presents an overview of issues related to medium access control (MAC), routing, and transport in wireless ad hoc networks and techniques proposed to improve the performance of protocols. Research activities and problems requiring further work are also presented. Finally, the paper presents a project concerning an ad hoc network to easily deploy Internet services on low-income habitations fostering digital inclusion.

1 Introduction

Wireless networks are being increasingly used in the communication among devices of the most varied types and sizes. Personal computers, handhelds, telephones, appliances, industrial machines, sensors, and others are being used in several environments, such as residences, buildings, cities, forests, and battlefields. Different wireless network standards and technologies have appeared in the last years to enable easy deployment of applications.

The deployment of wireless networks where there is no infrastructure or the local infrastructure is not reliable can be difficult. Ad hoc networks have been proposed in order to solve such problems. A wireless ad hoc network is a collection of wireless nodes that can dynamically self-organize into an arbitrary and temporary topology to form a network without necessarily using any

* Supported by CNPq, CAPES, FAPERJ, UOL, FUJB, FINEP, and FUNTTEL.

Please use the following format when citing this chapter:

Rubinstein, M.G., Moraes, I.M., Campista, M.E.M., Costa, L.H.M.K., Duarte, O.C.M.B., 2006, in IFIP International Federation for Information Processing, Volume 211, ed. Pujolle, G., Mobile and Wireless Communication Networks, (Boston: Springer), pp. 1–33.

pre-existing infrastructure. In ad hoc networks, each node may communicate directly to each other. Nodes that are not directly connected communicate by forwarding their traffic through intermediate nodes. Every ad hoc node acts as a router.

The main advantages of ad hoc networks are flexibility, low cost, and robustness. Ad hoc networks can be easily set up, even in desert places and can endure to natural catastrophes and war. These characteristics make ad hoc networks well suited for military activities, emergency operations, disaster recovery, large scale community networks, and small networks for interaction between meeting attendees or students in a lecture room.

The design of a wireless ad hoc network has to take into account several interesting and difficult problems. Traditional wireless communication problems related to the physical medium, such as low transmission rate, high bit error rates, noise, limited range, and significant variation in physical medium conditions, must be overcomed. In the MAC sublayer, the difficulty of collision detection and the hidden and the exposed terminal problems demand new medium access algorithms. Moreover, as wireless ad hoc nodes may move arbitrarily and the status of the communication links between the nodes may vary, routing protocols proposed for wired networks are not suited for operation in wireless ad hoc networks. Several routing protocols have been proposed to cope with the various challenges of ad hoc networks. At the transport layer, TCP-like transport protocols also present several problems when used on wireless networks. High bit-error rates and frequent route failures reduce TCP performance, demanding modifications to TCP or the design of new transport protocols.

Other issues are also important when designing a wireless ad hoc network. The uncontained shared medium creates difficult challenges for securing the wireless network. On the other hand, the use of mobile devices equipped with radio interfaces turns energy conservation an important issue. Additionally, peculiarities of the wireless technology used, such as multiple channels and directional antennas, may improve the performance of the network but have to be carefulley taken into account in redesigning some of the protocol layers.

This paper presents an overview of issues related to MAC, routing, and transport in wireless ad hoc networks and techniques proposed to improve the performance of protocols. Research activities and problems requiring further work are also presented. Finally, the paper presents a project concerning an ad hoc network to easily deploy Internet services on low-income habitations fostering digital inclusion.

This paper is organized as follows. Section 2 presents different MAC protocols designed for wireless ad hoc networks. Section 3 describes Bluetooth and IEEE 802.11, the most widespread technologies for wireless ad hoc networks. Section 4 compares the main routing protocols for ad hoc networks. In Section 5, we present protocol proposals to solve the TCP performance issues related to wireless networks. Section 6 presents the issues related to directional antennas and security and gives an overview of a project that investigates a community ad hoc network for underserved populations.

2 Medium Access Control Protocols

The design of a suitable Medium Access Control (MAC) protocol is an important issue for an ad hoc network. The protocol must deal with channel constraints, attenuation, and noise, whereas provide an efficient medium access considering requirements, such as quality of service (QoS), low energy consumption, fairness, and scalability.

MAC protocols for wireless networks can be classified as contention-free or contention-based, depending on the medium access strategy [1]. The contention-free schemes pre-define assignments to allow stations to transmit without contending for the medium, e.g., TDMA, CDMA, FDMA, polling, and token-based. Contention-free mechanisms are normally employed to provide bounded end-to-end delay and minimum bandwidth, privileging delay sensitive applications such as audio and video streams. Bluetooth personal area networks employ a master-slave MAC mechanism. On the other hand, contention-based schemes are more appropriate for sporadic data transfer on mobile networks due to the random and temporary nature of the topologies. Wi-Fi local area networks in their ad hoc mode employ contention-based MAC protocols.

ALOHA and Slotted-ALOHA are the pioneers contention-based schemes for medium access. In ALOHA, a station accesses the medium as soon as it has a frame to send. If two or more stations send data at the same time collisions occur. To decrease the collision probability, in the Slotted-ALOHA access scheme, a station must wait for the beginning of a pre-defined interval of time to start its transmission. Slotted-ALOHA doubled the efficiency of ALOHA, however, it introduced the necessity of synchronization. CSMA (Carrier Sense Multiple Access) is another access scheme that added carrier sensing before transmitting a frame to minimize the number of collisions. In CSMA, a station that has data to send becomes aware of current transmissions sensing the medium. If a carrier is sensed, the medium is considered busy and the station postpones its medium access. Nevertheless, if the medium is idle, the station transmits its data frame immediately. CSMA can be non-persistent or p-persistent depending on the scheme deployed to attempt a transmission after sensing the medium busy. The non-persistent CSMA sets a random period of time to perform another medium access. In the p-persistent CSMA the station transmits with a probability p as soon as the medium gets idle. The most famous access scheme for wired networks is a variation of CSMA persistent that detects collisions. This scheme is employed by Ethernet and is called Carrier Sense Multiple Access with Collision Detection. Unfortunately, in free space collision detection is not possible. Thus, a successful reception is not guaranteed because stations may not sense a collision at the receiver. The phenomenon known as the hidden terminal problem is depicted in Figure 1. In this figure, each station centers a dotted circle that represents its own transmission range. In the example of Figure 1, the station A is transmitting to B. As station C cannot sense the ongoing transmission, it may also transmit to B, resulting in a collision at B.

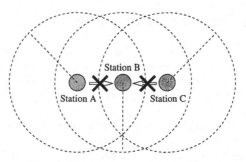

Fig. 1. The hidden terminal problem.

Unlike CSMA, the MACA (Multiple Access with Collision Avoidance) proto-col [2] does not perform carrier sensing. MACA assumes that performing carrier sense before transmitting is not an efficient approach because it reduces colli-sions but does not completely eliminate them. To cope with the hidden terminal problem, MACA introduced a three-way handshake for data transmissions. A station that wants to transmit must immediately send a RTS (Request-To-Send) frame containing the length of the following transmission. The stations within the transmission range of the sender will defer for the time announced in RTS. Upon receiving the RTS, the destination will send a CTS (Clear-To-Send) packet to the transmitter. The stations within the transmission range of the destination will defer as well for the time announced in CTS, which cor-responds to the length of the data frame. Thus, the medium will be reserved for the transmission of the upcoming frame, avoiding collisions. If the CTS is not received after a RTS transmission, a collision is inferred and the stations enter into a collision resolution phase. To resolve collisions, the stations per-form a binary exponential backoff. The MACAW (MACA for Wireless LANs) protocol [3] extends MACA by adding link level acknowledgment (ACK) for data frames. The data acknowledgment at link layer is an important improve-ment because it accelerates the loss frame recovery, which were only initiated at transport level. MACAW also altered the backoff scheme to improve fairness.

Although the RTS/CTS mechanism avoids the hidden terminal problem, it may accentuate another typical problem of ad hoc networks, the exposed ter-minal. Every station that is within the transmission range of a communicating node does not send frames. This happens even if the other potential destination is out of the former receiver range. In Figure 2, station C does not transmit to D even if its transmission will not interfere at destination A.

In opposition to MACA and its derivatives, the FAMA (Floor Acquisition Multiple Access) protocol [4] shows that carrier sensing must be used along with the RTS/CTS mechanism to improve medium access. Without carrier sensing, MACA behaves essentially as ALOHA, dropping down its overall performance when the medium is high loaded. It is also shown that MACA does not com-pletely solve the hidden terminal problem and collisions may occur between

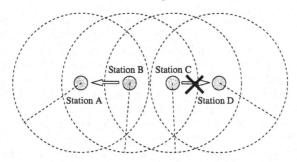

Fig. 2. The exposed terminal problem.

control and data frames. In Figure 1, depending on the propagation delays, a CTS from B to A may have already been received at A, but not at C. When A starts sending its data frame, C has not yet received the CTS, hence, it will simultaneously send a RTS to B. FAMA addresses this problem introducing intervals of time between a reception and a following transmission. These intervals, also known inter-frame spaces, must take into account the maximum propagation and processing delay of all stations within the network. This amount of time is enough to assure that the entire network is aware of the state of the current transmission. In the example above, if station B had waited some time before responding with the CTS, the RTS from C would have arrived. Thus, a collision would have been inferred between control frames, which is less harmful then a collision involving a data frame.

The CSMA/CA (CSMA with Collision Avoidance) combines characteristics of CSMA, MACA/MACAW, and FAMA. CSMA/CA senses the medium before transmissions, deploys RTS/CTS, acknowledges data frames, and uses inter-frame spaces to compensate propagation delays. Besides, CSMA/CA adds a random interval of time before transmissions to further avoid collisions from stations that were simultaneously contending for the medium. The concept of NAV (Network Allocation Vector) is also introduced in CSMA/CA. NAV is a timer maintained by each station that contains the interval of time which the medium is expected to be busy. Thus, the stations can only transmit after the expiration of the NAV. As CSMA/CA is used in the IEEE 802.11 standard, it will be examined in more details in Section 3.

Depending on the deployment of the ad hoc network, the design of the MAC protocol focus on a specific desirable characteristic. These characteristics are related to higher throughput, lower delay, lower power consumption, etc [1, 5, 6]. Next sections summarizes some existing protocols that use multiple channels, power-aware schemes, and QoS-aware schemes to achieve these goals.

2.1 Multiple Channel Protocols

The deployment of a single channel for the transmission of data and control frames increases the collision probability when a high number of nodes is actively accessing the medium. Using multiple channels, the overall performance of the network can be improved because each channel is a different collision domain and the available bandwidth increases with the number of channels. Additionally, differentiation among channels to support QoS is possible.

MAC protocols for multiple channels can be classified considering whether there is a dedicated control channel. When a dedicated control channel is used, the remaining channels are exclusive for data transmissions. In RI-BTMA (Receiver Initiated Busy Tone Multiple Access) [7] the transmitter sends a preamble to the intended destination. After receiving the preamble, the destination sets up an out-of-band busy tone to reserve the medium for the data frame. In the DBTMA (Dual Busy Tone Multiple Access) protocol [8] the transmitter emits a transmit-busy tone in the control channel after sending a RTS frame. Upon receiving an RTS frame, the receiver emits a receiver-busy tone to reserve the medium. When a dedicated control channel is not used, all traffic is shared among the multiple channels. In the Multi-Channel CSMA protocol [9] the total available bandwidth is divided by N distinct channels. Every station senses the last used channel before attempting a transmission. If the last channel used is idle, the station sends its frame. Otherwise, the station randomly chooses another channel to transmit. The Hop-Reservation Multiple Access (HRMA) protocol [10] employs frequency hopping to send data frames.

Multiple channel protocols must deal with distributed mechanisms to manage channel assignments. This requirement represents the major drawback of this approach. Contention-free schemes can also be used, however, these schemes introduce synchronization requirements and, as consequence, complexity and cost that are not desirable in ad hoc networks.

Currently, the deployment of multiple channels along with multiple interfaces is receiving especial attention in Wireless Mesh Networks (WMN) [11, 12]. Mesh Networks are a special case of hybrid ad hoc network, where fixed nodes are used to guarantee connectivity and interconnection to isolated nodes. The fixed nodes can be considered an infrastructure.

2.2 Power-aware Protocols

Mobile wireless devices are battery powered, therefore, energy constraints must be taken into account. In mobile ad hoc networks, stations must be able to save energy to extend their battery lifetimes. Power-aware protocols use three basic techniques: active and standby modes switching, power setting, and retransmissions avoidance. Switching between active and standby modes avoids wasting energy during idle periods. In addition, power must be set, during transmissions, to the minimum necessary for the receiver correctly receive the data frames. Finally, retransmissions are also power consuming due to successive transmissions of a single frame.

Currently, the power-aware proposals implement power management or power control mechanisms [13, 1]. In power management mechanisms, the stations must alternate between "wake" and "sleep" periods. In the PAMAS

(Power Aware Medium Access Control with Signaling) protocol [14] the destination sends a busy tone in the out-of-band channel when receiving a data frame to signalize that the medium is busy. The neighbors decide, upon listening to the busy tone, whether it is worth to power down their transceivers since they cannot transmit. The Dynamic Power Saving Mechanism (DPSM) protocol [15] uses beacons to divide the time in intervals. The beacons announce the status of the frame to be sent in the following interval. After participating on a communication in the prior interval, the transmitter and the destination may decide to sleep. In power management mechanisms, it is important to define when to sleep and when to be awake so as not to loose availability.

The control mechanisms adapt the transmission power according to the minimum necessary for a correct reception at the destination. In the Power Control MAC (PCM) protocol [16], besides avoiding the hidden terminal problem, the RTS/CTS mechanism is used to negotiate the transmission power of the data and the ACK frames. In the Power Controlled Multiple Access (PCMA) protocol [17] the power to send data and ACK frames is set similarly to PCM. Power control mechanisms face problems regarding accurate power measurements and the variability of medium conditions concerning noise and attenuation.

2.3 QoS-aware Protocols

Providing QoS in ad hoc networks means guarantee limited end-to-end delay and minimum bandwidth to specific flows. These requirements arise with delay sensitive applications such as video and audio streams. In a wireless environment, however, it is difficult to guarantee QoS given the medium unpredictability. Moreover, it is a major challenge to distinguish between frame losses due to collisions and congestions, or erroneous receptions because of high bit error rate. The distributed scheme and the dependency on other stations to forward data frames in multihop communications further aggravate the problem.

To guarantee QoS constraints, the whole protocol stack must be aware of the QoS requirements. There are some frameworks that aim to define guidelines to assure QoS in ad hoc networks using cross-layer models [18, 19, 20]. At the MAC layer, one possible approach involves synchronous schemes that are not suitable for distributed networks [21, 22, 23]. The asynchronous proposals can guarantee QoS by avoiding collisions and useless retransmissions or by adjusting inter-frame spaces and backoff periods according to the priority of the frame. In Real Time MAC (RT-MAC) protocol [24], the stations set a deadline to each frame. Upon reaching the deadline, the frame is discarded because it has become useless for the real-time application. RT-MAC avoids collisions by recording the next backoff value in the header of the frame. Thus, the neighbors will be able to choose a different backoff value for their own transmissions. In DCF with Priority Classes (DCF-PC) [25] the differentiation is done by setting different inter-frame spaces and backoff periods depending on the priority of the frames. Thus, using lower inter-frame spaces and backoff periods guarantee priority during medium access. The same idea is used in the IEEE 802.11 standard with QoS, which is presented in Section 3.

3 Enabling Technologies

Bluetooth and IEEE 802.11 are the main technologies for implementing wireless ad hoc networks [26]. In the following subsections, we give a brief overview of the MAC sub-layer and some physical layer characteristics of Bluetooth and IEEE 802.11.

3.1 Bluetooth

Bluetooth is a wireless technology that is being used to deploy personal area networks and adopted as IEEE 802.15.1 standard [27]. Most Bluetooth products are compliant with the 1.1 specification [28].

The Bluetooth architecture consists of a basic unit called piconet and of scatternets. A piconet is an ad hoc network formed by a master and slaves devices. A device can be a master or a slave, but not both at the same time. The master is the device that establishes the piconet and the slaves are the other devices that belong to the piconet. The master informs the slaves the logical addresses to be used, when the slaves can transmit and for how long and what frequencies must be used in transmission. Communication is always between a master and one or more slaves (point-to-point or point-to-multipoint). There is no direct communication between slaves.

A piconet is composed of a master and up to seven active slaves. Moreover, there may be up to 255 inactive devices in the network, in a low-power state.

The maximum number of active devices could limit the applicability of Bluetooth, but a Bluetooth network can be extended by the interconnection of piconets. In this case, the network is called a scatternet and the piconets are interconnected by bridge nodes. The bridge between the piconets can have the role of slave in all piconets to which they belong or of master in one piconet and slave on the others. A bridge cannot be master in more than one piconet, because the master is the unit that establishes the frequencies to be used in communication. Figure 3 shows an scatternet example in which the bridge node is a master in one piconet and a slave in the other piconet.

In order to separate master and slave transmissions, Bluetooth uses a Time Division Duplexing (TDD) scheme, with a 625 μs slot time. The master begins its transmission in even slots and slaves transmit in odd slots. Frames can be one, three or five slots long, depending on the frame type.

Frames are transmitted over links called logical channels between the master and one or more slaves. There are two kinds of links: ACL (Asynchronous Connectionless) and SCO (Synchronous Connection-Oriented). The ACL is a point-to-multipoint link between the master and all active slaves of the piconet. There is only one ACL link per piconet. Polling is used for medium access. A

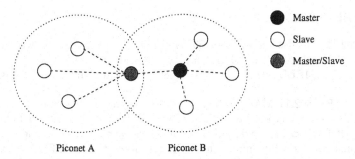

Fig. 3. Scatternet example.

slave can transmit data to the master only if the slave has been addressed in the previous master-slave slot. ACL frames not addressed to a specific slave are considered broadcast frames and are read by all slaves. In ACL, a best effort service is provided. This link is used to send asynchronous data. The maximum data rate to the master is 723.2 kbps. In symmetric links, the maximum data rate is 433.9 kbps. The SCO is a point-to-point link between the master and a slave. SCO uses slots reservation at regular intervals. This link is mainly used to transmit real-time data. SCO does not use retransmission but can use Forward Error Correction (FEC). A master can have up to three SCO links to the same slave or to different slaves. A slave can have up to three SCO links to the master or up to two SCO links to different masters. In each link, the data rate is 64 kbps. Figure 4 shows an example of an SCO link between the master and the slave 1 and the ACL link.

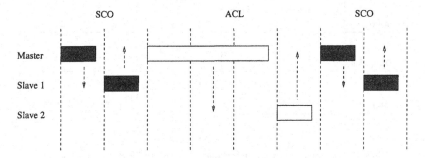

Fig. 4. SCO and ACL links example.

Bluetooth uses FHSS (Frequency Hopping Spread Spectrum) in the 2.4 GHz band and supports 1 Mbps physical data rate.

3.2 IEEE 802.11

IEEE 802.11 [29], also know by Wi-Fi (Wireless Fidelity), is the most widespread wireless technology. The 802.11 family includes several standards, e.g., IEEE 802.11b, IEEE 802.11a, and IEEE 802.11g, which differ in the physical layer.

The IEEE 802.11 MAC protocol specifies two medium access algorithms: Distributed Coordination Function (DCF) and Point Coordination Function (PCF). DCF is a distributed mechanism in which each node senses the medium and transmits if the medium is idle. On the other hand, PCF is a centralized mechanism where an access point controls medium access. Therefore, this mechanism is designed for infrastructured networks.

The DCF function uses Carrier Sense Multiple Access with Collision Avoidance (CSMA/CA) to control medium access (Figure 5). A station that wants to transmit first senses the medium. If the medium is idle for at least a time called Distributed Inter-Frame Space (DIFS), the station transmits. Otherwise, if the medium is busy, the transmission is postponed until a DIFS period after the end of the current transmission. After deferral, a backoff process is initiated. A station chooses a random number between zero and the Contention Window (CW) size and starts a backoff timer. This timer is periodically decremented by a slot time after the medium is sensed idle for more than DIFS. The backoff timer is paused when a transmission is detected. If the medium gets idle for DIFS again, the station resumes its backoff timer. When the timer expires, the station sends its frame.

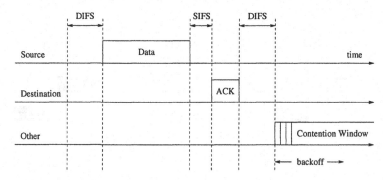

Fig. 5. Transmission of a data frame using the IEEE 802.11 protocol.

A Cyclic Redundancy Check (CRC) is used for error detection. If the frame seems to be correct, the receiver sends an acknowledgment frame (ACK) after sensing the medium idle for a period of time called Short Inter-Frame Space (SIFS). By definition, SIFS is smaller than DIFS to prioritize the access and reception of acknowledgment frames over data frames. If the sender does not receive the ACK frame, it schedules a retransmission and enters the backoff process since a collision is assumed. Hence, to reduce collision probability, the contention window starts with a minimum value given by CW_{min}. After each unsuccessful transmission, the contention window increases to the next power of 2 minus 1, until reaching a maximum predefined value called CW_{max}. CW_{min} and CW_{max} values depend on the physical layer used. Moreover, if a maximum number of retransmissions is reached, the frame is dropped. To avoid medium capture, prior to transmitting another frame the sending station will wait for DIFS and then enter the backoff phase.

The DCF method optionally uses Request to Send (RTS) and Clear to Send (CTS) frames to avoid the hidden terminal problem [29].

The original IEEE 802.11 uses the 2.4 GHz band and supports 1 and 2 Mbps physical data rates. IEEE 802.11b also uses the 2.4 GHz band and supports up to 11 Mbps using DSSS (Direct Sequence Spread Spectrum). IEEE 802.11a uses the 5 GHz band and defines up to 54 Mbps physical data rates using OFDM (Orthogonal Frequency Division Multiplexing). As the standards a and b use different frequency ranges, they are incompatible. To attain the same 54 Mbps physical data rate of IEEE 802.11a at the 2.4 GHz band of IEEE 802.11b, the standard IEEE 802.11g has been proposed.

IEEE 802.11e The original IEEE 802.11 does not support QoS. A best effort service is provided for all kinds of data traffic. Moreover, a great part of the medium access time is "wasted" by fragmentation, inter-frame spacing, and acknowledgments [30]. In order to deal with these problems, a new standard, called IEEE 802.11e [31], was published in 2005. This standard modifies IEEE 802.11 and its extensions.

IEEE 802.11e defines a Transmission Opportunity (TxOP) as a limited time interval in which a station is allowed to transmit a series of frames [32]. A TxOP is defined by the start time and a maximum duration, in order to avoid a large delay to the other stations.

IEEE 802.11e defines two access algorithms: Enhanced Distributed Channel Access (EDCA) and Hybrid Coordination Function Controlled Channel Access (HCCA). HCCA is a centralized mechanism that demands an infrastructured mode. EDCA provides QoS based on the medium access priority. Differentiation using different priorities is obtained by: varying the amount of time a station listens to the medium before backoff or transmission, the size of the contention window to be used during backoff, and the transmission duration of a station after obtaining the medium. The mechanism uses eight frame priorities assigned according to IEEE 802.1D [33], but there are four instances of the coordination functions that are executed in parallel in a station, as virtual MACs. These instances are associated to Access Categories (ACs) that identify the following traffic types: background, best effort, voice, and video. Differentiation between the ACs is performed by setting different values for ACs parameters. Each AC has an specific transmission queue, in which are used different values for AIFS (Arbitration Inter-Frame Space), CW_{min}, CW_{max}, and TxOP limit. AIFS corresponds to the smaller time interval between the time the medium gets idle and the start of a frame transmission, i.e., AIFS is analogous to DIFS for DCF. The TxOP has a maximum duration limit. ACs contend for TxOPs and perform the backoff procedure independently. An internal contention algorithm calculates the backoff based on AIFS, CW_{min}, CW_{max}, and random numbers. Backoff is similar to the one used on DCF, i.e., the AC with the smaller backoff wins the internal contention. Two or more ACs may have their timers expired at the same time. Station internally solves these conflicts between categories, offering the TxOP to the category of higher priority and forcing the categories with lower priorities to execute the backoff procedure. Then the winner AC contends externally for the medium.

4 Routing Protocols

A major challenge of wireless ad hoc networks is the design of efficient routing protocols that dynamically find routes between two communicating nodes [34, 35, 36, 37, 38]. In a mobile ad hoc network, nodes may move arbitrarily and the status of the communication links between the nodes is a function of several factors such as the position of the nodes, the transmission power level, and the interference between neighbor nodes. Therefore, the mobility of the nodes and the variability of the state of the links result in a network with fast and unpredictable topology changes. Due to this characteristic, protocols proposed for wired networks are not suited for operation in wireless ad hoc networks. These protocols are designed for operation in *quasi*-static networks with wired links and are based on periodical updates. Then, if the rate of topological changes in the network is high, the frequency of periodical updates must be fast enough to maintain the routing information consistent. Nevertheless, the action of only increasing the frequency of routing updates is prohibitive due to the limited energy of the nodes and the reduced capacity of the wireless links [39, 40].

According to the routing strategy, ad hoc routing protocols fall into two categories: topology-based and position-based protocols. Topology-based routing protocols find a route from a source to a destination according to the metrics of the network links. Networks that employ topology-based protocols forward packets based on the address of the destination node. On the other hand, position-based routing protocols do not require the establishment or maintenance of routes. Here, the idea is to obtain the information about the geographical position of the destination and find the best way to forward packets to this position.

4.1 Topology-Based Routing

Topology-based routing protocols rely on the status of the network links to compute a route from a source to a destination. Thus, every node of the network has to exchange routing information to maintain routing tables up to date. Topology-based protocols can be further divided into proactive and reactive protocols.

Proactive Routing Proactive routing protocols work like a classical Internet routing protocol. They share routing information even if there are no specific requests for a route to maintain consistent and up-to-date routes from each node to every other node in the network. Proactive protocols require that each node stores a routing table and responds to changes in network topology by propagating update messages throughout the network in order to maintain a consistent network state. This strategy continuously produces control traffic, which should be avoided for wireless networks. On the other hand, it provides low latency route access. The existing proactive protocols differ in the number of necessary routing-related tables and the methods by which changes in network topology are broadcasted. Examples of proactive protocols are DSDV and OLSR.

The Destination-Sequenced Distance-Vector(DSDV) routing protocol [41] is a modified version of the Bellman-Ford algorithm to guarantee loop-free routes. In DSDV, every node maintains a routing table in which the next-hop to all of the possible destinations is stored. The number of hops to each destination and a sequence number assigned by the destination node are associated to each routing table entry. The sequence numbers avoid the creation of routing loops once they enable the nodes to distinguish stale routes from new ones. Update packets are periodically sent throughout the network in order to maintain up-to-date the routing tables of the nodes. In order to reduce the control overhead, two types of update packets are used: a full dump and an incremental packet. The full dump packet contains all the available information in the routing table of a node. On the other hand, the incremental packet carries only the information changed since the last full dump was transmitted. Although this mechanism reduces the routing overhead, as the topological changes increase, the number of incremental packets transmitted by DSDV also increases. In this situation, update routing packets use a large amount of network bandwidth.

The Optimized Link State Routing (OLSR) protocol [42, 43] is based on the link-state algorithm. In OLSR, each node periodically exchanges routing information with other nodes to maintain a topology map of the network. In order to reduce the flooding during the routing update process and the size of the update packets, OLSR employs multipoint relays (MPRs). The reduction of flooding provided by the MPR mechanism is illustrated in Figure 6. In this mechanism, each node in the network selects a set of neighboring nodes to retransmit its update packets. For selecting the MPRs, a node periodically broadcasts *hello* messages to all one-hop neighbors to exchange its list of neighbors. From neighbor lists, a node calculates the nodes that are two hops away and computes the MPRs set which is the minimum set of one-hop neighbors required to reach the two-hop neighbors. The optimum MPRs computation is NP-complete [44], therefore heuristics are used by the OLSR protocol to compute the MPRs set. Each node notifies its neighbors about its MPRs set in the *hello* message. When a node receives the *hello*, it records the nodes that select it as one of their MPRs. These nodes are called MPR selectors. A routing update message transmitted by a node carries only information about its MPRs selectors. Thus, the size of a routing update message is reduced and a node can be reached only from its MPR selectors. The shortest path to a given destination is calculated using the topology map consisting of all of its neighbors and of the MPRs of all other nodes. The OLSR protocol is particularly suited for dense networks since if the network is sparse, most of the neighbors of a node becomes an MPR.

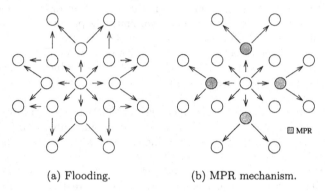

(a) Flooding.   (b) MPR mechanism.

Fig. 6. The efficiency of the MPR mechanism implemented by the OLSR protocol.

Reactive Routing Reactive, or on-demand, routing protocols operate only when there is an explicit request for a route. This strategy only creates routes when desired by a source node. When a node requires a route to a destination, it initiates a route discovery process within the network. This process is completed when a route is found or when all possible route permutations have been examined. Once a route has been established, it is maintained by a route maintenance procedure until either the destination becomes inaccessible because a link rupture or until the route is no longer needed. Reactive routing significantly reduces the memory consumption in the nodes and only generates control traffic when needed, but it typically floods the network with control messages to discover routes between two communicating nodes. In spite of providing fast route discovery, flooding has several inconveniences frequently observed, such as redundancy, contention, and collision [38]. In a typical mobile ad hoc network, the resource consumption caused by control packets has a significant impact because of the low-bandwidth links and power-limited terminals.

An example of reactive protocol is the Ad Hoc On-Demand Distance Vector (AODV) [45], which is based on the Bellman-Ford algorithm. In AODV, when a source node wants to send a packet to a destination and does not already have a valid route to that destination, the source initiates a route discovery process to find a route. Then, the source broadcasts a route request (RREQ) packet to its neighbors, which then forward the request to their neighbors. This process is repeated until either the destination or an intermediate node with a valid route to the destination is found, as shown in Figure 7(a). To guarantee that routes are loop free and contain the most recent information, AODV employs destination sequence numbers. Each node of the network maintains its own sequence number and a broadcast ID. Every time a node initiates a route discovery process, the broadcast ID is incremented. The address of the node and its broadcast ID uniquely identify an RREQ packet. The source also includes in the RREQ the most recent sequence number it has for the destination. Therefore, intermediate nodes can reply to the RREQ only if they have a route to the destination whose corresponding destination sequence number is greater than or equal to the sequence number of the RREQ. When intermediate nodes forward RREQs, they record in their route tables the address of the neighbor from which the first copy of the RREQ packet is received, thereby establishing a reverse path. Due to the flooding process, other copies of the same RREQ can be received later and all are discarded. When the RREQ reaches the destination or an intermediate node with a fresh enough route, the destination or the intermediate node sends, in unicast, a route reply (RREP) packet back to the neighbor from which it first received the RREQ. As the RREP is routed back through the reverse path, nodes along this path set up forward route entries in their route tables. The result of this process is illustrated in Figure 7(b). There is a timer for each entry in the routing table, which limits the lifetime of unused routes. It is worth noting that AODV only supports symmetric links once the RREP is forwarded along the path previously established by the RREQ. AODV also employs a route maintenance mechanism. When a node within a route moves, its upstream neighbor notices the move and propagates a route error (RERR) message to each of its active upstream neighbors to inform them of the route rupture. These nodes in turn propagate the RERR packet to their upstream neighbors. This process is repeated until the source node is notified. Then, the source is able to initiate a new route discovery process for that destination. A link failure is detected using *hello* messages, which are periodically broadcasted to maintain the local connectivity of a node. Nodes can also detect a link failure by information from the data link layer.

The Dynamic Source Routing (DSR) [46] is another reactive protocol which is based on the strategy of source routing. In DSR, each node of the network maintains a route cache that contains the source routes of which the node knows, as Figure 8 shows. Entries in the route cache are continuously updated as the node learns new routes. DSR employs route discovery and route maintenance processes similar to AODV. When a node has to send a packet to a given destination, it first verifies its route cache to determine whether it already has a route to the destination. If it has a valid route to the destination, it will use this route to send the packet. Otherwise, if the node does not have a valid route, it initiates a route discovery process by broadcasting a route request packet. The route request contains the address of the destination, the address of the source node, and a unique identification number. Each node that receives the route request verifies if it knows a route to the destination. If it does not, it adds its own address to the route record field of the packet header and then forwards the packet to its neighbors. To limit the number of route requests propagated to its neighbors, a node only forwards the route request if the request has not

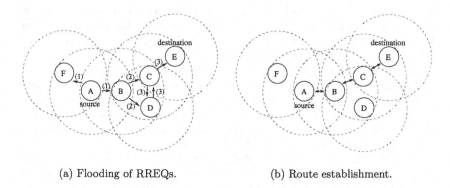

(a) Flooding of RREQs.   (b) Route establishment.

Fig. 7. An example of the route discovery procedure of AODV.

yet been seen by the node and if the address of the node does not already appear in the route record. A route reply is generated when the route request reaches either the destination or an intermediate node, which contains in its route cache a valid route to the destination. When the route request reaches the destination or an intermediate node, it carries a route record containing the sequence of hops traversed. If the node that generates the route reply is the destination, it places the route record contained in the route request into the route reply. If the responding node is an intermediate node, it will append its cached route to the route record and then generate the route reply. In order to send the route reply, the responding node must have a route to the source. If it has a route to the source in its route cache, it may use that route. Otherwise, if symmetric links are supported, the responding node may reverse the route that is in the route record. If symmetric links are not supported, the node may initiate a new route discovery process and piggyback the route reply on the new route request. The asymmetric links support is an advantage of DSR as compared to AODV. DSR employs a route maintenance process based on route error messages. These messages are generated at a node when the data link layer detects a transmission failure. When receiving a route error, a node removes the failed node from its route cache and all routes containing the failed node are truncated at that point.

4.2 Position-Based Routing

Position-based routing protocols require that information about the geographical position of the communicating nodes be available. Each node determines its own position using GPS (Global Positioning System) or some other kind of positioning system [47]. In position-based routing, nodes have neither to maintain routing tables nor to exchange routing messages since the packet forwarding is

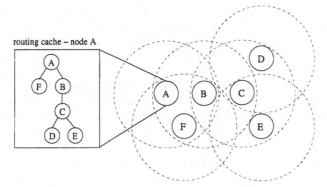

Fig. 8. An example of routing cache in DSR.

performed based on the position of the destination node, carried by each packet. Then, before sending a packet, it is necessary to determine the position of its destination. Thus, the source node needs to use a location service to determine the position of the destination node and to include it in the destination address of the packet. In the following sections, we describe two position-based protocols, DREAM and Grid.

DREAM The Distance Routing Effect Algorithm for Mobility (DREAM) protocol [48] is an example of position-based protocol that employs an all-for-all location service. In DREAM, each node stores position information concerning every node of the network in a position database. An entry of this database contains a node identifier, the direction of and distance to a node, and a time value, which indicates the age of the entry. For propagating its position, a node periodically floods the network. The advantage of exchanging position information is that it consumes significantly less bandwidth than exchanging complete routing tables even if the network is flooded. The efficacy of network flooding can be improved according to two factors. The first one is that the frequency of position updates is a function of the mobility of nodes. Thus, a node can locally control the frequency at which it sends position updates according to its own mobility rate. The higher is the mobility of a node, the higher is the frequency of position updates. The second factor is the distance separating two nodes. The greater the distance separating two nodes, the slower they appear to be moving with respect to each other. This is called the distance effect [49]. Therefore, nodes in the direct neighborhood must exchange position updates more frequently than nodes farther away. A node can employ this strategy by indicating the distance that a position update can cover before it is discarded.

The DREAM protocol also employs a restricted directional flooding to forward packets. A source sends a packet addressed to a certain destination to all its one-hop neighbors, which are within the direction toward the destination. In order to determine this direction, called the expected region, a node calculates the region where the destination is probably within. The expected region is a circle around the position of the destination node as it is known to the source, as shown in Figure 9. Since this position information may be outdated, the radius r of the expected region is set to $(t_1 - t_0)v_{max}$, where t_1 is the current time, t_0 is the timestamp of the position information of the destination which the source knows, and v_{max} is the maximum speed that a node can move in the network. Given the expected region, the direction toward the destination can be defined [48]. The neighboring nodes repeat this procedure using their information concerning the position of the destination. If a node does not have a one-hop neighbor in the required direction, a recovery procedure has to be initiated. This procedure is not implemented by DREAM.

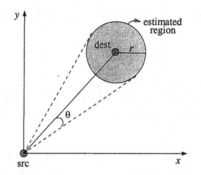

Fig. 9. The estimated region in DREAM.

Grid Grid is a routing protocol [50, 51] composed by the Grid Location Service (GLS) and a greedy strategy for forwarding packets.

The main idea of the Grid location service is to divide the area of an ad hoc network into several squares. Thus, GLS builds a hierarchy of squares where n-order squares contain four smaller $(n-1)$-order squares as shown in Figure 10. An n-order square does not overlap other square of the same order. Every node of the network knows the hierarchy of squares and its origin.

A node has a unique identification (ID) in the network defined by a hash function of one of its parameters such as the IP address or the MAC address. For identifying each node, GLS defines a circular identification space where the nearest ID of a given node is the smallest ID greater than the ID of the own node. For example, an ID space contains four IDs: 2, 12, 25, and 50. In this example, the nearest ID of 12 is 25 and the nearest ID of 50 is 2.

A node periodically broadcasts update messages that contain its position and ID. These messages are limited to the first-square where the node is. Thus, each node only knows the position and the ID of its one-hop neighbors, which are within its first-order square. For disseminating its position through the network, first, a node sends an update message toward its three adjacent first-order squares as Figure 11(a) shows. Then, the nodes within these squares,

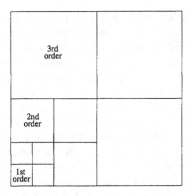

Fig. 10. Hierarchy of squares.

which have the nearest ID of the transmitting node ID, are elected to store the position information of the transmitting node. These nodes are called location servers of the transmitting node. In the example, nodes 11, 13, and 18 are elected first-order location servers of node 1. In Figure 11(a), the numbers in parenthesis are the ID of nodes that a given node knows the position. The process is repeated for all the n orders to cover the network area. Figure 11(b) illustrates the election of second-order location servers for node 1. It is worth noting that each node has only one position-server in an n-order square and, consequently, three position servers per order.

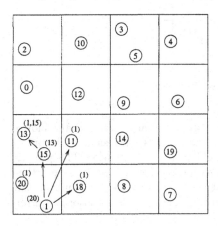

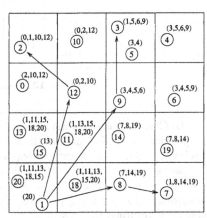

(a) First-order servers of node 1.   (b) Second-order servers of node 1.

Fig. 11. Election of location servers.

Suppose that a node wants to send a packet to a destination. If the destination is not within the first-order square of the source and the source is not a location server of the destination, the source does not know the destination ID and position. Figure 12 shows an example where node 10 wants to send a packet to node 1 and it does not know the position of node 1. Then, to find the ID and the position of the destination, the source, in this case node 10, sends a request toward the node with the smallest ID of which the source knows, node 0. If this node knows the position of the destination, it responds the request toward the source. Otherwise, it forwards the request to the node with the smallest ID in its position table. The process continues until the request reaches a node that has the position of the destination. In the example, node 0 does not know the position of node 1, then it forwards the request to node 2, the node with the smallest ID which node 0 knows. When node 2 receives the request it responds to node 10 since it is a second-order location server of node 1.

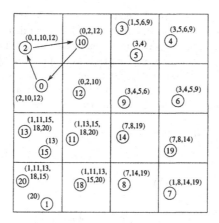

Fig. 12. Position discovery.

The Grid protocol uses the greedy strategy to forward packets. After finding the position of the destination, the source node sends a packet that ch carries this information to its closest one-hop neighbor to the destination. This process is repeated node-by-node until the destination receives the packet. Nevertheless, if there is no one-hop neighbor that is closer to the destination than the forwarding node itself, the packet forwarding fails. In this situation, an error message is returned to the source.

5 Transport Protocols

The Transmission Control Protocol (TCP) is a connection-oriented transport protocol designed to provide reliable, ordered, end-to-end delivery of data. TCP should be independent of the underlying layers and should not care if IP is running over a wired or wireless network. Wired networks are reliable and losses are mainly due to network congestion. On the other hand, wireless networks suffer from a high bit error rate that corrupts TCP-data segments or acknowledgments, and from frequent route failures. Thus, ignoring these specific characteristics of wireless networks can lead to poor TCP performance [52, 53].

The TCP protocol was designed for wired network with low bit error rate and assumes that data loss is due to congestion. Thus, when the sender transmits a TCP-data segment, it starts a retransmission timeout (RTO), and waits for a TCP acknowledgment from the receiver. When acknowledgments do not arrive at the TCP sender before the RTO goes off, the sender retransmits the segment, exponentially backs off its retransmission timer for the next retransmission, and closes its congestion window to one segment. Therefore, the exponential back-off retransmission and the congestion window mechanism prevent the sender from generating more traffic under network congestion. Repeated errors will ensure that the congestion window at the sender remains small, resulting in low throughput. Nevertheless, because of the high bit error rate of a wireless link, TCP-data segments and acknowledgments may be lost without congestion. In this case, the retransmission of the TCP-data segment in error should be done as fast as possible, instead of backing off and closing the congestion window. For mobile wireless networks the negative aspects of these mechanisms are even worse. Mobility and fading cause link failures and, as a consequence, path disruption. While the routing protocol is finding the new path the TCP recovery mechanism continues retransmitting new copies of the TCP-data segment and exponentially increasing its retransmission timeout. Therefore, the mobile node does not begin receiving data immediately after the new path establishment.

As outlined, the main problem that affects the TCP performance is to distinguish errors due to congestion from other errors such as: corrupted data, route failures, etc. Fixed RTO [54] uses a heuristic to distinguish route failures and congestion. When two timeouts expire in sequence, the Fixed-RTO TCP sender assumes that a route failure has occurred. The unacknowledged TCP segment is retransmitted but the timer is not doubled. This proposal is restricted only to wireless networks and does not fit well for combined wired and wireless networks. TCP Detection of Out-of-Order and Response (DOOR) [55] interprets out-of-order TCP segments as route failures.

Several proposals have been made to improve the TCP performance. We classify the proposals in two types: split of transport connection and cross-layer. To ensure TCP efficiency, it is necessary to prevent the sender from reducing the congestion window when TCP-data segments are lost either due to bit errors or disconnections in the wireless environment. For scenarios composed of wired and wireless networks, this can be done introducing an intermediate host in the wired network who "spoofs" the sender into thinking that the wireless link is working well. It must be noted that the end-to-end semantics of TCP is broken with the introduction of the intermediate host. The Snoop Module creates an intermediate host near the wireless user that inspects TCP-data segments and acknowledgments and buffers copies of TCP-data segments. Therefore, the intermediate host acknowledges TCP-data segments coming from the wired network and performs local retransmissions for the wireless network. An improved version of Snoop [56] adds selective retransmissions from the intermediate host to the wireless host. The Indirect-TCP (I-TCP) [57], MTCP [58], and M-TCP [59] protocols use similar strategies.

The interaction of with other layers can be useful to improve the performance of TCP. The key idea of cross-layer proposals is to provide lower-layer information to upper layers resulting in better performance of the overall system. The Explicit Link Failure Notification (ELFN) technique [60] uses a message to inform the TCP sender about a link failure. A ELFN message is piggybacked onto the route failure message sent by the routing protocol to the sender. On receiving the ELFN message, the TCP sender disables its retransmission timer and enters a standby mode. During standby, the TCP sender probes the network to verify if the route is restored. If the probe is successful, the TCP sender leaves the standby state, resumes its retransmission timers, and continues the normal operation. TCP Feedback (TCP-F) [61] similarly uses feedback messages from the network. The messages Route Failure Notification (RFN) and Route Re-establishment Notification (RRN) are used to freeze retransmission timers and congestion window size during route failures. Ad hoc TCP (ATCP) [62] also uses cross-layer information, but creates a new layer between the TCP and IP layers being compatible with other TCPs that do not implement ATCP. Another cross-layer optimization is proposed by Fu *et al.* [63], which show that there is an optimum value for the TCP congestion window size. If the congestion window is greater than this optimum value, packet losses increase and the TCP throughput decreases. Hence, the authors propose two link-level mechanisms: Link Random Early Discarding (Link RED) and adaptive spacing. Link RED tunes packet drop probability at the link layer to keep the TCP congestion window size near the optimum value. In association with Link RED, the adaptive spacing mechanism improves the spatial channel reuse through better coordination among contention for channel access. The idea is the introduction of extra backoff intervals to mitigate the exposed-terminal problem in a multihop communication.

6 Other Issues

6.1 Directional Antennas

Most of the work on ad hoc networks assume the use of omnidirectional antennas, which means that the range of a node's transmission covers a circular area around it. As a consequence, when two nodes are communicating, all nodes in the vicinity of them must remain silent for the duration of the communication. That vicinity may be defined by the union of the two transmission range circles. This assumption is made by MAC protocols such as IEEE 802.11 [29].

The advantage of directional antennas is twofold. First, the area covered by a node's transmission is no longer a circle, but may be approximated by a circular sector (Figure 13). Thus, spatial reuse may be potentially larger than with omnidirectional transmissions. Second, the transmission as well as the receiving gain are larger for directional than for omnidirectional antennas. Hence, the transmission range is larger with directional antennas.

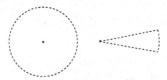

Fig. 13. Omni and directional antenna models.

The Friss Equation [64, 65] can be used to derive the maximum distance r between the communicating nodes, which is given by

$$r = \left(\frac{P_t G_t G_r}{K P_r} \right)^{1/\alpha} \tag{1}$$

where P_t and P_r are the transmitted and received powers, G_t and G_r are the transmit and receive gains, K is constant that accounts for atmospheric absorption and other losses, and α, $2 \leq \alpha \leq 4$, is the path-loss index. It is worthing note that the distance r increases with the transmit and receive gains, but in a non-linear way, because of the α parameter.

The first problem with the use of directional antennas as opposed to omni antennas in *mobile* ad hoc networks is to know where the receiver is. Depending on the antenna model, different solutions may arise. Obviously, if the locations of the stations are known or if the stations are stationary, the problem is leveraged.

The antenna model most commonly used is a system with two modes of transmission and reception, omni and directional. That system could be implemented by two antennas, an omnidirectional one and a directional one. Now, suppose a communication taking place from the viewpoint of the receiver. As the receiver does not know, *a priori*, where the communication will arrive from, the communication must start by receiving a signal in omni mode, i.e., with receive gain $G_r = g_o$. Then, if possible, the system can use the convenient directional antenna for the rest of the communication, by selecting the beam on which the incoming signal power is maximum. Then, suppose the opposite situation of a station willing to transmit a frame and not being aware of the location of the receiver. The transmitter must start the communication in omni mode, i.e. with gain $G_t = g_o$ and consequently with shorter range than with a directional transmission. Then, the communication can go on directionally. Alternately, the transmitter could try to start the communication directionally, probably by sending a starting signal in all the directional antennas in turn.

A station is said to be in either omni mode or directional mode. To be in directional mode is equivalent to say that the antenna is beamformed. When in omni mode, the station can sense signals coming from all possible directions, whereas when beamformed, the station can only send and only hears the signal coming from the sector corresponding to the chosen direction. The fact that the antenna is beamformed has two consequences: on the one hand, it reduces interference, because while being beamformed the system is not interfered by signals coming from other directions; on the other hand, the very fact that the system does not hear on the other directions produces a phenomenum called deafness, explained later.

MAC Most of the ad hoc network research and implementations are based on the IEEE 802.11 standard [29]. IEEE 802.11 is a CSMA/CA protocol which avoids collisions by physically sensing the medium before transmitting, and then by using a backoff mechanism. Additionally, IEEE 801.11 solves the hidden terminal problem by silencing all nodes in the vicinity of the sender and of the receiver [2]. The RTS/CTS control frames exchange occurs prior to the DATA communication. Both the RTS and CTS frames contain the proposed duration of the transmission. Nodes located in the vicinity of the communicating nodes can then construct a Network Allocation Vector (NAV) to implement virtual carrier sensing. As a consequence, the area covered by the transmission range of the sender and of the receiver is reserved for the duration of the transmission.

The design of IEEE 802.11 MAC assumed an omnidirectional antenna. Even if IEEE 802.11 can operate with a directional antenna at the physical layer, the potential gains of using a directional antennas may not be achieved and, actually, performance may be affected by the use of directional antennas [66].

A key advantage of using directional antennas is spatial reuse. Nevertheless, other issues arise. The first problem is, given a mobile ad hoc network where the nodes are not location-aware, how can spatial reuse be maximized. Assume the use of IEEE 802.11. If the sender does not know where the receiver is, the RTS must be sent in omni mode, hindering spatial reuse. Then, if RTS is sent omni and DATA is sent directionally, the communication ranges are different. The MAC protocol has to cope with such problems to maximize spatial reuse.

Choudhury et al. [65] summarize the main issues that arise from the use of directional antennas. The main problems are related to the phenomena called deafness and hidden terminal.

Consider two nodes, A and B, which are engaged in a communication. Suppose that A is beamformed in the direction of B, therefore, A can not be interfered by signals coming from other directions, we say that A is "deaf" in the other directions. Then, suppose that a third node, C, has a data frame to send to A. Node C then sends an RTS to A, who ignores it. As node C does not receive an CTS, it will eventually increase its backoff window. As long as A is beamformed and does not respond to C with an RTS, C will keep on backing off when it retransmits subsequent RTS frames. Suppose that B has a series of frames to be sent to A. It may actually pass a long interval before C gets access to the medium and sends a frame to A. When it does, A may now become deaf to B's frames, causing B MAC layer to retransmit and eventually B will give up. The upper layers of B will see a packet loss. That packet loss would be interpreted as congestion by TCP, even if this is not exactly the case. Therefore, the deafness phenomenum can affect the network performance by causing multiple packet drops, without congestion or link rupture and, at the same time, cause short-term unfairness between flows that have the same receiver.

Hidden terminal problems may actually be aggravated with the use of directional antennas. Consider the example scenario of Figure 14. Suppose that nodes A and B are both beamformed in the direction of each other, and that there is an ongoing communication between A and B. Now, suppose that node C sends an RTS to node D, which is followed by a directional CTS from D to C. Thereafter, C and D start to communicate directly. The RTS issued by C, whether omni or directional, as well as the directional CTS from D were not taken into consideration by A, which was beamformed in the direction of B. Now, suppose that the conversation between A and B ends, and that A tries to start a communication with D, or any other node in the direction of D. Node A may well send an RTS in the direction of D, since it is not aware of the ongoing communication. When it does, the RTS of A will cause a collision at D. That kind of hidden terminal problem would not be possible if all control frames had been sent omni directionally.

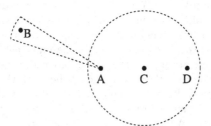

Fig. 14. RTS from C unheard by A.

The first adaptation proposed to IEEE 802.11 to support directional antennas is the use of a Directional Network Allocation Vector (DNAV) per sector, instead of a single NAV [67, 68]. The idea is to reserve a sector instead of a circular area if the reservation control frames (RTS and/or CTS) are sent directionally.

Directional MAC (DMAC) is a MAC protocol based on IEEE 802.11 with the basic modifications to support directional antennas [68]. DMAC supposes that an upper layer is capable of supplying transceiver profiles that describe the capabilities of each of the node neighbors. Basic DMAC reserves the channel using RTS/CTS frames which are both transmitted directionally. An idle node listens to the channel omnidirectionally, when it receives a signal, it beamforms in that direction. Basic DMAC has problems with hidden terminals due to gain assimetry and unheard RTS/CTS, as explained previously.

Multihop RTS MAC (MMAC) [65] enhances basic DMAC by using RTS frames which can be retransmitted traversing multiple hops. The objective is to exploit the longer range possible with directional antennas. Assume that the idle node is in omni mode. Thus, a RTS sent directionally can only form a link whose gain is $g_d \times g_o$, that is, the receiver of the RTS will be at a distance as long as the one defined by $g_d \times g_o$. Nevertheless, if both the emitter and the receiver were beamformed, the gain would be $g_d \times g_d$ and the range would be larger. The basic idea of MMAC is to have protocol that allows the RTS to travel multiple hops and form longer links.

Ko et al. [69] investigated the use of directional RTS frames and omnidirectional CTS frames. The basic idea is that, when an idle node receives a CTS, it will block that antenna to not interfere with ongoing communications. Nevertheless, it can use the other unblocked directions to start other communications, increasing spatial reuse.

To reduce the deafness problem caused by directional antennas, Korakis *et al.* [70] propose the use of a circular RTS, or sweeping. The main idea is that the emitter sends the RTS frame in all the directional antennas, to notify the nodes in all the possible directions about the upcoming communication.

Routing The routing layer may also be affected by the use of directional antennas. Choudhury and Vaidya [71] evaluate the impact of directional antennas over the performance of the omnidirectional routing protocol DSR and propose different strategies for directional routing. Using directional transmissions, the request message broadcast used in DSR must be implemented by sweeping at the MAC layer, i.e., retransmitting the frame for each of the directional antennas. The authors show that there is a tradeoff between the latency added by sweeping and the narrowidth of the antenna beam. Intuitively, the narrower the beam, the greater is the spatial reuse, but also the sweeping latency.

Utilizing Directional Antennas for Ad hoc Networking (UDAAN) [72] is a complete solution for wireless ad hoc networks using directional antennas. The routing protocol used by UDAAN is a link-state proactive routing protocol. UDAAN is based on the HSLS (Hazy Sighted Link-State) routing protocol. To improve scalability, the basic idea of HSLS is to reduce the amount of link-state updates as the distance from the originating node increases. This is done by setting a time-to-live of the link-state updates such that the frequency of updates with n hops is inversely proportional to n. Additionally, UDAAN routing protocol supports ToS-based routing and uses a table of radio profiles to forward packets.

Directional antennas may also be used to improve the routing protocol operation. Saha and Johnson [73] propose a modification of the DSR protocol where the larger transmission range of the directional antenna is used to find longer links and locally repair a broken route.

6.2 Security

Securing a wireless ad hoc network is a challenging task [74, 75, 76]. The broadcast nature of the radio transmission, the absence of an infrastructure, the dynamical topology, the collaborative multihop communication, and the self-organizing characteristic increase the vulnerabilities of an ad hoc network.

Free-space radio communication exposes ad hoc networks to jamming denial of service (DoS) attacks. Jamming is simple and effective in narrow-band wireless networks. Defenses against jamming involve spread spectrum communication, or detection and isolation of the affected jammed region and reroute of the traffic.

Eavesdropping in wireless communication is another threat usually impossible to detect. Hence, the use of cryptography algorithms is mandatory if privacy is required in the wireless ad hoc network.

Conventional solutions to secure communications are the use of symmetric (or secret) or asymmetric (public-private) cryptographic keys. Asymmetric algorithms require more processing than symmetric algorithms. Furthermore, asymmetric algorithms require certification, which is difficult to implement in ad networks because of the lack of infrastructure. Ad hoc nodes can easily join and leave the network. Moreover, ad hoc nodes seldom reside in safe places, and hence can fall under attackers' control. Conventional intrusion detection solutions based on certification authorities and servers are inappropriate due to the absence of infrastructure. The Techniques for Intrusion-Resistant Ad Hoc Routing Algorithm (TIARA) [77] were proposed to limit the damage caused by intrusion attacks.

Multihop ad hoc networks assume that every node is also a router that can forward messages. This makes secure routing a difficult task because a malicious node can easily join the network and modify or fabricate routing information and impersonating other nodes. Several routing attacks were identified, such as:

- Selective Forwarding - an attacker selectively drops some packets;
- Sinkhole - an attacker forges routing information claiming falsified shorter distances to attract packets and then discard some or all of them;
  - Blackhole - a variation of sinkhole where all packets are discarded;
  - Greyhole - similar to the blackhole, but selectively drops some packets but not others.
- Wormhole - a pair of attackers, nodes A and B, linked via a private network connection;
- Selfishness - a node that simply does not contribute in the network operation, not forwarding packets. A selfish node is not necessarily an attacker and do not intend to damage other nodes; it may only aim to save its battery life;
- Gratuitous Detour - an attacker forges routing information with the objective of not forwarding packets for other nodes, by adding virtual nodes and making a route through itself appear longer;
- Isolation - an attacker forges routing information to cause a node to use a route detour preventing one set of nodes from reaching another;

– Rushing - used against on-demand routing protocols that use duplicate message suppression at each node - an attacker quickly disseminates route requests throughout the network, thus causing the nodes to suppress any later legitimate route requests;
– Sibyl - an attacker presents multiple identities to other nodes.

Several secure routing protocols were proposed. The Secure Efficient Ad Hoc Distance (SEAD) [78] is a proactive secure routing protocol, based on the DSDV protocol, that avoids modification of routing-table update messages. The basic idea is to use a one-way hash function to authenticate the sequence number and the metric fields of the messages.

The Secure Routing Protocol [79] is proposed to improve the DSR reactive protocol using an extension header that is attached to the route request and the route reply messages. A node that requests a route to a destination is able to identify and discard false routing information messages. Ariadne [80] is another secure protocol based on DSR and TESLA, which is an efficient broadcast authentication scheme that requires loose time synchronization. It assumes that each pair of communicating nodes has one secret key in each direction, and no assumption is made regarding the forwarding, which may exhibit malicious behavior.

To implement security in the AODV protocol, the Secure AODV (SAODV) protocol [81] was proposed. The authors assume that there is a key management system that makes it possible for each node to obtain public keys from the other nodes of the network, and that each node is capable of verifying the association between the identity of a given node and the public key of that node. Given these assumptions, the proposal secure important fields of the AODV messages. The SAODV uses a digital signature to authenticate the fixed fields of the messages, and hash chains to secure the hop count information, which is the only changeable information in the messages.

Most of the proposals try to secure existing protocols and do not succeed against all possible attacks. Securing ad hoc networks is still an open issue. Some researchers argue that all protocols for ad hoc networks must be designed thinking in security from the beginning.

6.3 Underserved Communities

The Brazilian government intends to use the Interactive Digital TV technology as a vehicle for fostering the social inclusion of less-privileged social groups, which live on underserved communities, by using information and communication technologies as tools to encourage active citizenship. It is worth mentioning that more than 90% of the Brazilian residences have a TV set, but less than 10% have Internet access. Some initiatives promoted by non-governmental organizations show that people, when start using computers, experience a positive change in their daily lives, as returning to schools, meeting people, talking about issues regarding to their communities, such as human rights, environment, sexual information, and health. Computers can also keep people away from drugs and violence.

One low-cost, scalable, and easy solution to implement the return channel is an ad hoc community network. Every set top box is a node of the community network. The set top boxes generate traffic that is routed to a gateway, which then forwards the traffic over the Internet to the TV station. Thus, the community networks have specific characteristics: the presence of a gateway and the low mobility of the nodes. Moreover, the presence of a gateway plays an important role in the return channel because all the traffic forwarded to the Internet converges to it. A node is connected only if it has a path to the gateway. Consequently, the availability of the nodes must be higher near the gateway. Campista *et al.* [82] showed that if 20% of the nodes are turned on in an ad hoc return channel, a high connectivity is already reached in typical urban scenarios.

References

1. S. Kumar, V. S. Raghavan, and J. Deng, "Medium access control protocols for ad hoc wireless networks: A survey," *Ad Hoc Networks*, vol. 4, no. 3, pp. 326–358, May 2006.
2. P. Karn, "MACA - a new channel access protocol for packet radio," in *ARRL/CRRL Amateur Radio Computer Networking Conference*, pp. 134–140, Sept. 1990.
3. V. Bharghavan, A. J. Demers, S. Shenker, and L. Zhang, "MACAW: A media access protocol for wireless LAN's," in *ACM SIGCOMM*, pp. 212–225, Aug. 1994.
4. C. L. Fullmer and J. J. Garcia-Luna-Aceves, "Floor acquisition multiple access (FAMA) for packet-radio networks," in *ACM SIGCOMM*, pp. 262–273, Aug. 1995.
5. I. Chlamtac, M. Conti, and J. J.-N. Liu, "Mobile ad hoc networking: imperatives and challenges," *Ad Hoc Networks*, vol. 1, no. 1, pp. 13–64, Jan. 2003.
6. A. C. V. Gummalla and J. O. Limb, "Wireless medium access control protocols," *IEEE Communications Surveys and Tutorials*, pp. 2–15, Sept. 2000.
7. C. Wu and V. O. K. Li, "Receiver-initiated busy-tone multiple access in packet radio networks," in *ACM SIGCOMM*, pp. 336–342, Aug. 1987.
8. Z. J. Haas and J. Deng, "Dual busy tone multiple access (DBTMA)-A multiple access control scheme for ad hoc networks," *IEEE Transactions on Communications*, vol. 50, no. 6, pp. 975–985, June 2002.
9. A. Nasipuri, J. Zhuang, and S. R. Das, "A multichannel CSMA MAC protocol for multihop wireless networks," in *IEEE Wireless Communications and Networking Conference (WCNC)*, pp. 1402–1406, Sept. 1999.
10. Z. Tang and J. J. Garcia-Luna-Aceves, "Hop reservation multiple access (HRMA) for ad-hoc networks," in *IEEE Conference on Computer Communications (INFO-COM)*, pp. 194–201, Mar. 1999.
11. I. A. Akyildiz and X. Wang, "A survey on wireless mesh networks," *IEEE Communications Magazine*, vol. 43, no. 9, pp. S23–S30, Sept. 2005.
12. A. Raniwalaa and T.-C. Chiueh, "Architecture and algorithms for an IEEE 802.11-based multi-channel wireless mesh nertwork," in *IEEE Conference on Computer Communications (INFOCOM)*, pp. 2223–2234, Mar. 2005.

13. D. de O. Cunha, L. H. M. K. Costa, and O. C. M. B. Duarte, "Analyzing the energy consumption of IEEE 802.11 ad hoc networks," in *IFIP/IEEE International Conference on Mobile and Wireless Communications Networks (MWCN)*, Oct. 2004.

14. S. Singh and C. S. Raghavendra, "PAMAS-power aware multi-access protocol with signaling for ad hoc networks," *ACM Computer Communications*, vol. 28, no. 3, pp. 5–26, July 1998.

15. E.-S. Jung and N. H. Vaidya, "An energy efficient MAC protocol for wireless LANs," in *IEEE Conference on Computer Communications (INFOCOM)*, pp. 1756–1764, June 2002.

16. E.-S. Jung and N. H. Vaidya, "A power control MAC protocol for ad hoc networks," in *ACM International Conference on Mobile Computing and Networking (MobiCom)*, pp. 36–47, Sept. 2002.

17. J. Monks, V. Bharghavan, and W. Hwu, "A power controlled multiple access protocol for wireless packet networks," in *IEEE Conference on Computer Communications (INFOCOM)*, pp. 219–228, Apr. 2001.

18. H. Xiao, W. K. G. Seah, A. Lo, and K. C. Chua, "A flexible quality of service model for mobile ad hoc networks," in *IEEE VTC-Spring*, pp. 445–449, Apr. 2000.

19. G. S. Ahn, A. T. Campbell, A. Veres, and L. H. Sun, "SWAN: Service differentiation in stateless wireless ad hoc networks," in *IEEE Conference on Computer Communications (INFOCOM)*, pp. 457–466, June 2002.

20. S. B. Lee and A. T. Campbell, "INSIGNIA: In-band signaling support for QoS in mobile ad hoc networks," in *International Workshop on Mobile Multimedia Communication (MoMuc)*, pp. 12–14, Oct. 1998.

21. M. Gerla and J. T.-C. Tsai, "Multicluster, mobile, multimedia radio network," *Journal of Wireless Networks*, vol. 1, no. 3, pp. 255–265, Feb. 1995.

22. C. R. Lin and M. Gerla, "Adaptive clustering for mobile wireless networks," *Journal of Selected Areas in Communications*, vol. 15, no. 7, pp. 1265–1275, Sept. 1997.

23. C. W. Ahn, C. G. Kang, and Y. Z. Cho, "Soft reservation multiple access with priority assignement (SRMA/PA): A novel MAC protocol for QoS-guaranteed integrated services in mobile ad hoc networks," in *VTS-Fall IEEE VTC*, pp. 942–947, Sept. 2000.

24. R. O. Baldwin, N. J. D. IV, and S. F. Midkiff, "A real-time medium access control protocol for ad hoc wireless local area networks," *ACM SIGMOBILE Mobile Computing and Communications Review*, vol. 3, no. 2, pp. 20–27, Apr. 1999.

25. D. J. Deng and R. S. C. and, "A priority scheme for IEEE 802.11 DCF access method," *IEICE Trans. Commun.*, vol. 82-B, no. 1, pp. 96–102, Jan. 1999.

26. D. Remondo, "Tutorial on wireless ad hoc networks," in *International Working Conference in Performance Modelling and Evaluation of Heterogeneous Networks (HET-NET)*, pp. T2/1–T2/15, July 2004.

27. IEEE, "Part 15.1: Wireless medium access control (MAC) and physical layer (PHY) specifications for wireless personal area networks (WPANs)." IEEE Standard 802.15.1, 2002.

28. Bluetooth SIG, "Specification of the bluetooth system." Core Specification Version 1.1, Feb. 2001.

29. IEEE, "Wireless LAN medium access control (MAC) and physical layer (PHY) specifications." IEEE Standard 802.11, 1999.

30. S. Chung and K. Piechota, "Understanding the MAC impact of 802.11e: Part 1," *Communication Systems Design Magazine*, Oct. 2003. http://www.commsdesign.com/design_corner/OEG20031029S0009.

31. IEEE, "Wireless LAN medium access control (MAC) and physical layer (PHY) specifications: Medium access control (MAC) quality of service enhancements." IEEE Standard 802.11e, 2005.
32. S. Chung and K. Piechota, "Understanding the MAC impact of 802.11e: Part 2," *Communication Systems Design Magazine*, Oct. 2003. http://www.commsdesign.com/design_corner/OEG20031030S0005.
33. IEEE, "Media access control (MAC) bridges." IEEE Standard 802.1D, 1998.
34. E. M. Royer and C.-K. Toh, "A review of current routing protocols for ad-hoc mobile wireless networks," *IEEE Personal Communications Magazine*, vol. 6, no. 2, pp. 46–55, Apr. 1999.
35. X. Hong, K. Xu, and M. Gerla, "Scalable routing protocols for mobile ad hoc networks," *IEEE Network*, vol. 16, no. 4, pp. 11–21, July 2002.
36. M. Abolhasan, T. Wysocki, and E. Dutkiewicz, "A review of routing protocols for mobile ad hoc networks," *Ad Hoc Networks*, vol. 2, no. 1, pp. 1–22, Jan. 2004.
37. M. Mauve, J. Widmer, and H. Hartenstein, "A survey on position-based routing in mobile ad hoc networks," *IEEE Network*, vol. 1, no. 6, pp. 30–39, Dec. 2001.
38. L. H. M. K. Costa, M. D. Amorim, and S. Fdida, "Reducing latency and overhead of route repair with controlled flooding," *ACM/Kluwer Wireless Networks*, vol. 10, no. 4, pp. 347–358, July 2004.
39. S.-M. Senouci and G. Pujolle, "Energy efficient routing in wireless ad hoc networks," in *IEEE International Conference on Communications (ICC)*, June 2004.
40. H. Badis, A. Munaretto, K. A. Agha, and G. Pujolle, "Qos for ad hoc networking based on multiple-metric: Bandwidth and delay," in *IFIP/IEEE International Conference on Mobile and Wireless Communications Networks (MWCN)*, Oct. 2003.
41. C. Perkins and P. Bhagwat, "Highly dynamic destination-sequenced distance-vector routing (DSDV) for mobile computers," in *ACM SIGCOMM*, pp. 234–244, Aug. 1994.
42. T. Clausen and P. Jacquet, "Optimized link state routing protocol (OLSR)." IETF Request for Comments 3626, 2003.
43. T. Clausen, G. Hansen, L. Christensen, and G. Behrmann, "The optimized link state routing protocol, evaluation through experiments and simulation," in *IEEE Symposium on Wireless Personal Mobile Communications*, Sept. 2001.
44. L. Viennot, "Complexity results on election of multipoint relays in wireless networks," tech. rep., INRIA, France, 1998.
45. C. Perkins, E. Belding-Royer, and S. Das, "Ad hoc on-demand distance vector (AODV) routing." IETF Request for Comments 3561, 2003.
46. D. Johnson, D. Maltz, and J. Broch, *DSR: The Dynamic Source Routing Protocol for Multihop Wireless Ad Hoc Networks*, ch. 5, pp. 139–172. Addison-Wesley, 2001.
47. J. Hightower and G. Borriello, "Location systems for ubiquitous computing," *IEEE Computer*, vol. 34, no. 8, pp. 57–66, Aug. 2001.
48. S. Basagni, I. Chlamtac, V. R. Syrotiuk, and B. A. Woodward, "A distance routing effect algorithm for mobility (DREAM)," in *ACM International Conference on Mobile Computing and Networking (MobiCom)*, (Dallas, USA), pp. 76–84, Oct. 1998.
49. S. Basagni, I. Chlamtac, and V. R. Syrotiuk, "Geographic messaging in wireless ad hoc networks," in *Annual IEEE International Vehicular Technology Conference*, (Houston, USA), pp. 1957–1961, May 1999.

50. J. Li, J. Jannotti, D. De Couto, D. Karger, and R. Morris, "A scalable location service for geographic ad-hoc routing," in *ACM International Conference on Mobile Computing and Networking (MobiCom)*, (Boston, USA), pp. 120–130, Aug. 2000.

51. R. Morris, F. Kaashoek, D. Karger, D. Aguayo, J. Bicket, S. Biswas, D. De Couto, and J. Li, "The grid ad hoc networking project." http://pdos.csail.mit.edu/grid/, 2003.

52. A. A. Hanball, E. Altman, and P. Nain, "A Survey of TCP over Ad Hoc Networks," *IEEE Communications Surveys and Tutorials*, vol. 7, no. 3, no. 3, pp. 22–36, 2005.

53. R. Hsieh and A. Seneviratne, "A comparison of mechanisms for improving mobile IP handoff latency for end-to-end TCP," in *ACM International Conference on Mobile Computing and Networking (MobiCom)*, pp. 29–41, Sept. 2003.

54. T. D. Dyer and R. V. Boppana, "A comparison of TCP performance over three routing protocols for mobile ad hoc networks," in *ACM International Symposium on Mobile Ad Hoc Networking and Computing (MobiHoc)*, pp. 56–66, Oct. 2001.

55. F. Wang and Y. Zhang, "Improving TCP performance over mobile ad-hoc networks with out-of-order detection and response," in *ACM International Symposium on Mobile Ad Hoc Networking and Computing (MobiHoc)*, pp. 217–225, June 2002.

56. H. Balakrishnan, V. N. Padmanabhan, S. Seshan, and R. H. Katz, "A comparison of mechanisms for improving TCP performance over wireless links," in *ACM SIGCOMM*, pp. 256–269, Aug. 1996.

57. A. V. Bakre and B. R. Badrinath, "Implementation and Performance Evaluation of Indirect TCP," *IEEE Transactions on Computers*, vol. 46, no. 3, pp. 260–278, Mar. 1997.

58. R. Yavatkar and N. Bhagawat, "Improving end-to-end performance of TCP over mobile internetworks," in *IEEE Workshop on Mobile Computing Systems and Applications (Mobile)*, pp. 146–152, Sept. 1994.

59. K. Brown and S. Singh, "M-TCP: TCP for mobile cellular networks," in *ACM SIGCOMM*, pp. 19–43, July 1997.

60. G. Holland and N. Vaidya, "Impact of Routing and Link Layers on TCP Performance in Mobile Ad Hoc Networks," in *IEEE Wireless Communications and Networking Conference (WCNC)*, pp. 1323–1327, Sept. 1999.

61. K. Chandran, S. Raghunathan, S. Venkatesan, and R. Prakash, "A feedback-based scheme for improving TCP performance in ad hoc wireless network," *IEEE Personal Communications*, vol. 8, no. 1, pp. 34–39, Feb. 2001.

62. J. Liu and S. Singh, "ATCP: TCP for mobile ad hoc networks," *IEEE Journal on Selected Areas on Communications*, vol. 9, no. 7, pp. 1300–1315, July 2001.

63. Z. Fu, H. Luo, P. Zerfos, S. Lu, L. Zhang, and M. Gerla, "The impact of multihop wireless channel on TCP performance," *IEEE Transactions on Mobile Computing*, vol. 4, no. 2, pp. 209–221, Mar. 2005.

64. T. S. Rappaport, *Wireless Communications: Principles and Practice.* Prentice Hall, 2002.

65. R. R. Choudhury, X. Yang, R. Ramanathan, and N. H. Vaydia, "On designing MAC protocols for wireless networks using directional antennas," *IEEE Transactions on Mobile Computing*, vol. 5, no. 5, pp. 477–491, May 2006.

66. Z. Huang and C.-C. Shen, "A comparison study of omnidirectional and directional MAC protocols for ad hoc networks," in *IEEE GLOBECOM*, pp. 57–61, 2002.

67. M. Takai, J. Martin, A. Ren, and R. Bagrodia, "Directional virtual carrier sensing for directional antennas in mobile ad hoc networks," in *ACM International Symposium on Mobile Ad Hoc Networking and Computing (MobiHoc)*, pp. 183–193, June 2002.

68. R. R. Choudhury, X. Yang, N. H. Vaydia, and R. Ramanathan, "Using directional antennas for medium access control in ad hoc networks," in *ACM International Conference on Mobile Computing and Networking (MobiCom)*, pp. 59–70, Sept. 2002.

69. Y.-B. Ko, V. Shankarkumar, and N. H. Vaidya, "Medium access control protocols using directional antennas in ad hoc networks," in *IEEE Conference on Computer Communications (INFOCOM)*, Mar. 2000.

70. T. Korakis, G. Jakllari, and L. Tassiulas, "A MAC protocol for full exploitation of directional antennas in ad-hoc wireless networks," in *ACM International Symposium on Mobile Ad Hoc Networking and Computing (MobiHoc)*, pp. 98–107, June 2003.

71. R. R. Choudhury and N. H. Vaidya, "Impact of directional antennas on ad hoc routing," in *IFIP International Conference on Personal Wireless Communication*, Sept. 2003.

72. R. Ramanathan, J. Redi, C. Santivanez, D. Wiggins, and S. Polit, "Ad hoc networking with directional antennas: A complete systems solution," *IEEE Journal on Selected Areas in Communications*, vol. 23, no. 3, pp. 496–506, Mar. 2005.

73. A. K. Saha and D. B. Johnson, "Routing improvement using directional antennas in mobile ad hoc networks," in *IEEE GLOBECOM*, pp. 2902–2908, Dec. 2004.

74. H. Yih-Chun and A. Perrig, "A survey of secure wireless ad hoc routing," *IEEE Security & Privacy Magazine*, vol. 2, no. 3, pp. 28–39, May 2004.

75. C. Karlof and D. Wagner, "Secure routing in wireless sensor networks: Attacks and countermeasures," *Ad Hoc Networks*, vol. 1, no. 2-3, pp. 293–315, Sept. 2003.

76. A. D. Wood and J. A. Stankovic, "Denial of service in sensor networks," *IEEE Computer*, vol. 35, no. 10, pp. 54–62, Oct. 2002.

77. R. Ramanujan, A. Ahamad, J. Bonney, R. Hagelstrom, and K. Thurber, "Techniques for intrusion-resistant ad hoc routing algorithms (TIARA)," in *IEEE Military Communications Conference (MILCOM)*, pp. 660–664, Oct. 2000.

78. Y.-C. Hu, D. B. Johnson, and A. Perrig, "SEAD: Secure efficient distance vector routing for mobile wireless ad hoc networks," in *IEEE Workshop on Mobile Computing Systems and Applications (WMCSA)*, pp. 3–13, June 2002.

79. P. Papadimitratos and Z. Hass, "Secure routing for mobile ad hoc networks," in *SCS Communication Networks and Distributed Systems Modeling and Simulation Conference (CNDS)*, Jan. 2002.

80. Y.-C. Hu, A. Perrig, and D. B. Johnson, "Ariadne: A secure on-demand routing protocol for ad hoc networks," in *ACM International Conference on Mobile Computing and Networking (MobiCom)*, pp. 12–23, Sept. 2002.

81. M. G. Zapata and N. Asokan, "Securing ad hoc routing protocols," in *ACM Workshop on Wireless Security (WiSe)*, pp. 1–10, Sept. 2002.

82. M. E. M. Campista, I. M. Moraes, P. M. Esposito, A. A. Jr., D. de O. Cunha, L. H. M. K. Costa, and O. C. M. B. Duarte, "Wireless ad hoc network on underserved communities: An efficient solution for interactive digital TV," in *IFIP/IEEE International Conference on Mobile and Wireless Communications Networks (MWCN)*, Aug. 2006.

HIT: A Human-Inspired Trust Model *

Pedro B. Velloso[1], Rafael P. Laufer[2], Otto C. M. B. Duarte[3], and Guy Pujolle[1]

[1] Laboratoire d'Informatique de Paris 6 (LIP6) - Paris VI
Paris, France
[2] Computer Science Department - UCLA
California, USA
[3] Grupo de Teleinformática e Automação (GTA) - UFRJ
Rio de Janeiro, RJ, Brazil

Abstract. This paper presents a new approach to assign trust levels in ad hoc networks. Our system is inspired by the human concept of trust. The trust level considers the recommendation of trustworthy neighbors and their own experience. For the recommendation computation, we take into account not only the trust level, but also its accuracy and the relationship maturity. We also propose the Recommendation Exchange Protocol (REP), which minimizes the number of exchanged messages. The results show the efficacy of the system and the influence of main parameters.

1 Introduction

Ad hoc networks rely on collaborative behavior of nodes to work properly. Therefore, nodes must trust each other at some level to allow distributed applications, including routing and admission control. A naive trust model might lead to low efficiency, high energy consumption, and network attacks. The behavior of the nodes is dynamic and depends on their goals and constraints, which might lead to distinct behaviors. Nodes must decide what is best for themselves but in a context of minimum collaboration, like in a society. We believe that the first step towards a self-learning and collaborative system is defining whether neighbors are reliable or not, because trust allows the information exchange and stimulates cooperation among nodes. Moreover, trust can also be used to minimize the effect of malicious nodes

Our work aims at building a trust relationship inspired on the human concept of trust among nodes of an ad hoc network. Each node must assign trust levels to other nodes based on the recommendation of trustworthy neighbors and its own experiences. There are already some effort in bringing trust to ad hoc networks [1–8], but most of them are concerned solely about routing aspects.

Liu *et al.* [1] propose a trust model to ad hoc networks based on the distribution of threat reports to interested nodes. The goal is to make security-aware routing decisions, where nodes use the trust level as an additional metric for

---

* This work has been supported by CNPq.

Please use the following format when citing this chapter:

Velloso, P.B., Laufer, R.P., Duarte, O.C.M.B., Pujolle, G., 2006, in IFIP International Federation for Information Processing, Volume 211, ed. Pujolle, G., Mobile and Wireless Communication Networks, (Boston: Springer), pp. 35–46.

routing packets. The authors present different approaches for the trust level calculation. Nevertheless, they assume that nodes cooperate with each other which is not always the case. They also assume that all nodes are capable of detecting malicious behavior by means of Intrusion Detection Systems (IDS). This assumption leads to high energy consumption, which is clearly not an appropriate option for ad hoc networks. All the trust level dynamics is based on the reports provided by the IDS.

Yan et al. [2, 3] propose a security solution for ad hoc networks based on a trust model. They suggest using a linear function to calculate the trust according to a particular action. The function considers different factors that can affect the trust level, including intrusion black lists, previous experience statistics, and recommendations. Nonetheless, the influence of such factors on the trust evaluation is not defined. Although mentioning general trust concepts, the work focus on specific routing issues.

Pirzada and McDonald [4] propose another trust model for ad hoc networks to compute the reliability of different routes. Nodes can use this information as an additional metric on routing algorithms. The authors propose an extension to DSR protocol which applies their trust model in order to find trustworthy routes. Although the authors present an interesting approach, the model presents several disadvantages. For instance, it is restricted to DSR so far, it relies on using promiscuous mode ignoring the energy constrains of mobile nodes, and it stores a significant amount of information, since it keeps information for all nodes in the network.

Virendra et al. [5] present an architecture based on trust that allows nodes to make decisions on establishing keys with other nodes and forming groups of trust. Their scheme considers trust self-evaluation and recommendation of other nodes to compute trust. Although we have a similar approach, our trust model differs in the following way. Their trust self-evaluation is based on monitoring nodes and a challenge-response system. We propose a self-learning and context-based approach in which nodes evaluate their neighbors based on their own goals, current state, present location, and network conditions.

We focus on providing nodes with a trust level regarding their direct neighbors. The goal is to make nodes capable of gathering information to reason, learn, and make their own decisions. Different from most related works, our work improves scalability by restricting nodes to keep and exchange trust information solely with direct neighbors, that is, neighbors within the radio range.

The contributions of this paper are twofold. First, we propose a trust model that takes into account time-space parameters of each node, such as its current state and its location, the network conditions, and mobility parameters to compute the trust level. Accordingly, nodes rely on a self-learning mechanism to set some parameters in our model. Finally, we propose the Recommendation Exchange Protocol (REP), which allows nodes to build and update their trust table.

The paper is organized as follows. Our self-learning approach to build trust is presented in Section 2. Section 3 shows our simulation results. In Section 4 we present our conclusions.

2 Trust model

The basic idea consists of building a trust information system that allows nodes to learn based on the information exchanged with other nodes. The main goal is to make nodes self-configuring, self-adaptive, self-optimized. As a result, nodes are capable of making their own decisions. Moreover, nodes might use the trust information to detect and isolate malicious nodes.

The proposed model can be divided in two distinct layers. The Learning layer is responsible for gathering and converting information into knowledge. The Trust layer defines how to assess the trust level using knowledge information provided by the Learning layer. Both layers can interact with all other layers. In this paper, we only describe the Trust layer.

The level of trust is based on both the previous experiences of nodes and the recommendation of others. Previous experiences allow nodes to judge the actions performed by other nodes. These actions can lead to three types of verdict. An action affects negatively, positively, or does not affect other nodes at all. The first two types of effect will generate a reaction that begins with a trust level update, but can also change the node behavior. The Learning layer is the responsible for the evaluation of other nodes actions and for choosing the appropriate reaction.

The recommendation of other nodes can be taken into account while calculating the trust level. For that, we introduce the concept of relationship maturity, which is based on the age of the relationship between two nodes. This concept allows nodes to give more importance to recommendations sent by long-term neighbors than recommendations sent by new neighbors. Nodes willing to consider the recommendation of other nodes can use the proposed Recommendation Exchange Protocol (REP) to keep updated the trust level of each neighbor.

Each node is responsible for computing and storing the trust level of each neighbor. For that purpose, nodes keep a so-called trust table which contains the trust level of all direct neighbors. Additionally, a node might also store the trust table of its neighbors whenever it is possible.

In our model, nodes can also keep an additional table that is not mandatory. The Auxiliary Trust Table (ATT) contains the confidence of the trust level and the so-called relationship maturity for each neighbor. The confidence of the trust level represents the accuracy of this measure whereas the relationship maturity represents the time that the node has met this specific neighbor. The goal of ATT is to supply nodes with additional information that can improve the trust-level evaluation.

Nodes with power or storage constrains can choose not to implement the entire trust system. We define three operation modes. Nodes with low power/storage capacity can operate in the simple mode, where they only use the main trust table. Nodes with a medium capacity operate in the intermediate mode, where nodes exchange trust information using the REP protocol and store the trust table of neighbor nodes. In the advanced mode, nodes implement the same features used in intermediate mode and also use the ATT to keep track of additional parameters.

We divide the trust scheme in two distinct phases. An initial phase is used when nodes first meet. At this phase, nodes assign an initial trust level to each other. The second phase is triggered by trust level updates, which assumes that the nodes have already met. We propose a continuous representation for the trust level, ranging from 0 to 1 where 0 means the least reliable node and 1 means the most reliable node.

2.1 First Trust Assignment

When a node first meets a specific neighbor, it must assign an initial level of trust for this neighbor. The first trust assignment depends on several network parameters, such as mobility, location of nodes, and its current state. We can classify the first trust assignment strategy as prudent or friendly/naive. In the prudent strategy the node does not trust strangers and considers that every new neighbor might be a threat to the network. As a consequence, the node assigns a low value of trust for the new neighbor. Following the friendly/naive strategy means that every node is considered reliable until proven otherwise. In such case, the node associates a high level of trust for new neighbors. When a node adopts this strategy based on previous experience, we consider it friendly and if the node chooses this strategy due to lack of options it is considered naive. Right in the middle of these two strategies one could think of a moderate strategy, in which the node assigns an intermediate level of trust for strangers.

Different situations might demand distinct strategies. For example, if a node has already a significant number of reliable neighbors it can adopt a prudent strategy because it does not need new reliable neighbors. Further, the addition of a new neighbor might not significantly increase the probability of augmenting its satisfaction level. On the other hand, in a network where topology periodically changes and neighbor relationships are ephemeral, a node can opt for the naive strategy. In hostile environments, nodes might want to adopt the prudent strategy whereas in well-known cordial environments nodes can select the friendly strategy.

The first trust assignment occurs during the initial phase. The first trust level can also take into account the recommendation of known neighbors weighted by their trust levels. In order to a node a calculate the first trust level of node b, we propose the following equation

$$T_a(b) = (1 - \alpha)F_a + \alpha C_a(b), \tag{1}$$

where F_a is the value used by node a according to the chosen strategy, $C_a(b)$ is the contribution of the trust level of other nodes about node b, and and α is the weight factor that allows us to give more relevance to the desired parameter. The group K_a defines the nodes from which recommendations will be considered. It is a subset of the neighbors of node a comprising all nodes that satisfy certain conditions. We consider two basic conditions for selecting K_a. The first one selects the nodes whose trust level is above a certain threshold (T_{th}). Let N_a be the set of neighbors of node a that includes all nodes known for a period of time longer than the relationship maturity threshold (M_{th}). The subset K_a can be defined as follows

$$K_a = \{\forall i \in N_a | T_a(i) \geq T_{th}\}. \tag{2}$$

Another option would be selecting r nodes in N_a with the highest trust levels.

Deciding the best strategy to derive F_a is not a simple task. For instance, F_a must take into account the level of mobility, the current satisfaction, the number of reliable neighbors. As choosing the best strategy evolves several parameters, we suggest a learning approach to select the strategy. This means that the Learning layer is responsible for selecting the best strategy.

2.2 Recommendation Computation

All nodes are qualified to contribute in the trust assignment. Therefore, the trust level evaluation might consider the recommendations of other nodes. The variable $C_a(b)$ is the contribution of all nodes $i \in K_a$ about node b weighted by the trust level of node a about node i, as follows

$$C_a(b) = \frac{\sum_{i \in K_a} T_a(i) M_i(b) X_i(b)}{\sum_{j \in K_a} T_a(j) M_j(b)}. \tag{3}$$

The relevance of the recommendation of other nodes is strongly related to the selection of K_n. The more trustworthy K_n is the more useful the recommendation of others is. The contribution considers not only the trust level of others but also the accuracy and the relationship maturity. The accuracy of a trust level is defined by the standard deviation, similar to Theodorakopoulos and Baras [8]. The relationship maturity is defined by $M_a(b)$ and it is expressed in hours by a continuous variable and X is a random variable with a normal distribution, which can be expressed as

$$X_i(b) = N(T_i(b), \sigma_i(b)). \tag{4}$$

The value in the trust level table of node a regarding node b is associated to a standard deviation $\sigma_a(b)$, which refers to the variations of the trust level that node a has observed. After a trust level update of node a about node b, node a must update $\sigma_a(b)$. The vaule of $\sigma_a(b)$ is defined as

$$\sigma_a(b) = \sqrt{\frac{\sum_{j=1}^{k} (\overline{S} - s_j)^2}{k - 1}}, \tag{5}$$

where S represents the set of the k last trust level samples about a specific node, for $2 \leq k \leq 10$. The value of $\overline{S}$ represents the average of these k samples. The parameter $\sigma_a(b)$ tells us the confidence of the trust level. A high value fot $\sigma_a(b)$ has two meanings. Either the node is not able to assess the trust value with accuracy or the node whose trust level is being estimated is unstable.

Malicious nodes might try to fake trust levels for several reasons. One can try to slander a trustworthy node, to make other nodes believe that a specific malicious node can be trusted, or just to confuse other nodes. In order to minimize this effect, each node must define a maximum relationship maturity value M_{max}, which represents an upper bound for the relationship maturity. This value is based on the average time for which a node knows its neighbors. Accordingly, we can express $M_i(b)$ as

$$M_i(b) = \begin{cases} M_i(b), & \text{if } M_i(b) < M_{max} \\ M_{max}, & \text{if } M_i(b) \geq M_{max}. \end{cases} \tag{6}$$

2.3 Trust Level Updating

After assigning a trust level to a specific neighbor a node must be able to change it whenever an event triggers this change. Updating the trust level imply two different steps. First, a node must know when to change a certain trust level. Second, a node must define how to calculate the new value of trust level.

We consider that every update is triggered by an event, but the occurrence of an event does not imply an automatic trust level update. The definition of event consists of the reception of a new recommendation or an action performed by a neighbor. The second type of event, which is related to the actions performed by a neighbor, is the most difficult to evaluate.

We first define the trust level update as a sum of its own trust and the contribution of other nodes, in the same way as defined by Virendra et al. [5]. The fundamental equation is

$$T_a(b) = (1 - \alpha)Q_a(b) + \alpha C_a(b), \tag{7}$$

where α permits choosing the most relevant factor. The variable $Q_a(b)$ represents the capability of a node to evaluate the trust level of their neighbors based on its own information. In order to obtain $Q_a(b)$, we propose the following equation

$$Q_a(b) = \beta E_T + (1 - \beta)T_a(b), \tag{8}$$

where E_T represent the value obtained by the judgment of a neighbor actions, β allows choosing which is the factor more relevant at a given moment. It means that α depends on which event has triggered the trust level update. For example, supposing node a starts a trust level update about node b, triggered by a new recommendation from neighbor c, but node a has noticed nothing strange in the behavior of node b. Thus, node a can ignore the first factor of Equation 8.

2.4 Recommendation exchange protocol

The Recommendation Exchange Protocol (REP) includes three basic messages and is not mandatory for every node. Nodes can choose weather to use it or not according to their current goals and constrains. When two nodes first meet they can broadcast a Trust Request (TREQ) with TTL equals to 1. Accordingly, the TREQ will not be forwarded by its neighbors. The other nodes must answer TREQ with a Trust Reply (TREP) message after waiting for a random period of time t_{REP} to avoid collisions and to wait for receiving other TREQs. The TREP message contains the recommendation of a specific node. If the replying node has received more than one TREQ, it might choose between sending different unicast messages and sending a broadcast message with all the requested recommendations. A node might set a TREP threshold under which it will not answer the TREQ. The threshold is based on the trust level of the requesting node. Before sending a TREQ message, a node might wait for a specific period of time t_{REQ} trying to gather the maximum number of new neighbors. After t_{REQ}, the node will request the recommendations of all the q new neighbors it has collected. Thus, instead of sending q TREQ messages it will send just one with q node IDs.

After sending a TREQ, the trust requesting node will wait for a specific timeout period to receive the TREPs from its neighbors. If a node does not receive any TREP, it ignores the recommendation of its neighbors by choosing $\alpha = 1$ in Equation 7. The Trust Advertisement (TA) message is an unsolicited recommendation. A Node only send a TA message when the recommendation about a particular neighbor changes due to a reaction. Receiving a TA does not necessarily mean a recalculation of the trust level.

The recommendation includes the trust level for a particular node, its accuracy and for how long they know each other. For a node that does not implement the auxiliary trust table the recommendation includes just the trust level.

3 Results

This section presents the results and the main characteristics of the simulator we have implemented to evaluate the proposed scheme. In the simulator, each node has a particular nature which defines its behavior. The nature of a node ranges from 0 to 1. Most reliable nodes have nature equals to 1 while nodes not reliable have nature equals to 0.

All events that might happen with a node, like a route request not answered, a packet correctly forward, a useful information received, among others, are represented by "actions". Therefore, each node performs good actions or bad actions. Bad actions are represented by the value -1 and good actions by 1. Nodes perform actions according to an exponential distributed variable. The kind of action that will be performed depends solely on the nature of the node. A node with a nature equals to 0.8 means that it performs eight good actions out of ten.

Another important characteristic introduced in our simulator is the perception of a node. The perception indicates the probability of noticing a certain action. Therefore, a node with 0.4 of perception is able of noticing 40% of all the actions performed by its neighbors. This parameter simulates an interaction between the learning layer and the trust layer, since the perception and the judgment of an action is the responsibility of the Learning layer.

The term that considers the experiences of the own node in Equation 8 is calculated using the last i perceived actions. It implies the existence of a minimum number of actions i that a node must notice from each neighbor to be able of having an opinion about them, based on its own experience. This means that during the initial phase of first contact, nodes use just the recommendations of its neighbors to evaluate the trust level of the new one.

Each neighbor might assume three different conditions. When nodes have not yet identified the existence of each other, they consider each other as an "unknown" neighbor. Nodes sense the presence of each other upon the reception of a message or the perception of an action. From this moment on, neighbors are considered "acquaintance" until the first trust level is assigned. Meanwhile, the trust level of an acquaintance is set to -1.

Our main goal in this paper is to evaluate and analyze the influence of the number of neighbors, the first trust assignment strategy, and the variation of parameters α and perception. All results are presented with a confidence interval of 95%.

The simulation scenario consists of 16 nodes with 250 m transmission range, which are randomly placed in a 150 m × 150 m area. Under these circumstances, all nodes can communicate directly to each other, characterizing a single hop ad hoc network. We chose this scenario to make easier the evaluation of the effect of the basic parameters already mentioned. All nodes operate in the advanced mode, which means that they implement all the features of the proposed system. We defined three values for the first trust assignment: 0.1 for the prudent, 0.5 for the moderate, and 0.9 for the friendly/naive strategy, also called optimistic strategy. All nodes adopt the same strategy. We also chose $\alpha = \beta = perception = 0.5$. These are the standard values for the simulations. For each specific configuration, the parameters that differ from its standard values are outlined. At last, in each configuration, all nodes have the same nature.

Figure 1 presents the time response of the average trust level from all neighbors about a specific node. In this specific scenario, the simulation time is 6,000 seconds. We observe in Figure 1(a) that the trust level value begins in a certain level but tends to the expected trust level. The expected (correct) level is the nature of the node that is being analyzed. After a specific amount of time $t_1 \approx 5\text{min}$, the curve oscillates around the correct value. Thus, we verify the existence of a transient period and stationary period. In the transient period (Figure 1(a)), nodes are trying to approximate to the expected value, while in the stationary period, the trust level is almost stable, very close to the correct value, varying like a smoothed sine function.

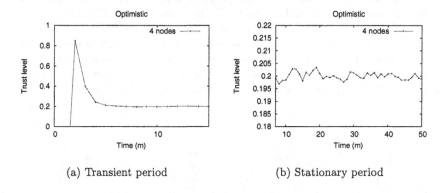

(a) Transient period   (b) Stationary period

Fig. 1. Variation of trust level during time.

In the other figures, instead of presenting the average trust level, we present the average error of the trust value evaluated, that is, the difference between the trust level and the correct value. At the end, the ideal result is a curve that reaches the value zero, which means that there is no error between the average trust values calculated by the neighbors and the value of the nature of the node.

In Figure 2, nodes adopt an optimistic strategy and we vary the number of neighbors. The nature is set to 0,2. We can notice that the greater is the number of neighbors the closer to zero is the error. It occurs due to the fact that augmenting the number of neighbors means increasing the number of recommendations, which implies a greater probability of receiving recommendations closer to the correct value.

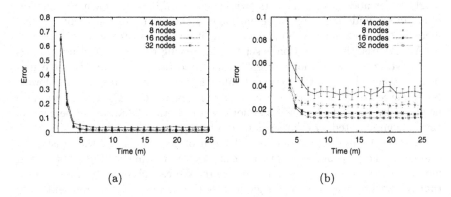

(a)   (b)

Fig. 2. Influence of the number of neighbors.

Figure 3 shows the influence of the parameter *alpha* on the trust level evaluation. Decreasing *alpha* implies that the contribution of other nodes has a minor effect in the trust level calculation. The first observation from Figure 3(a) is that the convergence to the correct value is faster with a higher *alpha*, namely, the transient is longer. Therefore, although the global opinion about a specific node changes slower when *alpha* is larger, the convergence value is closer to the expected one and presents a smaller variation, as shown by Figure 3(b).

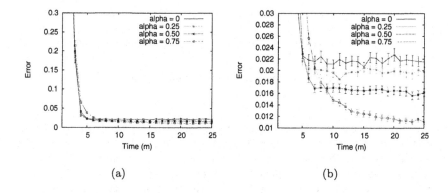

(a)   (b)

Fig. 3. The influence of *alpha*.

The perception is the fraction of actions a node can notice from its neighbors. Figure 4 shows the impact of the perception on the trust level evaluation. It is clear that the perception is strong related to the duration of the transient period. It occurs due to the existence of a minimum number of actions from each neighbor for nodes to consider its own experiences. If we augment the number of actions a node must notice before judging the nature of a neighbor, it will increase the precision of the judgment, but it will also increase the transient.

Afterwards, the perception is set to 0.2, varying the number of nodes. Figure 5 reveals that with a low perception the importance of the number of neighbors to reach closer to the expected value is clearer. It means that the lowest is the perception, the lowest is the probability of noticing the real nature of a neighbor by the judgment of its actions. On the other hand, a low perception can be compensated by a larger number of neighbors.

At last, Figure 6 presents the influence of the nature on the trust level evaluation. For this purpose, we set the strategy to optimistic (Figure 6(a)) and moderate (Figura 6(b)), varying the nature. We can observe, by Figure 6(a), that the nature does not affect significantly the duration of the transient, only the peak, according to the chosen strategy. On the other hand, Figure 6(b) shows that it is easier for nodes to find the correct value when the nature is in

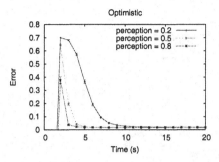

Fig. 4. The influence of perception.

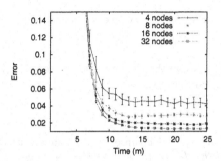

Fig. 5. Number of neighbors with a low perception.

the extremities. It happens because when a node produces the same amount of good and bad actions, the probability of sensing the exact proportion of good and bad actions decreases, considering that perception is less than 1.0.

4 Conclusion

In this paper, we propose a trust assignment model for ad hoc networks. We aim at building a trust relationship among nodes inspired by the human concept of trust. Our concern is different from other works that focus strictly on security issues. We focus on providing nodes a way of having an opinion about their neighbors. This opinion governs the interaction among nodes. The goal is to make nodes capable of making their own decisions based on the autonomic paradigm. The proposed model results in a utterly distributed trust system for ad hoc networks based on the recommendation of other nodes and on the own experiences of the nodes. Our approach considers not only the trust level but also its accuracy and the relationship maturity. We also define the Recommendation Exchange Protocol (REP) that allows nodes to exchange recommendations in an efficient way. The system performance is analyzed through

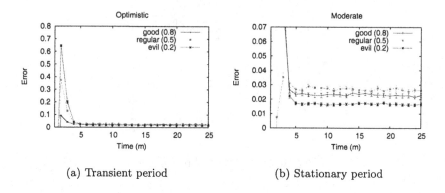

(a) Transient period   (b) Stationary period

Fig. 6. The influence of the nature.

simulations The results reveal the efficacy of the proposed system and show the influence of the main parameters.

References

1. Z. Liu, A. W. Joy, and R. A. Thompson, "A dynamic trust model for mobile ad hoc networks," in *IEEE International Workshop on Future Trends of Distributed Computing Systems (FTDCS'04)*, (Suzhou, Chine), May 2004.
2. Z. Yan, P. Zhang, and T. Virtanen, "Trust evaluation based security solution in ad hoc networks," in *Proceedings of the Seventh Nordic Workshop on Secure IT Systems, (NordSec'03)*, (GjÃ¸vik, Norway), Oct. 2003.
3. H. Deng, W. Li, and D. P. Agrawal, "Routing security in wireless ad hoc networks," *IEEE Communiations Magazine*, pp. 70–75, Oct. 2002.
4. A. A. Pirzada and C. McDonald, "Establishing trust in pure ad-hoc networks," in *Proceedings of 27th Australasian Computer Science Conference (ACSC'04)*, (Dunedin, New Zealand), Oct. 2004.
5. M. Virendra, M. Jadliwala, M. Chandrasekaran, and S. Upadhyaya, "Quantifying trust in mobile ad-hoc networks," in *Proceedings of IEEE International Conference on Integration of Knowledge Intensive Multi-Agent Systems (KIMAS'05)*, (Waltham, USA), Apr. 2005.
6. S. Buchegger and J.-Y. Le Boudec, "The effect of rumor spreading in reputation systems for mobile ad-hoc networks," in *Modeling and Optimization in Mobile, Ad Hoc and Wireless Networks (WiOpt03)*, (Sophia-Antipolis, France), Mar. 2003.
7. K. Ren, T. Li, Z. Wan, F. Bao, D. Robert H, and K. Kim, "Highly reliable trust establishment scheme in ad hoc networks," *Computer Networks*, vol. 45, no. 6, pp. 687–699, Aug. 2004.
8. G. Theodorakopoulos and J. S. Baras, "Trust evaluation in ad-hoc networks," in *Proceedings of the ACM Workshop on Wireless Security (WiSE'04)*, (Philadelphia, USA), Oct. 2004.

Privacy and Location-Aware Service Discovery for Mobile and Ubiquitous Systems

Leonardo Galicia Jiménez, J. Antonio García-Macías

Computer Science Department
CICESE Research Center
Ensenada, Baja California, México
{lgalicia, jagm}@cicese.mx

Abstract. Wireless networks play a major role in allowing the deployment of ubiquitous distributed systems. In these networks, service discovery should not only allow finding available networked services, but should also take into account the physical proximity of the entities requesting these services. However, physical proximity is not a sufficient criteria for service search and selection, as close attention should be paid to privacy issues. In this paper we present the design issues that should be considered in order to properly support service discovery based on the physical location of clients; these issues are taken into account for the proposal of an architecture for context-aware distributed systems that consider privacy concerns.

1. Introduction

As mobile technologies get cheaper and more widely available, demand for networked services has rapidly increased. Therefore, it is very important to provide users the possibility to find and make use of the services available in the network. Service discovery has been addressed by many commercial and academic entities and many proposals for solving related problems have been made, for instance SLP (Service Location Protocol) **Erreur ! Source du renvoi introuvable.**Jini [4] and UPnP (Universal Plug and Play) [5] However, some issues have been left out from these proposals, such as the selection of services based on their physical proximity; this particular issue is important because it is needed for supporting location-based and context-aware systems [3]

In order to support service discovery taking into account the physical location of the clients, it is necessary to have mechanisms to estimate this location and based on that search for the services. This type of search has the purpose of finding those entities –static or dynamic– that are within the space defined as proximal. Such entities can be devices or persons that the user wishes to interact with. However, when these mechanisms are used for finding persons, it is important to consider crucial factors related to the privacy of these persons. It is therefore of the utmost importance to include mechanisms that allow the protection of such privacy.

In this paper we present several aspects that need to be considered when designing systems that allow the discovery of services based on physical proximity; an

Please use the following format when citing this chapter:

Jiménez, L.G., García-Marcías, J.A., 2006, in IFIP International Federation for Information Processing, Volume 211, ed. Pujolle, G., Mobile and Wireless Communication Networks, (Boston: Springer), pp. 47–59.

architecture that includes these factors is presented and a proof-of-concept prototype is implemented. In section 2 we present an overview of some of the related work, and section 3 deals with the design issues for developing this architecture, taking into account experiences gathered in public health institutions; privacy is an important issue here. Then in section 4, the architecture and its main components are presented. Some functional tests for the architecture are presented in section 5. Finally, section 6 offers some concluding remarks and outlines future developments.

2. Related Work

Previous work has been made regarding the provision of user support in location-based services. However, most lack features to address privacy concerns and to minimize the client's devices in order to automatically access an available network infrastructure and related services. Also, they do not provide the means to control and filter responses to service discovery requests, according to who issues the requests.

Some of these previous works offer a class framework [11] on top of which applications can be developed; others present architectures [10] [12] oriented toward location-based services. Most of these proposals rely on notification of events to the client that registers to a given service; they also use different technologies such as CORBA, RMI, Java Messaging Service (JMS), or Publish/Subscriber mechanisms. Our approach is event-based using the instant messaging and presence awareness (IMPA) paradigm.

Perhaps the proposal that is the most closely related to ours is Splendor [16] . However, there are some notable differences: first, Splendor has provisions for locating users, but we go farther than that and closely integrate local mobility issues by providing representation of physical spaces, proximity models, and other aspects that will be detailed later; second, with our approach, services are extended beyond the traditional device-centric view and even persons can be represented as service providers, according to their role or currently enforced policies; third, we not only rely on technical schemes (e.g., public and private keys, etc.) to provide security and privacy, but also take into account administrative policies defined by the authorities (persons) within certain scopes; also, we base our work on accepted standards such as XMPP, SLP, IETF´s Geopriv, etc.

3. Design considerations

As previously stated, current proposals do not appropriately handle service selection based on their physical proximity, and so they do not support very well ubiquitous computing systems. Another important aspect left out by these proposals is privacy issues, which become particularly important when the discovered entities are persons. In this section we analyze these and other issues that should be considered for the design of systems that support service discovery based on physical proximity.

3.1 Local mobility

Some of the so called "knowledge workers" present a high degree of mobility in their daily activities. Local mobility refers to dynamic patterns of mobility that take place close to the worker's office, or even within a building, when a worker is carrying out her duties, collaborating with colleagues, etc. [1] A clear example of this is the kind of work performed in a hospital [7] [6] [9] as it involves a high degree of mobility of patients, equipment, resources and personnel within the hospital facilities.

3.2 Localization of artifacts and persons

In order to provide location-based service discovery, it is first necessary to have some mechanisms to estimate the location of artifacts and persons through some device. Usually, location of devices is basically categorized as device-centered and network-centered. The first one allows the device, through some mechanism, to estimate its own position; that is, it is only the device and no other which can estimate and know its physical location. Meanwhile, network-based mechanisms require that a different entity within the network perform the estimation of a device's physical location; this way, when a device want to know its location, it has to consult the entity in the network which is in charge of determining it. Some good examples of device-centered systems are RADAR [13] Cricket [14] and AeroScout[1]. In this type of systems the estimation is usually performed by a PDA, mobile phone, or some other type of mobile device. So, in some way the estimation is person-centered, as the devices are normally carried by persons; but only the device is fully in control of the calculations for determining the current position and if the device is turned off for some reason, the location can not be determined. Some examples of network-centered systems are Active Badge [15] Ubisense[2], and Exavera[3]. In these types of systems, objects and persons can carry small devices to aid the network in determining their location.

We think that the network-centered model is more appropriate for the type of scenarios that take place in hospitals, which are our focus for technological development. In a hospital environment some artifacts, such as wheelchairs, stretchers, portable EKG equipment, and others, are good candidates to be located. Moreover, the network-centered model allows the possibility of continuous tracking.

3.3 Representation of physical spaces

It is necessary to have a computational model to represent all those artifacts and persons that are moving within a physical space. This model should represent, at least, the physical space, the entities that move within it, as well as those that are static.

---

[1] http://www.aeroscout.com

[2] http://www.ubisense.com

[3] http://www.exavera.com

There are currently different models that allow the representation of physical spaces [12] including the geometric model, set theory, graphs, and the semantic model. The geometric model includes definitions based on Euclidian geometry, through coordinates in a Cartesian plane; this plane is a direct consequence of cartographic representation, where information and participating entities are superposed on maps, planes or images. The semantic model offers descriptive information about the geometric areas that represent physical spaces. Under these considerations, both the geometric and semantic models are appropriate for the requirements and technological needs identified in the type of environments that we are interested in (*i.e.*, hospitals). These models have been previously used in the projects and commercial systems mentioned above, namely Cricket, RADAR, Exavera, Ubisense and Radianse.

3.4 Proximity model

A fundamental concept for proximity-based service discovery is, not surprisingly, proximity. The key for a correct association between services and physical spaces is the geographical criterion to be used when services are searched based on their proximity. Two models are widely used for the selection of services: the distance-based model and the scope-based model. In the distance-based model, clients select the services that are within a certain distance from the current position. Given that proximity is a relative value and what is perceived as proximal can vary drastically according to the activities being performed by the client, some mechanism should be present to dynamically change the proximity range.

In a scope-based model, each service is associated with a scope that explicitly represents the context of use of the service within a physical space. The client selects those services whose scopes include the location of the requesting client; that is, a client can discover services if it is inside a certain scope, as well as the services. The main characteristic of this model is that the correlation between context and proximity is assured. When services are discovered, no matter what their distance, they have a high probability of being relevant for the requesting client.

We consider that the scope-based model better suits our needs, mainly because it allows the representation of physical sub-spaces as geometric shapes; this is very adequate for indoors environments such as hospitals where the definition of rooms, working areas, etc. is very useful.

3.5 Definition of services

A service is an entity that can be used by a person, a computer program, or any other entity [4] examples of services are files, a storage device, a printer, a server, etc. When service discovery is performed within a physical space or scope, it is not enough to know the available services, but also the persons within it, in order to be able to interact with them. Thus, it is convenient to consider artifacts and persons as services associated to a given scope; it should be noted that some of these entities will not strictly provide a service, but it is necessary to know their attributes (type, role, etc.), in order to know what kind of entities there are and where they are in a certain space.

3.6 User identification

In a ubiquitous computing environment, the search for services responds to contextual variables such as the location of the user and its identification. While the location allows obtaining those services near to the user, the identification allows the user to access them. This way, a user could make an anonymous request for available services within a scope and she may obtain a list of them, however, it could be possible that more services would exist; this is because some of those services may require additional information about the user (such as her role, an ID, etc.) in order to be possible to discover them. This way, services are discovered not only based on their location or proximity, but also based on who is requesting them.

3.7 Access control to location information

In spite of the benefits that ubiquitous computing environments offer, one of the main barriers for the adoption of related technologies is the privacy concerns of users. A clear example is shown in the results obtained by Intel Research Berkeley through a series of interviews and scenarios [7] where users manifested concerns regarding being located. Recently the IETF[4], through the Geopriv[5] working group, has been studying privacy issues that arise when the geographical information of people and resources is used. The focus of the group, as stated in their charter, is "to assess the authorization, integrity and privacy requirements that must be met in order to transfer such information, or authorize the release or representation of such information through an agent". Then, attention is paid to presence and geospatial information, commonly used in instant messaging systems, location-based services and others. Up to date, the Geopriv working group has generated a couple of RFCs (request for comments) and recommendations aimed at proposing a standard that guarantees the privacy of users. Much of this work is currently under review, but rules and mechanisms have already been defined (represented in XML formats); these control when, to whom, in what place, and under what circumstances geolocation information can be released. The Geopriv group uses formats and architectures previously approved by the IETF, for instance, XMPP (Extensible Messaging and Presence Protocol) or SIMPLE (SIP for Instant Messaging and Presence Leveraging Extensions).

The user should be able to define when (day and time), to whom, where (place), and under what circumstances (status of the user) location information can be released. The mechanisms for this are defined by the Geopriv group, and can be easily applied to artifacts, not for protecting their privacy as this would not make much

---

[4] http://www.ietf.org
[5] http://www.ietf.org/Geopriv

sense, but for extending service discovery and indicate who and under what circumstances can be discovered. This way, artifacts and persons (viewed more generally as services) can be discovered based not only on their location, but also taking into account who is requesting them.

4. An architecture for privacy and location-aware service discovery

Considering the issues presented in the preceding section, we have designed an architecture that allows the discovery and selection of services based on their physical location and considering privacy concerns. A key component for implementing a functional prototype incorporating the elements of this architecture is SALSA (Simple Agent Library for Seamless Applications). SALSA is a framework that provides a set of abstract classes and mechanisms for the development of autonomous agents that represent users and services [7] SALSA agents can be executed on PDAs, cell phones, servers, or any other computing device. XMPP (Extensible Messaging and Presence Protocol) is used for communication of XML messages between clients and servers (implemented with Jabber). Basically, a SALSA agent contains a Jabber server and a subsystem that implements the autonomous behavior of the agent. Many components are present in the agent: a protocol for registration in an agent directory; a Jabber client through which users, and agents representing users and services, interact via XML messages; and finally, a subsystem including components for perception, reasoning and actions.

We outline the main components of the proposed architecture:

- **Location system.** We assume the presence of a system that estimates the current location of entities on a physical space; we have previously given examples of these systems. Then, each entity (person or artifact) is represented as a SALSA object and gathers its (x,y) coordinates from the location estimation system; of course, this information may vary with time. Each SALSA agent representing an entity is autonomous and independent from others. Also, each agent resides in a centralized server.
- **Physical space server.** Physical spaces or areas of interest are geometrically represented through polygons. These have a semantic value for the user, such as a floor, a room, a department, etc. These polygons are centrally stored in an entity (the physical space server) which is responsible for translating from geometric coordinates to semantic values more understandable by the final user; so, in a way it acts similarly to a DNS server. The physical space server is represented by a SALSA agent that is loaded on a different computer than the location system. It is the main entity to be discovered by the rest of the system's entities, as without it the scope of the services is lost.
- **Policies generator.** We have previously discussed the importance of controlling the release of location information, and we have also mentioned the efforts of the IETF Geopriv group in this regard. The policy generator is the entity charged with presenting an interface for editing the policies that control when, where, and

who has the right to discover particular services. This entity can be on a mobile device for allowing editing policies for that device, or it can be centralized for editing the policies of a set of services.

- **Location server.** This server, contrary to the physical space server, is optional. The location server is an entity represented by a SALSA agent, and it has the purpose of containing information about the location of entities that subscribe to this server. When an entity requests a subscription it first gets validated, and after that it will periodically send location information to the server. During the validation process the entities indicate the policies that will restrict access from non-authorized entities. The location server has two auxiliary components: a policy container and a location container. The first one serves as a temporary storage for policies that are sent during the subscription process. The second one stores, information about the location of an entity (which is periodically updated).
- **General purpose SALSA agents.** In the SALSA framework, agents can represent services, devices, and users. Thus, any entity represented by an agent can potentially search for services. A SALSA agent can reside in a user's computer and perform a service search, consume location information from other entities, or have an associated scope and receive requests for service discoveries.

4.1 Control policies for service discovery

These policies are inspired mainly by RFC 3669 of the Geopriv working group, as well as by the policy and common policy working drafts of that same group. RFC 3669 deals with the authorization, integrity and privacy involved in releasing information about the location of users. The Geopriv group is currently exploring how to represent information about location and presence, as well as how to protect this information.

In its Common Policy draft, the Geopriv group defines the base mechanisms for delivering location information in presence messages; these mechanisms, which allow access control form information regarding presence and location of users, can be extended and translated easily to other application domains. These mechanisms define an XML document (figure 1) that represents policies associated to an entity. Requests from entities contain policy rules, and these are checked against the policies defined in the entity that receives the request; if one or more of the rules match, then the location and presence information are released, else it is denied. Each rule is composed by three sections: conditions, actions, and transformations. The conditions section defines all the restrictions that should be satisfied by an entity in order for it to obtain the requested information. The actions section is a set of processes that the user requests to an entity to perform; these actions have not been defined by Geopriv and are meant to be defined at the application (and not at the user) level. The transformation section indicates those modifications that should be made to the location information before being released. For instance, even if a user complies with all the rules imposed by an entity, a transformation could be imposed to reduce the precision of the geographic location, or to indicate the floor where the entity is located but without saying in what room it is. These mechanisms are used on our proposed architecture.

```
<rule id="f3g44r1">
    <conditions>
        <identity>
            <id>bob@example.com</id>
        </identity>
        <validity>
            <from>2003-12-24</from>
            <to>2003-12-24</to>
        </validity>
    </conditions>
    <actions/>
</rule>
```

Figure 1. XML document showing a rule with the conditions section defined by the Geopriv working group.

4.2 Discovery of the Jabber server

The proposed architecture utilizes a IMPA (Instant Messaging and Presence Awareness) paradigm, so for implementation purposes we used a Jabber system. In fact, the SALSA framework relies on Jabber, so each SALSA agent should have a Jabber identifier and normally has to be manually configured to indicate to which server it will connect. This last point goes against the idea of automatic service discovery. With this in mind, our architecture incorporates the SLP API so SALSA agents can automatically be configured to find the Jabber server to which they should connect. Although other service discovery protocols could have been used, we think that SLP offers an important advantage: it allows the integration with DHCP; this means that a device can automatically send a request to a DHCP server and obtain not only the network parameters for autoconfiguration, but also the information regarding the SLP server to which it should connect.

4.3 Interaction of components

When an architectural component is initialized it sends a multicast request for a SLP server. Once this server is located, the component locates the Jabber server to which it should connect. Then, the SALSA agent representing the component is initialized. The first interaction of a SALSA agent is made with the physical space server in order to obtain all the spaces that it contains. This way, the agent can determine to which space it belongs and can be associated to a certain scope. As its (x,y) coordinates change with time, the agent can detect these changes and translate them to semantic values, meaning that it can determine at all times to which scope it is associated. The scopes have an associated identifier which is also used for joining conference rooms in the Jabber server. This way, all agents within the same scope are also present in the same conference room. A consequence of this design feature is that service discovery is greatly simplified, as all involved messages are sent to only one conference room (and to all agents within it), and not to all services system-wide.

There are also other characteristics of conference rooms that motivated their use in this architecture. One is that every time that a Jabber entity enters a conference room, a presence message is sent to all entities participating in that room. Likewise, when an entity leaves a room, all entities are notified of it. These way, all SALSA agents within a conference room are aware at all times of which other entities are within a conference room (which in turn represents a scope), guaranteeing the integrity of services within a scope. Another characteristic is that every time a Jabber entity enters a conference room, it enters with a pseudonym, and not with its Jabber-ID. This means that the Jabber-ID for an agent will not be disclosed, thus allowing for complete anonymity. Of course, when an agent leaves one room and enters another, its pseudonym also changes.

4.4 Service discovery

Once a SALSA agent is aware of its scope, and once it is associated to a conference room, it is capable of discovering other agents (representing entities) within that scope. The discovery process can be performed in a proactive or reactive way. When performed proactively, each time a SALSA agent detects that a new entity has entered the room it requests to know the service(s) associated to that entity and this information is stored in its cache. When the entity leaves the room, the SALSA agent eliminates the information from its cache. On the other hand, with a reactive approach, an explicit request for a list of the entities in a room is made. This list reflects the entities present at the time when the request is made, and for each entity the SALSA agent can request its associated services. No matter what method (proactive or reactive) is used, the mechanism for service discovery works in the same way (figure 2). Each SALSA agent has a discovery policy, and when a service discovery request is made, the SALSA agent issuing the request can either provide its Jabber-ID or make an anonymous request (providing "anonymous" as its identifier).

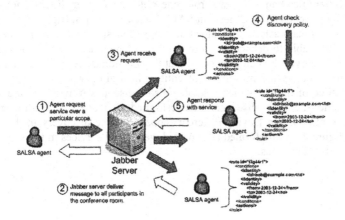

Figure 2. Service discovery mechanism within a certain scope, represented by a Jabber conference room.

5 Functional tests

The proposed architecture is supported by two key elements: the physical space server and the location server. The physical space server, the location server, the mechanisms for service discovery, as well as the policies for this discovery, have all been implemented by extending the SALSA framework. However, we have left out the implementation of the location estimation subsystem to third parties, in order to provide more flexibility; the only restriction here is to obtain standard (x,y) geographic coordinates.

For the purpose of testing the functionality of our architecture, we implemented a prototype. The SALSA agents of this prototype were given (x,y) coordinates from a simulator, which simulated the random movement of entities within a predefined physical space. We then conducted functional tests in order to determine the differences between the functional requirements and the actual system. These functional requirements are derived from the design considerations presented in section 3. For the evaluation of these functional requirements we used the following configuration:

5.1 Location system

The location system implemented is able to run a number of independent SALSA agents. These agents were assigned a random lifetime between 10 and 60 minutes. Likewise, random services are defined between five predefined ones: doctor, patient, nurse, assistant, and artifact. The location system used a uniform distribution to randomly assign (x,y) coordinates each second, taking care of making continuous movements (entities can not jump from one point to another distant one). For the tests, 40 simultaneous and independent SALSA agents were run (figure 3).

We observed that each SALSA agent determined its space from the physical space server, and was able to deduce its corresponding scope. Also, each agent subscribed to the location server. It should be noted that the location server provided a graphical interface to visualize the movement of entities in a simulated 2-D physical space during the time of the simulation, showing also the scopes were the entities are and their interactions. Service discovery was performed proactively for each agent in the simulation, entering and leaving different scopes. Service discovery in the scenario shown in figure 2 was performed as expected, getting all services in the scope during intervals of 0 to 2 seconds.

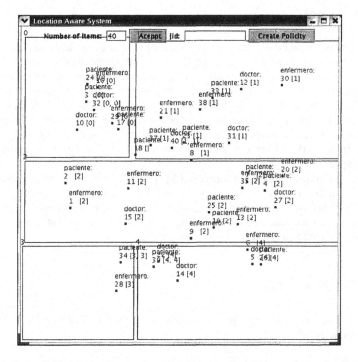

Figure 3. Forty SALSA agents moving simultaneously within a given physical space. Each point represents a mobile SALSA agent identified by a number from 1 to 40. Numbers between braces represent the current scope of the agent. The physical space is divided in fives scopes named from 0 to 4. They represent rooms, divisions, etc.

5.2 Physical space server

Five scopes (figure 2) were defined arbitrarily as regular geometric shapes through the physical space server. For the determination of the scope to which a SALSA agent belongs, and taking into account (total or partial) intersections between scopes, the prototype implemented R-trees [2] The evaluation platform was developed using Java2 SE, a Jabber v2.2 Jive Jive Messenger[6] on a Pentium II computer running Linux RedHat v2.4.20-8, and of course using the SALSA framework.

---

[6] http://www.jivesoftware.com

6. Conclusions

We have presented the design considerations that should be taken into account for the design of ubiquitous distributed applications that allow the discovery of service based on their physical proximity and considering important privacy concerns. These considerations were modulated by the requirements of ubiquitous computing applications to be used in public health facilities such as hospitals. With these design considerations, an architecture was proposed and later evaluated through the development of a functional prototype. This prototype uses an extension of the SALSA framework, which defines autonomous agents that represent entities in a physical space.

The use of privacy policies, as proposed by the IETF Geopriv working group, were applied in order to restrict the way in which services are discovered and the potentially sensitive information is disclosed. Even if the proposed architecture supposes a network-centered model for the location of persons and artifacts, it can easily be extended to adopt a device-centered model.

Acknowledgements

Financial support for this project was provided by the Mexican Council for Science and Technology (CONACyT).

References

[1]   Belloti, V., and S. Bly. Walking Away from the Desktop Computer: Distributed Collaboration and Mobility in a Product Design Team. In Proceedings of CSCW, ACM Press. 209-218 p. (1996).

[2]   Guttman, A. R-trees: A dynamic index structure for spatial searching. ACM SIGMOD Conference on Management of Data, 47-57 p. (1984).

[3]   Hodes, T., Katz, R., Servan-Schreiber, E. and Rowe, L. Composable ad-hoc Mobile Services for Universal Interaction. In Third ACM/IEEE International Conference on Mobile Computing. 1-12 p. (1997).

[4]   Johansen, T. Jini Architectural Overview. White Paper Sun Microsystem. (1999).

[5]   Microsoft Corporation, Universal Plug and Play Device Architecture Reference Specification, Version 1.0. Technical report. Microsoft Corporation.

[6]   Muñoz, M., Rodriguez, M., Favela, J., Gonzalez, V.M., and Martinez-Garcia, A.I. Context-aware mobile communication in hospitals. IEEE Computer. 36(8):60-67 p. (2003).

[7]   Barkhuus, L., and Anind D. Location-Based Services for Mobile Telephony: a study of users' privacy concerns. INTERACT 2003, 9th IFIP TC13 International Conference on Human-Computer Interaction. (2003).

[8]   Rodríguez, M., and   Favela, J. Autonomous Agents to Support Interoperability and Physical Integration in Pervasive Environments. Atlantic Web Intelligence Conference, AWIC 2003, Springer-Verlag. 278-287 p. (2003).

[9]   Santana, P., Castro, L.A., Preciado, A., Gonzalez, V.M., Rodríguez, M. D. and Favela, J. Preliminary Evaluation of Ubicomp in Real Working Scenarios. 2nd Workshop on Multi-User and Ubiquitous User Interfaces (MU3I). (2005).

[10]   Chen, X., Chen, Y. and Rao, F. An efficient spatial publish/subscribe system for intelligent location-based services, Proceedings of the 2nd international workshop on Distributed event-based systems. (2003).

[11]   Coulouris, G., Naguib, H. and Sanmugalingam, K. FLAME: An Open Application Framework for Location-Aware Systems, UbiComp Adjunct Proceedings. (2002).

[12]   José, R., Moreira, A., Rodrigues, H., and Davies, N. The AROUND architecture for dynamic location-based services. Mobile Networks and Applications. 4(8): 377-387 p. (2003).

[13]   Bahl P. and V.N. Padmanabhan, RADAR: An In-Building RF-Based User Location and Tracking System, IEEE INFOCOM, Vol. 2, Tel-Aviv, Israel (March 2000), pages 775-784. (2000).

[14]   Nissanka B. Priyantha, Anit Chakraborty, and Hari Balakrishnan. The cricket location-support system. In Proceedings of MOBICOM, pages32-43, Boston, MA. (2000).

[15]   R. Want et al., The Active Badge Location System, ACM Trans. Information Systems, pp. 91-102. (1992).

[16]   Zhu, F. et al., Splendor: A Secure, Private, and Location-Aware Service Discovery Protocol Supporting Mobile Services. In Proceedings of the First IEEE international Conference on Pervasive Computing and Communications, p 235. (2003).

An Adaptive Approach to Service Discovery in Ad Hoc Networks

Carlos Henrique Pereira Augusto and José Ferreira de Rezende

Grupo de Teleinformática e Automação - PEE - COPPE
Universidade Federal do Rio de Janeiro (UFRJ)
{chenrique,rezende}@gta.ufrj.br

Abstract. Service discovery allows the interaction between network nodes to cooperate in activities or to share resources in client-server, multi-layer, as well as in peer-to-peer architectures. Ad hoc networks pose a great challenge in the design of efficient mechanisms for service discovery. The lack of infrastructure along with node mobility makes it difficult to build robust, scalable and secure mechanisms for ad hoc networks. This paper proposes a scalable service discovery architecture based on directory nodes organized in an overlay network. In the proposed architecture, directory nodes are dynamically created with the aim of uniformly covering the entire network while decreasing the query latency for a service (QoS) and the number of control messages for the sake of increased scalability.

1 Introduction

Ad hoc networks are characterized by the lack of infrastructure and spontaneous topologies. This complicates the use of previous configured and specific servers to perform service discovery, as occurs when a DNS server is used. In addition, the use of directory servers, such as LDAP or X.500, is not a simple task in an infrastructureless environment. Some solutions are available for service discovery in wired networks, such as SLP[1], Jini[2] and Upnp[3]. However, they assume the existence of special nodes acting as servers.

Nonetheless, there are proposals for wired networks and Internet that do not rely on specific servers, and are already used in Peer-to-Peer (P2P) environments. Researches are being performed in these environments, which present great challenges in scalability and dynamic behavior. Some proposals are Pastry[4], Tapestry[5], CAN[6], Chord[7] and Symphony[8], and there are some successful applications, such as Gnutella[9] and JXTA[10]. However, in P2P, scalability indicates from thousands to millions of nodes, and dynamic behavior refers to the ingress and egress of nodes in the network in a timescale from minutes to hours of sojourn without changing of location.

In contrast, ad hoc networks, due to their lack of infrastructure and scarcity of resources, present scaling challenges to attain a few hundreds of nodes collaborating in an efficient way. Further, dynamic behavior is replaced by mobility that leads to link breakages and even network partition.

Please use the following format when citing this chapter:

Augusto, C.H.P., de Rezende, J.F., 2006, in IFIP International Federation for Information Processing, Volume 211, ed. Pujolle, G., Mobile and Wireless Communication Networks, (Boston: Springer), pp. 61–75.

This paper proposes a mechanism to service discovery in ad hoc networks, using concepts of P2P networks. However, it is not made a direct use of a P2P solution in ad hoc network due to their distinct scope. The proposed architecture makes use of three abstractions planes: the real ad hoc network; the overlay network, composed of directory nodes only; and the service table ring.

This paper presents the general design concepts involved in the proposal, and details and evaluates the first abstraction plane and the mechanism of construction of second plane. The reminder of the paper is organized as follows. Section 2 presents related works, firstly in P2P and after in ad hoc networks. Section 3 makes a theoretical description of the proposal. In Section 4, an analytical model for the second plane construction is presented. Section 5 discusses implementation details of first and second planes, and present some simulation and analytical results. Finally, the Section 6 draws conclusions and discusses the future of this work.

2 Related Works

This section presents some works related to the proposal presented in this paper. Firstly, a brief overview of service discovery schemes used in P2P architectures are presented with the purpose of clarifying some design choices made in this proposal. Next, we describe some service discovery schemes specially tailored to mobile ad hoc networks (MANETs).

2.1 In P2P

In P2P systems, such as Chord [7], Symphony [8], CAN [6], Pastry [4], and Tapestry [5], a service or resource description is hashed to a key that is used in the lookup for that particular service or resource. The ownership of the keys, i.e. the responsibility over the location of the associated services, is partitioned among participating nodes using the concept of DHT (Distributed Hash Table). In these systems, when a query is issued, it is routed through an overlay network formed by the DHT nodes to the node responsible for that key. The geometry structure of the overlay network, i.e. the DHT nodes organization, is the key difference between the existing proposals. In Chord and Symphony, nodes are organized in a virtual ring. Pastry and Tapestry maintain a tree-like data structure, and CAN uses a d-dimensional Cartesian coordinate.

Therefore, a great challenge is how to distribute keys, consistently and efficiently, among the nodes of the network. In Chord and Symphony, each node should have at least the knowledge about its successor and predecessor nodes in the ring. However, a query using only this information may cause a circular search in the entire ring. A lookup should traverse on average $N/2$ nodes when random variables are uniformly distributed and N is the number of DHT nodes.

Chord[7] creates connections between nodes nearly located to the $N/2$, $N/4$, $N/8$ positions of the ring in order to diminish the search space. These connections enable jumps in the ring, and decrease the search space to $O(logN)$, making the query more efficient. However, when there are many ingress and egress of nodes in the network, the cost associated to the management of these connections largely increases.

Alternatively, Symphony[8] proposes the establishment of random connections, using a probability distribution function in a similar way of the small-world Kleinberg's work[11]. Since there is no need of recalculating ring fractions when nodes ingress or egress to the network, the overhead cost due to a dynamic behavior does not increase.

2.2 In Ad Hoc Networks

In this subsection, we describe some proposals for service discovery in ad hoc networks. These works are organized in two types, the ones that are independent of ad hoc routing protocols being used and the ones that rely on a specific routing protocol with the purpose of improving scalability.

Independent of Routing Protocol In [12], it is proposed Nom, where clients actively flood the network with service query messages that are handled by passive servers. This approach is normally referred as *pull method*. In opposition to this method, there is the *push method*, where servers broadcast service advertisements, and clients cache it for later invocation. It is possible to merge these two methods in a hybrid one, where both, servers and clients, participate actively, advertising or registering their services, or sending queries, respectively.

The Card proposal[13] uses *small world* concepts to establish long-range contacts in the ad hoc network. However, since it has not any location mechanism, contacts are established in a random way, contradicting the Kleinberg work[11]. Further, it requires a routing protocol that permits to know an H-hops neighborhood of a node.

[14] can be classified as orthogonal to the above approaches, since it does not rely on any routing protocol, but still can use cross-layer mechanisms to enhance performance and scalability. It models each server instance as an electrostatic charge that produces a field in the network, and it models each query message as a charge with inverse polarity that is attracted to the service by the field gradient. However, for the field information to be propagated to every node, it needs a network flooding, as in the *push method*. A proposed solution to this problem [14] is to cache information in intermediate nodes. However, this solution is only effective when multiple instances of the same service exist. Considering that a network can make available several distinct services, there will be a field value to each service type. Further, some services, such as file sharing or Web Services, require the announcement of file name descriptions, what leads to a large increase in the service per node ratio.

In [15], despite it has been classified as independent, the mechanism strongly uses typical OLSR protocol information, such as MultiPoint Relays (MPR) selection, to perform a two-hops bordercast, making it more complex to be implemented with another routing protocol. This restriction is in part overcome by the use of an overlay network. Applying a typical concept from P2P networks, some nodes are elected as directory nodes, which are responsible for services registering. Thus, queries are driven to them, which will answer the queries, acting as super peers.

Routing Protocol Dependent A good option in terms of scalability for service discovery in ad hoc networks is the use of routing protocol functions. The main reason is the similarity between both tasks. In this approach, register and query messages may be piggybacked on control messages of the routing protocol or may be routed through paths expressly maintained by the routing protocol for service discovery. However, the main distinction between these tasks is that in service discovery the search is not univocal as in routing, i.e. service discovery aims to find some of the available instances of queried services. In addition, there is no need to find the best path to these instances, since this task is lately achieved by the routing protocol.

In [16], service queries are piggybacked on route discoveries launched by the AODV routing protocol. In [17], it is proposed the Konark protocol to service discovery and delivery, where services are described through XML, increasing the flexibility. However, the discovery process is dependent on a previously established multicast tree in the ad hoc network.

3 Proposed Architecture

In this section, it is made a brief description of the entire service discovery architecture proposed in this work. The design of this architecture is influenced by the following evaluation of work presented in [14]. The average sending rate of control traffic per node ($NrMsg/(node \times s)$) has a linear increase with the number of service instances (see Figure 2(a)). Therefore:

$$NrMsg/(node \times s) = O(Nrofservers) \qquad (1)$$

Considering that the number of service providers is a constant ratio of the nodes in the network, i.e. $Nrofservers = K \times Nrofnodes$, then:

$$NrMsg/(node \times s) = O(K \times Nrofnodes) = O(Nrofnodes) \qquad (2)$$

This implies a scalability constraint. Further, for some service types, according to considerations in Section 2.2, one can have a high number of services per node ratio. This claim supports the use of an overlay network and suggests the use of a single service type - the directory node service - in a similar way of the proposal in [15]. An advantage of directory nodes adoption is the multiple answer possibility. If there are several service instances, the directory node can answer with all possible instances, leaving to the client the choice of the more adequate one.

In this model, a service query must arrive at a directory node, which will answer or forward this query to another node in the directory nodes overlay network. This mechanism assumes that each client node has knowledge of at least one directory node, and that each directory node has knowledge of other directory nodes to forward messages to them.

Our proposal avoids flooding the whole network with control messages. Each directory node floods their neighborhood for H hops, so that every node within this neighborhood has knowledge about its existence. Then, each node computes the field contribution of this directory node, which is the charge announced by this directory node divided by the hop distance from it. The messages used to this purpose are called announcement messages.

In a similar way of the work in [14], each node computes a sum of all contributions of all those directory nodes that advertise to it. This sum is inserted in a hello message and sent to 1-hop neighbors. When there is a query or subscribe message needing to be forwarded, each node sends it to its neighbor that has the highest contribution value advertised. This way, this message follows the gradient to the target, such as in an anycast routing.

However, directory nodes should provide a full coverage of the network and maintain a certain degree of connectivity between them in the overlay network. Otherwise, some client nodes will not be able to send their queries. In our proposal, common nodes within uncovered areas (or with small contributions) should get promoted to directory nodes. We choose to call this procedure as *promotion process* to differ from an election process as performed in the proposal in [15]. Our promotion process does not require the exchange of extra messages to this purpose and each node makes a local decision. Further, the process is adaptive in the sense that it seeks to uniformly cover the entire network with a limited number of directory nodes, as proved in Section 4.

Nodes may establish a willingness to be promoted, which could be set by configuration or according to the residual energy, processing power, mobility, or interest of the node (e.g., a node with a large number of services). In the promotion process, the node willingness affects the window time within which a random value is chosen. At the end of this random time, the node verifies whether an announcement message was received from other nodes. Otherwise, it becomes a directory node. Nodes that are not willing to become directory nodes should wait for larger times. In our initial implementation, we did not make any distinction between nodes willingness.

Each directory node keeps two tables, namely the virtual neighbors table and the service table. The first one is composed by neighbors in the overlay network, and is maintained through the reception of announcement messages. This table is used to forward queries that a directory node cannot answer in a similar process used in P2P network solutions. The service table maintains the services registered in the directory nodes by the service providers. The distribution of the service table is made through a simplification of the proposal in [8], which is explained below.

By these definitions, the proposed architecture has three planes of abstraction. First, the real ad hoc network composed by nodes in a topographic distribution. Second, the overlay network composed by a subset of the nodes, i.e.

directory nodes. Finally, the DHT ring. Using the idea presented in [8], this ring is divided in: sectorial communities, or directory nodes into the same ring sector that keep the same DHT fragment; ring neighborhood, between nodes of adjacent sectors; and the long-range contacts that are nodes from far sectors used to aid in the ring search. However, this long-range contacts are also virtual neighbors in the overlay network, and, hence, they are H hops neighbors in the first abstraction plane, i.e. the real network.

Service providers must subscribe their services in a directory node using registering messages, which are also forwarded by field gradient. So, a service is subscribed in a directory by proximity. However, with DHT utilization an associated entry must be inserted in directory nodes of the corresponding sector. Then, the directory node, upon the reception of a subscribe request, must forward it to nodes in the adequate sector, using the procedure in [8], but keeping a local cache to make easier a local search. Therefore, each directory node keeps two service tables: a sector services table and a neighborhood services table.

Directory nodes must know their virtual neighbors and their respective sectorial community in the ring. Selective flooding in the overlay network is used to this purpose. Note that this network has much fewer nodes than the real network. Thus, flooding can be performed by unicast messages exchanged between directory nodes. All tables maintained by directory nodes are soft-state.

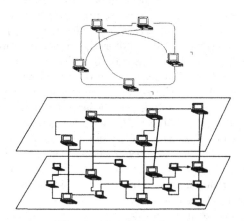

Fig. 1. Abstraction layers

These three network planes can be seen in Figure 1, where the real network is the bottom plane. The middle plane is the overlay network that is composed by directory nodes only, in this example they are named A, B, C, D and E. In the higher plane is the DHT ring, where the nodes are arranged according to a sector sequence. However, they establish long-range contacts as reported in [8], but these long-range contacts are only created when these nodes are virtual neighbors in the second plane. For example, the A-C link in the ring is created because there is a virtual neighborhood between A and C in the overlay network, since these nodes are H-hops neighbors in the first plane.

4 Analytical model

This section presents an analytical model for the process of directory nodes promotion, which is used to construct the overlay network. This model uses parameters of the network and table 1 presents the adopted notation. The network topology is modeled as a circular area.

Table 1. Adopted notation for directory nodes distribution

N	total number of nodes
R	network radius
$A = \pi R^2$	network area
$\delta = \frac{N}{A}$	density
r	transmission range radius
H	TTL of DN flooding
Nv_H	number of H hops neighbors
N_{DN}	total number of directory nodes
$\delta_{DN} = \frac{N_{DN}}{A}$	directory nodes density
$f(\delta, H, r)$	average area of H hops neighborhood of a node
Tx	rate of announcement messages per second sent by a DN

Considering that directory nodes are uniformly distributed in the network, we can assume that DN is a random variable with binomial distribution expressed by:

$$P(x = k) = \binom{n}{k} p^k (1 - p)^{n-k} \tag{3}$$

where p is the probability of a node to be a directory node, that is equal to $\frac{N_{DN}}{N}$, k is the number of directory nodes (N_{DN}) and n is the total number of nodes (N) in the area. Considering as a sample the number of nodes distributed in an area of H hops, the average number of nodes in this sample is:

$$Nv_H = f(\delta, H, r) \times \delta = f(\delta, H, r) \times \frac{N}{\pi R^2} \tag{4}$$

By letting $k = 0$, we have the probability that there is not any DN in the H-hops neighborhood of a node:

$$P(x = 0) = (1 - \frac{N_{DN}}{N})^{Nv_H} \tag{5}$$

However, if a node has not encountered a DN within its H-hops neighborhood, it must launch a promotion process. Assuming that the mechanism converges, we should not have other nodes being promoted, then:

$$(1 - \frac{N_{DN}}{N})^N v_H \times N < 1 \tag{6}$$

Solving this inequality:

$$N_{DN} > N(1 - (\frac{1}{N})^{\frac{1}{N v_H}}) \tag{7}$$

In this case, we have less than one node without DN in its H-hops neighborhood, and no more promotions should occur. Then, this equation gives a close approximation of the number of DN nodes in the network. Each DN sends Tx messages per second, and they are forwarded by each $H - 1$ hops neighbors. Then, the total announcement messages transmitted per second is:

$$AnnouncementMsg/s = (N(1 - (\frac{1}{N})^{\frac{1}{N v_H}}) \times Tx \times \delta \times f(\delta, H - 1, r) \tag{8}$$

Substituting (4) and δ:

$$AnnouncementMsg/(s \times N) = f(\delta, H-1, r) \times Tx \times \frac{N}{\pi R^2} \times (1-(\frac{1}{N})^{\frac{1}{f(\delta, H, r) \times \frac{N}{\pi R^2}}})) \tag{9}$$

Since we can prove that:

$$\lim_{N \to \infty} \frac{N \times (1 - (\frac{1}{N})^{\frac{k}{N}})}{Ln(N)} = k \tag{10}$$

Then, $AnnouncementMsg/(s \times N) = O(Ln(N))$, and for high values of N:

$$AnnouncementMsg/(s \times N) = \frac{f(\delta, H - 1, r)}{f(\delta, H, r)} \times Ln(N) \times Tx \tag{11}$$

and

$$N_{DN} = \frac{\pi R^2}{f(\delta, H, r)} \times Ln(N) \tag{12}$$

To estimate the area given by $f(\delta, H, r)$ observe that its maximum value occurs when the nodes are in the border of the transmission range (r). Then:

$$f(\delta, H, r) = \pi(rH)^2 \tag{13}$$

On the other hand, we can consider as an inferior limit to $f(\delta, H, r)$ when the nodes are placed in $\frac{r}{2} + dr$. Despite this is not being the worst case, we can admit this as an inferior limit to $f(\delta, H, r)$ in a network with a random distribution and a density not too small. Then:

$$f(\delta, H, r) = \pi(\frac{r}{2}H)^2 \tag{14}$$

Using the maximum value for f and $H > 1$:

$$AnnouncementMsg/(s \times N) = \frac{(H-1)^2 r^2}{R^2} \times N \times (1 - (\frac{1}{N})^{\frac{R^2}{NH^2 r^2}}) \times Tx \quad (15)$$

And, for large N, we have:

$$AnnouncementMsg/(s \times N) = \frac{(H-1)^2}{H^2} \times Ln(N) \times Tx \quad (16)$$

To obtain the total number of control messages in the first plane, to these announcement messages should be added the hello messages sent by all nodes at a Tx rate.

The N_{DN} is more dependent on $f(\delta, H, r)$, but it can be approximated by:

$$N_{DN} = \frac{R^2}{r^2 H^2} \times Ln(N) \quad (17)$$

In (16) and (17) the product $H \times r$ cannot be much higher than R since not the network is entirely flooded. In this case, these fractions should be replaced by 1.

5 Performance Evaluation

We use the ns-2 simulator, version 2.29, to evaluate our architecture. We made two implementations, both using IEEE 802.11 standard at MAC layer configured with its default parameters. The first one is equivalent to the proposal in [14]. Using this implementation, we obtain similar results to the original work in the same scenario of 1300×1500 meters, 100 nodes, 10 clients sending 4 queries per second, random way point mobility with velocity up to 20m/s without pause and 1000 seconds of simulation.

With this specification, we have the following values applicable to our analytical model:

Table 2. Values used in simulations

$N \ = 100 \ nodes$
$A \ = 1300 \times 1500 = 1950000 \ m^2 = 1.95 \ km^2$
$\delta \ = 51.28 \ nodes/km^2$
$r \ = 250 \ m$
$Tx = 1 \ message/5s = 0.2 \ messages/s$

In addition, we run some other simulations with different scenarios to understand the detailed behavior of this mechanism. We used a simulation time of 200 seconds with clients sending queries after an initial convergence time, estimated in 16 seconds, when DNs get promoted and state tables are constructed. Figures 2(a), 2(b) and 3 show the overhead imposed by control messages, the discovery success rate and the average response time when the number of service instances is varied, respectively. The discovery success rate is the ratio of the number of service query messages that arrive at directory nodes to the total number of query messages sent. The control message overhead is measured as the sending rate of control messages per node. Finally, the average response time is the time interval between sending a query message and receiving it at directory nodes or service instances. This metric is different from search time, which must include the transmission in the overlay network plus the latency of the query response to the requesting node.

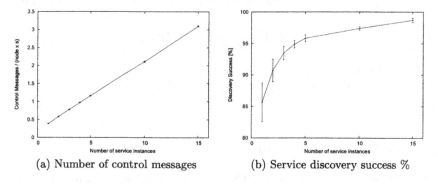

(a) Number of control messages   (b) Service discovery success %

Fig. 2. Control messages overhead and discovery success rate per service instances

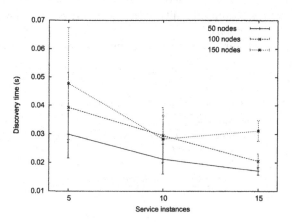

Fig. 3. Average response time

These curves show that their proposal suffers with the decrease of the number of service instances, presenting a smaller service discovery rate with a greater confidence interval. Therefore, we conclude that the proposal in [14] has a better performance to a specific number of service instances/nodes ratio. If the number of instances is too low, the efficiency in service discovery decreases. Otherwise, if it is high, there is a large increase in network overload. This happens even when the mechanism of flooding reduction (cache information in intermediate nodes) is used. In this case, the number of messages is limited but the number of overhead bytes increases linearly to the number of service instances.

The second implementation applies to our architecture. In this implementation the flooding control is made by a time to live (ttl) in each packet, as H variable of analytical model, which defines a flooding area. The same performance metrics defined above are evaluated.

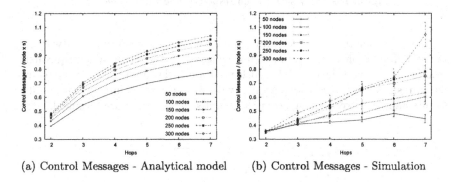

(a) Control Messages - Analytical model   (b) Control Messages - Simulation

Fig. 4. Analytical and simulation results

In the first simulations, we used the same parameters of table 2, but without mobility and varying the number of nodes (N). The control message overhead obtained by the analytical model and simulations are presented in Figures 4(a) and 4(b), respectively. The correspondence between the results demonstrates the effectiveness of our analytical model.

In the same simulations we obtained the two other metrics, discovery success rate and average response time, shown in Figures 5(a) and 5(b). These figures show that the first plane of our architecture presents coherent values, when compared to Figures 3 and 2(b), in a scenario without mobility.

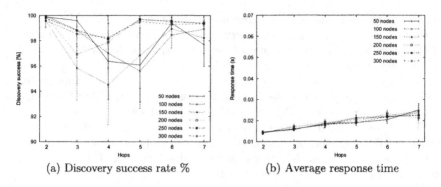

(a) Discovery success rate %   (b) Average response time

Fig. 5. Discovery success and response time without mobility

In second simulation runs, we evaluate geometrical aspect of the network. In the first simulations, we used an almost square area and we obtained equivalent results to the analytical model, which used a circular area. In Figure 6, simulation results using a rectangular area with $3000m \times 650m$ are shown. Similar results and a control message overhead limited to $O(LnN)$ are obtained.

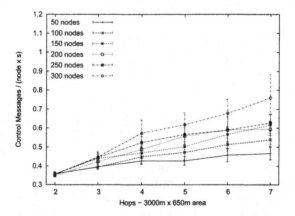

Fig. 6. Control Messages - 3000m x 650m area

After these validations, we made new simulations in scenarios with all nodes using random waypoint mobility with velocity up to 20m/s, without pause. Despite the fact that our analytical model do not consider mobility aspect, we can see in Figure 7 only a small increase of control message overhead when compared to the static scenario. This increase occurs because neighborhood changes, provoking new DN promotions. However, the overall behavior is similar to the previous results and they demonstrate the effectiveness of our model.

We also measured discovery success rate and average response time, shown in Figures 8(a) and 8(b), respectively. These results show a great robustness to mobility of the mechanisms proposed, since they are very similar to the ones obtained with static scenarios.

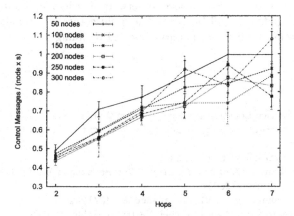

Fig. 7. Control Messages

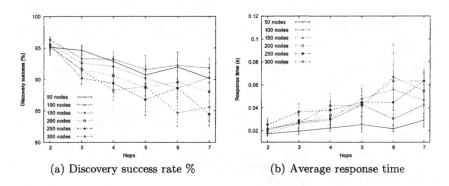

(a) Discovery success rate %   (b) Average response time

Fig. 8. Discovery success and response time with mobility

6 Conclusion

From analytical and simulation results, we conclude that our architecture for service discovery on ad hoc networks presents a good performance. The control message overhead in the first abstraction plane of this architecture is $O(Ln(N))$, which implies a good scalability and efficiency. Another main feature of our proposal is its independence from network parameters, as number of nodes, number of service instances and density. Besides, the proposed architecture achieve a good robustness against nodes mobility even when moderate to high degrees of mobility are used

A future work is the implementation of the second plane and its validation. With this implementation, a performance evaluation in different scenarios, adjusting the promotion process to several network densities and different mobility models and patterns will be done. The architecture will be also evaluated against node removal, network partitioning and rejoining.

References

1. RFC2608. Service Location Protocol, Version 2 (1999).
   `ftp://ftp.rfc-editor.org/in-notes/rfc2608.txt` - Último acesso em 13/12/2005.
2. Jini. Jini Network Technology (2005).
   `http://www.sun.com/software/jini/` - Último acesso em 13/12/2005.
3. UPnP. UPnP Forum (2005).
   `http://www.upnp.org/` - Último acesso em 13/12/2005.
4. Antony Rowstron and Peter Druschel. Pastry: Scalable, decentralized object location, and routing for large-scale peer-to-peer systems. *Lecture Notes in Computer Science*, 2218:329 (2001).
5. B. Y. Zhao, J. D. Kubiatowicz, and A. D. Joseph. Tapestry: An infrastructure for fault-tolerant wide-area location and routing. Technical Report UCB/CSD-01-1141, UC Berkeley (2001).
6. Sylvia Ratnasamy, Paul Francis, Mark Handley, Richard Karp, and Scott Shenker. A scalable content addressable network. Technical Report TR-00-010, Berkeley, CA (2000).
7. Ion Stoica, Robert Morris, David Karger, Frans Kaashoek, and Hari Balakrishnan. Chord: A scalable Peer-To-Peer lookup service for internet applications. In *Proceedings of the 2001 ACM SIGCOMM Conference*, pages 149–160 (2001).
8. G. Manku, M. Bawa, and P. Raghavan. Symphony: Distributed hashing in a small world. In *Proc. 4th USENIX Symposium on Internet Technologies and Systems (USITS 2003)* (2003).
9. Gnutella. Gnutella Protocol Development (2005).
   `http://rfc-gnutella.sourceforge.net/` - Último acesso em 13/12/2005.
10. JXTA. JXTA technology (2005).
    `http://www.jxta.org/` - Último acesso em 13/12/2005.
11. Jon Kleinberg. The small-world phenomenon: An algorithmic perspective. In *STOC '00: Proceedings of the 32nd ACM Symposium on Theory of Computing*, pages 163–170 (2000). ISBN 1-58113-184-4.
12. D. Doval and D. O'Mahony. Nom: Resource location and discovery for ad hoc mobile networks. In *1st Annual Mediterranean Ad Hoc Networking Workshop, Medhoc -Net* (2002).
13. Ahmed Helmy, Saurabh Garg, Priyatham Pamu, and Nitin Nahata. Contact-based architecture for resource discovery (card) in large scale manets. In *IPDPS '03: Proceedings of the 17th International Symposium on Parallel and Distributed Processing*, page 219.1 (2003).

14. Vincent Lenders, Martin May, and Bernhard Plattner. Service discovery in mobile ad hoc networks: A field theoretic approach. In *IEEE International Symposium on a World of Wireless, Mobile and Multimedia Networks (WoWMoM)*, pages 120–130 (2005).

15. Françoise Sailhan and Valérie Issarny. Scalable service discovery for manet. In *3rd IEEE International Conference on Pervasive Computing and Communications (PerCom'2005)*, pages 235–244 (2005).

16. J. Antonio Garcia-Macias and Dante Arias Torres. Service discovery in mobile ad-hoc networks: better at the network layer? In *ICPP 2005 Workshops. International Conference Workshops on Parallel Processing*, pages 452–457 (2005).

17. Sumi Helal, Nitin Desai, Varun Verma, and Choonhwa Lee. Konark - a service discovery and delivery protocol for ad-hoc networks. In *Third IEEE Conference on Wireless Communications and Networking (WCNC)*, volume 3, pages 2107–2113 (2003).

Performances of geographical routing protocols combined with a position estimation process in wireless heterogenous networks

Erwan Ermel, Anne Fladenmuller, and Guy Pujolle

Laboratoire d'Informatique de Paris 6
Université Pierre et Marie Curie
Paris, France
{erwan.ermel@, anne.fladenmuller@, guy.pujolle@}lip6.fr

Abstract. This paper addresses the performance of geographical routing protocol in wireless networks, where only few nodes possess self-locating capability such as GPS. To be able to apply end-to-end geographical routing protocols, it is necessary every node know their position coordinates. We propose a method to infer such positioning information to any node, based only on connectivity and localization information obtained from the neighborhood. Three metrics are used to evaluate the performance of such a scheme: the density of useful nodes for geographical routing protocol, the reachability and the path length.

Index Terms— **ad hoc network, localization, positioning, wireless network, self-locating.**

1 Introduction

Wireless systems are widely spread all around the world, but many problems remain to offer ubiquitous access. In internet networks, the routing process is based on the IP address of a destination, which uniquely identifies a node and contains a network prefix used to locate the node in the network. In case of mobile user, the node keeps its IP address but the network prefix looses its significance. This problem becomes even more crucial in Ad Hoc or Sensor Networks, as no dedicated routing infrastructure exists, leaving each node in charge of its auto-configuration and of routing issues. As the number of wireless terminals grows, the complexity of the routing process also increases and the main difficulty for such systems is to remain scalable.

One proposition to deal with this scalability issues consists of using a geographical routing protocol. Such a protocol bases the routing decision only on the geographical position - coordinates - of the destination node, thus suppressing the need for routing tables.

For example, the nearest node to the destination is chosen as the next hop node. These routing alternatives raise their own problems such as how to store

Please use the following format when citing this chapter:

Ermel, E., Fladenmuller, A., Pujolle, G., 2006, in IFIP International Federation for Information Processing, Volume 211, ed. Pujolle, G., Mobile and Wireless Communication Networks, (Boston: Springer), pp. 77–88.

and retrieve the mapping between an IP address - still required by applications - and the localization coordinates. Many research work is currently undertaken to overtake this problem, a survey proposed in [1] references some of the papers dealing with localization issues for ubiquitous computing. Another issue raised by geographical routing is that it requires that every node knows its position, therefore they can not be integrated by the geographical routing process.

Most of the papers in this research field deals with geographical routing in an homogenous networks, where all nodes have got self-location capability - like GPS - [2, 3]. We argue that this assumption is somehow restrictive as a wireless network is more likely to be composed of heterogeneous than homogenous devices.

For these reasons, we focus our work on evaluating the performances of geographical routing protocols in heterogeneous wireless networks. *Simple nodes* - nodes with no self-locating capability - could not be used in such scheme until they can estimate their own position. Some approaches try to overcome this problem by using IP routing solutions when nodes don't know their position [4]. This nonetheless leads to mix routing protocols which may not be adapted to low resources Sensor networks. Other proposals get the nodes to estimate their position based on physical measurements such as an angle of arrival (AOA) [5], signal strength [6], time of arrival (TOA) [7] or based on connectivity based approach [8]. The latter proposal has for main advantage that no specific devices is requested to infer a position.

We argue in this paper that although the position precision obtained when nodes get their position from their neighborhood is not always great, it is sufficient to operate routing operations.

Thus we combine geographical routing protocols with a simple position estimation process, based on a connectivity approach.

This paper is organized as follows : Section 2 will present our approach followed in Section 3 by our results. Section 4 will conclude the paper.

2 Context

We propose in this article to evaluate the performances of geographical routing protocol combined with our localization process for *simple nodes* (Fig. 1).

A greedy approach has been chosen for the geographical routing protocol, like [2] due to its simplicity: the next forwarding node is the nearest in distance to the destination.

The position estimation process is based on the connectivity approach [9]. With a convex hull selection method among the neighbor nodes, only useful nodes remain for the position estimation process. The estimated position is then a simple average of the position of selected nodes.

The main contribution of this position estimation proposal comes from the fact that we do not require any specific equipment to get a node to estimate its position. To run our solution we require that only a few nodes in the topology

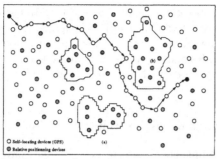

(a) Simple nodes with no position estimation process

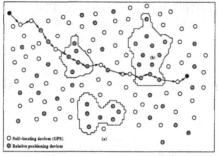

(b) Simple nodes with a position estimation process

Fig. 1. Geographical routing in heterogeneous wireless networks.

have self-locating capability. The position information of a node (coordinates and the estimated accuracy of the position) is then simply exchanged in "Hello Messages" adding no particular overhead in terms of the information propagation. Each time a node receives a "Hello Message", it decides or not to update its position and it forwards it to its own neighborhood. This process is done continuously to take into account the modifications of the environment. It allows step-by-step to infer a position to a node distant of x-hops from self-located nodes - the self-located nodes being the only ones with a very precise position information. The position estimation process is independent of the underlaying network technologies and protocols. Thus no further considerations will be made on the underlaying routing protocols in this paper.

In some previous work [10], we have shown that our position estimation proposal gives optimal results when selecting some neighbors. Obviously, our resulting estimated position is not always precise, as it depends on the network topology and the distribution and number of self-located nodes in the network.

The aim of this paper is first to evaluate the convergence of position information based on the number of time "Hello Messages" are exchanged. First we want to confirm that the estimation process will tend to become more and more precise as the number of "Hello Messages" propagated in the network increases. This point is not obvious, as divergences could appear if estimation errors propagate in the network. Second, we want to evaluate the impact of the topology density on the node reachability depending on the number of self-located nodes in the network.

2.1 Convergence time of the position estimation

We first consider a simple static case to evaluate the convergence time of the position estimation process (Fig. 2). We define five nodes $N1, N2, N3, N4, N5$, where only $N1$ and $N5$ are self-located. The real positions of the nodes are $N1_x(0)$, $N2_x(45)$, $N3_x(70)$, $N4_x(100)$ and $N5_x(130)$. R_{max} , the theoretical transmission range is set to 50m. $N5_x(130)$ emits its first "Hello message" at iteration 3.

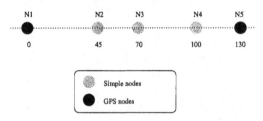

Fig. 2. Simple topology case.

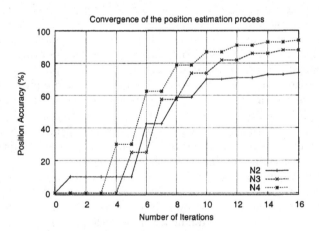

Fig. 3. Convergence time of the position estimation process

Fig. 3 shows the convergence time of the position estimation process combined with a geographical routing protocol. From 0 iteration to 3which also correspond to the number of position messages exchanged or broadcasted by the neighbor nodes - only $N1$ broadcasts its "Hello Message". Simple nodes $N2, N3, N4$ can't estimate their position until $N5$ broadcast its 'Hello Message" at iteration 3. in this example a simple node has a good estimation of its positions after 4-5 iterations - and the maximum precision of position is reached after 10 steps.

Before reaching the stationary state, the precision of position increases by steps. For example, between iteration 3 and 4, nodes $N2$ and $N4$ get position messages from $N1$ and $N5$ while $N3$ receives nothing. $N2$ and $N4$ estimate their position and then broadcast it. Then $N3$ estimates its position between steps 4 and 5, and broadcasts the result. And so on...

We showed that with a simple position estimation process, simple nodes can estimate their position with a simple connectivity approach.

Even if this example is basic, we observe that the convergence time of the precision of position is linked to the number of self-located nodes present in the neighborhood: as the density of SLN nodes increases, the convergence time decreases.

2.2 Definitions

We will now define the metrics we use to evaluate the performance of a geographical routing protocol combined with a position estimation process.

Useful density We define the useful density $\mathcal{D}_{useful}$ as the density useful for a geographical routing protocol i.e. only nodes with a position are taken into account. Thus $\mathcal{D}_{useful}$ of a node represents the number of SLN nodes and the number of SN nodes with a position in its neighborhood.

We also define $\mathcal{D}_{max}$ the maximum density of useful nodes. $\mathcal{D}_{max}$ is obtained when all the nodes are self-located i.e. 100% of the nodes are GPS nodes.

Accessibility As simple nodes gets a position, new paths can be found and used by the geographical routing protocol. Thus, a node can "discuss" with more nodes. We call *accessibility* or *reachability* the percentage of nodes that can be reached by another one with a geographical routing.

To estimate $\mathcal{R}$, we divide the number of real paths found by the theoretical number of paths. By construction $\mathcal{R} \in [0; 1]$ with $\mathcal{R} = 0$ when no path has been found and $\mathcal{R} = 1$ when the network is a connected graph. The higher $\mathcal{R}$ is, the higher the connectivity of the network is.

Path length We define by *average path length* $\mathcal{L}_{mean}$ the average number of hops necessary to establish a path between two nodes. If no path is found, it will not have a length since it does not exist and it will be discarded for the estimation of $\mathcal{L}_{mean}$.

Homogeneous and Heterogeneous routing We define two geographical routing protocol cases : the first one consists of a geographical routing protocol without a position estimation process. In such case, only SLN nodes are useful in the routing process, and SN nodes are purely ignored. We called such an approach a *homogeneous geographical routing protocol*. Inversely, when a geographical routing protocol is combined with a position estimation process, all nodes of the network can be used to achieve the routing and we call this approach a *heterogeneous geographical routing protocol*.

3 Results

As our position estimation process is independent from the underlayer technologies, we choose not to use NS2 or Glomosim and we have developed our own Java code simulator for its simplicity. 50 nodes are randomly placed in a 1000m x 1000m square. Self-locating nodes and simple nodes are also randomly elected. The maximum theoretical transmission range R_{max} is set to 170m. We consider only static cases. Mobility will be considered in future works.

3.1 Useful density and accessibility

We first study the impact of the percentage of SLN nodes from 0 to 100% for a 50 nodes topology (Fig. 4).

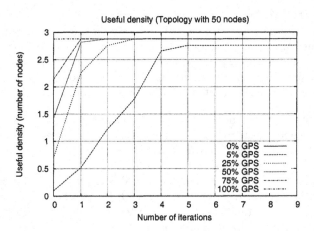

Fig. 4. Performance of $\mathcal{D}_{useful}$ for different percentage of GPS nodes and as a function of the number of iterations of the position estimation process

With 100% of SLN nodes, the useful density reaches the maximum density with $\mathcal{D}_{max} = 2.8$ (every node has got 2.8 neighbor nodes). Fig. 4 shows that as the percentage of SLN nodes increases, the convergence time of $\mathcal{D}_{useful}$ decreases.

With 5% of GPS nodes (2 SLN), $\mathcal{D}_{useful}$ never reaches $\mathcal{D}_{max}$ mostly due to the sparse topology. Several nodes are alone and won't be able to participate to the network and then won't be useful at all.

Focus now on the worst possible case : low density (50 nodes) with a low percentage of SLN nodes (5%) (Fig. 5).

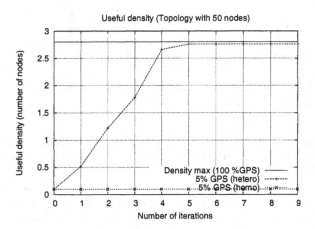

Fig. 5. Performance of $\mathcal{D}_{useful}$ for a topology of 50 nodes with 5% GPS

For a homogeneous routing, the number of useful nodes is equal to 0.1 and doesn't vary in time (the number of SLN is constant), whereas in the case of a heterogeneous routing, $\mathcal{D}_{useful}$ increases in time to reach a maximum of 2.8. The $\mathcal{D}_{useful}$ of a heterogeneous routing converges toward the maximum density $\mathcal{D}_{max}$ but never equals it due to the pathology of the network topology. Nevertheless heterogeneous routing performs better than homogeneous routing.

With a position estimation process, a geographical routing protocol can use more nodes to achieve its goals than in the case of using only SLN nodes.

We now study the reachability of a node into a heterogeneous network. This is an important performance factor because it determines if a path exists between every node of the network. $\mathcal{R}$ is a good indicator of the connectivity of the network.

Fig. 6 shows the impact on the reachability according to the number of iterations of the position estimation process. We varied the percentage of GPS nodes from 0 to 100%.

The study of the Fig. 6 is very similar to that which we have just done for the density Fig. 4. As the number of iterations of the position estimation process increases, $\mathcal{R}$ grows and converges towards a maximum value depending

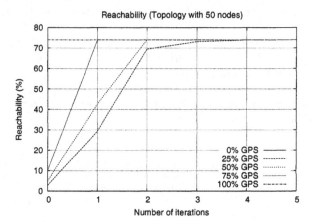

Fig. 6. Reachability for a given percentage of GPS nodes and as a function of the number of iterations of the position estimation process.

on the density of the topology. As the simple nodes estimate their position, the useful density grows, and as the useful density of nodes increases, the feasibility of roads increases as well.

As the simple nodes acquire a position, the connectivity of the network increases to reach a maximum. Here $\mathcal{R}_{max}(50) = 73\%$. We also see that the more the percentage of self-locating nodes in the network is, the faster the convergence is. $\mathcal{R}(50) < 100$ implies that the graph representative of the network is not complete but composed of under complete graphs.

As the useful density, the reachability (accessibility of the nodes) benefits from the packing of a position estimation process to a geographical routing protocol.

3.2 Path length

The figure Fig. 7 shows the average path length according to the number of iteration of the position estimation process. We looked at $\mathcal{L}_{mean}$ in topologies of 50 and 200 nodes. For each particular topology, we varied the percentage of SLN from 0 to 100%.

These curves comprise two phases: one *transitory* and the other one *stationary*:

- The stationary phase is reached when $\mathcal{L}_{mean}$ becomes constant. It is observed in every case.
- The transitional phase is the stage before the stationary phase. A difference of *pathology* of the results can be noticed according to the total number of

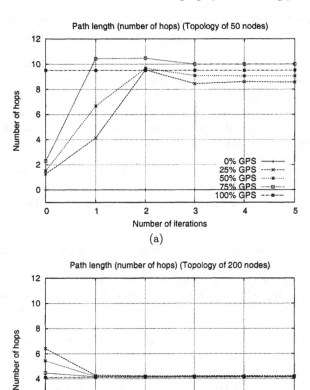

Fig. 7. Average path length in function of the percentage of SLN nodes and in function of the number of iteration od the positions estimation process.

nodes of topologies. Two types of transitional stages are defined: the *progressive transitory phase* and the *regressive transitory phase*.

The progressive transitional stage is observed when the theoretical density and the percentage of SLN nodes are low. In this case, the average path length increases quickly as the density and/or the percentage of SLN nodes is low. Increasing connectivity increases the probability of existence of a way between two nodes. In a spare topology case (50 nodes), the increase of connectivity is the result of the union of under complete graphs, as the simple nodes estimate their position. Thus the average path length can only be longer than before. But that also implies that news paths can be found to reach new destinations.

The regressive transitional stage is observed when the theoretical density and/or the percentage of SLN nodes are significant enough. In this case, $\mathcal{L}_{mean}$ decreases gradually towards the optimum path length. This decrease is all the more significant as the percentage of nodes GPS is weak. These cases of figures are the concrete example of a *Swiss-Cheese topology* as shown in Fig. 1(b).

At the beginning, when the simple nodes do not have a position, the geographical routing can not use them: the routing path has to circumvent all the empty zones of position information, which implies a longer path. As soon as simple nodes acquire their position, geographical routing protocol uses these nodes. Thus the *hole* grow blurred. Fig. 1(a) and Fig. 1(b) illustrate these remarks.

Now let us compare the average path length in the case of a homogeneous and/or heterogeneous routing.

The Fig. 8 compares $\mathcal{L}_{mean}$ obtained by a homogeneous and heterogeneous geographical routing. Moreover we have to study $\mathcal{L}_{mean}$ in the cases of progressive transitional stage Fig. 8(a) and regressive transitional stage Fig. 8(b).

In the case of a progressive transitional stage - Fig. 8(a) - the average path length in a homogeneous routing is constant. Within a topology of 50 nodes, $\mathcal{L}_{mean} \simeq 1.2$. Thus the average path length is no more than a hop. Routing in such topology is not very useful since a node can discuss only with its immediate neighbors and no further.

When simple nodes have a position, an important growth of the path length is noticed; $\mathcal{L}_{mean} \simeq 7$ is almost 6 times greater than for the homogeneous routing. Indeed this increase average path length is only a translation of the increase in probability of finding a road between two nodes. Thus when two under complete graphs are linked - by the means of simple nodes - the average path length increases.

In the case of a regressive transitional stage - Fig. 8(b) - the average path length in a homogeneous routing is constant, $\mathcal{L}_{mean} = 6.5$, whereas for a heterogeneous geographical routing, $\mathcal{L}_{mean}$ decreases quickly before being stabilized towards 4.3. These results confirm our idea to use simple nodes with position into geographical routing in order to largely minimize the path length.

In these two figures - Fig. 8(b) and Fig. 8(a) - the *theoretical curve* represents the theoretical average path length between different nodes. In the case of a progressive transitional phase, the theoretical average length is the upper limit, whereas in the decreasing transitional phase, it undervaluates the lengths obtained by the mean of the homogeneous and heterogeneous geographical routings. In all cases, the heterogeneous routing converges towards this theoretical

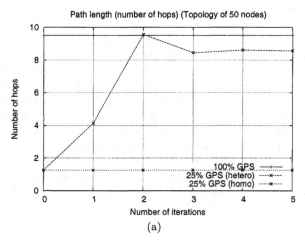

(a)

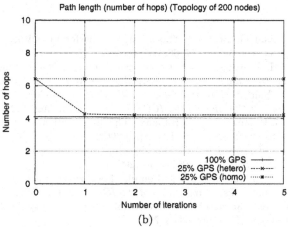

(b)

Fig. 8. comparison between average Length of roads in a number of jumps of a heterogeneous routing and a homogeneous routing for two topologies of 50 and 200 nodes including 25% of which autolocalized nodes.

length, without however reaching it. The path length, when using our approach becomes closer to the theoretical path length when the density of the nodes increases.

4 Conclusion

The addition of a position estimation process improves the total performances of a geographical routing in a heterogeneous wireless network.

We showed that despite the fact our position estimation process may not be precise, it allows ti increase nodes connectivity and reachability. The average path length reflect the benefices of such a routing for a heterogeneous network. This work underlines the possibility to use a simple geographical routing protocol, in an environment with a very little constraints, as it only requires that some nodes in the topology possess a precise position information.

We will focus our future works on the position estimation process and specially simple techniques to enhance the precision of estimated position to study the impact of the position precision on the performance of geographical routing for a heterogeneous network.

References

1. J. Hightower and G. Borriello, "Location systems for ubiquitous computing," *IEEE Computer*, vol. 34, pp. 57–66, August 2001.
2. B. Karp and H. T. Kung, "Gpsr : Greedy perimeter stateless routing for wireless networks," in *Proceedings of ACM/IEEE MOBICOM'00*, Aug. 2000.
3. Y. Ko and N. Vaidya, "Locaton-aided routing (lar) in mobile ad hoc networks," in *Proceedings of ACM/IEEE MOBICOM'98*, pp. 66–75, Aug. 1998.
4. S. Capkun, M. Hamdi, and J. P. Hubaux, "Gps-free positioning in mobile ad-hoc networks," *Cluster Computing*, vol. 5, April 2002.
5. D. Niculescu and B. Nath, "Ad hoc positioning system (aps) using aoa," in *Proceedings of IEEE INFOCOM'2003*, April 2003.
6. C. Savarese, J. M. Rabaey, and J. Beutel, "Localization in distributed ad-hoc wireless sensor networks," *Proceedings of the ICASSP*, May 2001.
7. A. Savvides, C.-C. Han, and M. B. Strivastava, "Dynamic fine-grained localization in ad-hoc networks of sensors," July 2001.
8. L. Doherty, K. S. J. Pister, and L. E. Ghaoui, "Convex optimization methods for sensor node position estimation," in *Proceedings of IEEE INFOCOM'2001*, (Anchorage), April 2001.
9. E. Ermel, *Localisation et Routage géographique dans les réseaux sans fil hétérogènes*. PhD thesis, Laboratoire Informatique de Paris VI, Université Pierre et Marie Curie (Paris VI), France, 2004.
10. E. Ermel, A. Fladenmuller, G. Pujolle, and A. Cotton, "Improved position estimation in wireless heterogeneous networks," in *Networking 2004*, May 2004.

Event-Driven Field Estimation for Wireless Sensor Networks

Daniel de O. Cunha[1,2], Otto Carlos M. B. Duarte[1], and Guy Pujolle[2] *

[1]Grupo de Teleinformática e Automação
Universidade Federal do Rio de Janeiro - UFRJ
Rio de Janeiro, Brazil

[2]Laboratoire d'Informatique de Paris 6 (LIP6)
Université Pierre et Marie Curie - Paris VI
Paris, France

Summary. This paper introduces and analyzes a field estimation scheme for wireless sensor networks. Our scheme imitates the response of living beings to the surrounding events. The sensors define their periphery of attention based on their own readings. Readings differing from the expected behavior are considered events of interest and trigger the data transmission to the sink. The presented scheme is evaluated with real-site-collected data and the tradeoff between the amount of data sent to the sink and the reconstruction error is analyzed. Results show that significant reduction in the data transmission and, as a consequence, in the energy consumption of the network is achievable while keeping low the average reconstruction error.

1 Introduction

Recent advances in MEMS technology and wireless communications made possible to embed sensing, processing, and communication capabilities in low-cost sensor nodes. As a consequence, the use of hundreds or thousands of nodes organized in a network [1] becomes an alternative to conventional sensing techniques. The resulting sensor network has the advantage of being closer to the sensed process, being able to acquire more detailed data.

Field estimation is an important application of wireless sensor networks. This type of application deploys sensor nodes in a specific region to remotely sense space-temporally variable processes, such as temperature or UV exposure. It is a continuous data-delivery application [2] and the simplest approach of such a system is based on deploying the sensors in the area of interest and requiring all the nodes to transmit data to the sink at a prespecified rate. The quality of the estimation depends of the spatial and temporal frequencies of sampling.

* This work has been supported by CNPq, CAPES, FAPERJ, FINEP, RNP and FUNTTEL.

Please use the following format when citing this chapter:

de O. Cunha, D., Duarte, O.C.M.B., Pujolle, G., 2006, in IFIP International Federation for Information Processing, Volume 211, ed. Pujolle, G., Mobile and Wireless Communication Networks, (Boston: Springer), pp. 89–98.

These frequencies must be high enough to avoid the aliasing problem [3]. Nevertheless, higher frequencies generate a larger amount of data to transmit. As the data transmission is the most consuming task of a sensor node [4], it is interesting to trade some data transmission for local processing.

The spatial sampling frequency is related to the number and position of the nodes. A higher spatial sampling frequency results in a larger number of nodes transmitting data to the sink. Without any prior analysis, it is necessary to deploy the nodes in such a way that the entire field is sampled with the highest required spatial frequency in the field. This required frequency is a function of the process and the field. As a consequence, the typical sensing field is not uniform. It is composed by areas where the sensed process varies smoothly and areas where the process varies sharply from one position to other. Usually, sharp-variation areas are *borders* between different smooth-variation areas. Some works aim at identifying such smooth-variation areas and deactivate some of the nodes in these regions [5, 6, 7]. The main idea is to reduce the amount of transmitted data by avoiding the transmission of redundant information. Nevertheless, these approaches are unable to save energy at the borders, which remain with a high spatial density of active nodes. The temporal sampling frequency is related to the period between consecutive samples. The required temporal sampling frequency is dictated by the sensed process and reducing this frequency may result in the lost of important information about the process. Typical solutions to reduce transmission time of a node to send the amount of data is the codification of the resulting temporal series [8, 9] in a more efficient way.

We have propose an event-driven field estimation scheme for wireless sensor networks [10]. Differing from the above discussed approaches, our scheme reduces the amount of transmitted data by sending only part of the samples. The assumption behind our scheme is that although we have to sample the process with its required temporal frequency to avoid losing important data, not all the samples will bring interesting information. Hence, the proposed scheme exploits specific features of the monitored processes in order to reduce the amount of data transmitted to the sink. Each sensor node collects the samples and decides to only send to the ones considered an event of interest to itself. This mimics an event-driven system over a continuous-data transmission application.

In this paper we evaluate the proposed scheme with real-site-collected data. Furthermore, we take a new metric, the average reconstruction error, into account and analyze the tradeoff between the average reconstruction error and the total amount of data transmitted.

The rest of the paper is structured in the following way. In Section 2, we introduce the proposed field-estimation scheme. Then, the simulations are then presented in Section 3, showing the efficiency of the scheme. Finally, conclusions and future research work are discussed in Section 4.

2 The Field Estimation Scheme

Our field-estimation scheme is bio-inspired, based on how living beings respond to the surrounding events. People and animals are continually receiving *stimuli*; however, it is impossible to handle consciously all these *stimuli*. The organisms develop the notion of periphery and center of attention [11]. While the periphery is handled in a sub-conscious manner, the center of attention is the event consciously treated. Generally, an event migrates from the periphery to the center of attention when it differs much from the periphery as a whole.

In practice, the sensor identifies a recurrent pattern in the process and defines an expected behavior, or the periphery of attention, for the next readings. Based on this expected behavior, the sensor decides whether a sample is important or not. If it decides that the sample will aggregate useful information, it sends the sample to the sink. These samples sent to ensure the quality of the estimation are called *refining samples*. Otherwise, the sample is still used to calculate the expected behavior of the process in the future, but is not transmitted. As we discussed earlier, the data transmission is the most energy consuming task in a sensor network and the reduction in the number of transmitted samples impacts signicantly the energy consumption of the network.

Originally, we proposed two different ways for implementing the proposed scheme, a sample-bounded algorithm and an error-bounded algorithm [10]. The sample bounded algorithm limits the maximum number of samples transmitted to the number of samples collected by the sensor, no matter how badly the scheme is configured. On the other hand, the error-bounded algorithm ensures that no event of interest will be lost by limiting the maximum reconstruction error at the sink. However, this algorithm must be well tuned or may result in the transmission of more samples than the originally collected by the sensor. As we want to ensure a correct estimation of process all the time, we will only consider the error-bounded algorithm in this paper. The first step is to determine the periodicity of the recurrent pattern. The algorithm must run once at the end of each period, after the collection of all samples. The physical process used in our analysis is the temperature, which clearly has a daily periodicity. It presents a regular behavior where the temperature is low in the morning and rises near noon. The temperature falls in the afternoon and reaches low values again at night. Temperature also presents annual periodicity, but our analysis is based only on daily periodicity. Thus, the sensor nodes must identify a daily-expected behavior, updated every day. The decision about refining samples is made based on this behavior. Additionally, the sink must have enough information to successfully reconstruct the remotely sensed process. Therefore, the sink needs to know an expected behavior, which is assumed to occur when no refining samples are received. The node must periodically send an updated expected behavior to the sink. The sink then assumes the process behaves exactly like the most recent expected-behavior vector, whenever no refining samples are received. These refining samples replace part of the expected behavior as informed by the sensor. The sensor node must decide on sending or not refining samples based on the last expected behavior vector sent to the sink. This procedure maintains the consistency between the measured and the reconstructed information. Therefore, the sensor verifies whether the measured value differs above a certain threshold from the corresponding sample of the last expected-behavior vector sent. If this difference is higher than the configured threshold, the sensor sends the refining sample to the sink.

Assuming that the daily periodicity is already known, Fig. 1 shows the daily procedure, where DB_j is the vector with the expected behavior during day j, D_i the vector with the measurements of day i, *last_update* is the vector with the most recent expected behavior sent to the sink, and the notation $X(k)$ is used to represent the k-th element of vector X.

DB $_i$ = α D $_i$ + (1−α) DB $_{i-1}$
If update time
    last_update = DB $_i$
    Send last_update
For all k samples in D $_i$ do
    If |D $_i$(k) − last_update(k)| > |last_update(k)| * configured_error
        Send D $_i$(k)

Fig. 1. Daily procedure.

As we can see in Fig. 1, the algorithm has three important parameters: the α factor, the *update* specification, and the *configured_error* limitation. The α factor weights the importance of the recent samples in the generation of the expected-behavior vector. The *update* parameter specifies the interval between the transmission of expected-behavior vectors to the sink. The *configured_error* is used to limit the reconstruction error at the sink. The performed simulations are detailed in the next section.

3 Simulations

We analyze the proposed scheme by simulating the local processing of one sensor node. The field-estimation scheme is evaluated considering two distinct metrics: the reduction in the total number of samples sent to the sink and the average reconstruction error at the sink. We use the percentage samples sent as an index to estimate the energy conservation. This preserves the generalization of the results by avoiding specific-MAC-layer biases. The average reconstruction error is used to evaluate how well the scheme performs the field estimation and is calculated as

$$AE = \frac{\sum_{i=1}^{N} \frac{sample(i)' - sample(i)}{sample(i)} \cdot 100}{N}, \tag{1}$$

where $sample(i)$ is the value sensed by the sensor for a given sample, $sample(i)'$ is the value for this sample after the reconstruction at the sink, and N is the total number of samples collected.

The simulations are performed with different configurations of the scheme. These configurations results from the variation of the three parameters highlighted in Section 2: the α factor, the *update* specification, and the *configured_error* limitation. Furthermore, the scheme is evaluated with real-site-collected data. We analyze the performance of the scheme in a temperature monitoring application based on the measurements of a Brazilian meteorological station. The next section details the data preprocessing.

3.1 Data Treatment

The field-estimation scheme is analyzed based on data available at the web page of the Department of Basic Sciences of the Universidade de São Paulo, Brazil [12]. The web-site maintains a history of meteorological data from the last eight years. The temperature measurements used in this paper presents the evolution of the temperature at an interval of 15 minutes, which results in 96 samples per day. We performed a preprocessing of the data to avoid the use of corrupted data. A small part of the daily files skipped one or two temperature measurements. A few files had three or more measurements missing. In the cases where only one measurement was missing, we replaced the missing measure by the linear interpolation between the preceding measurement and the measurement immediately after the missing measurement. Files with more than one measure missing were discarded.

After the elimination of corrupted data, the measurements of each day were arranged in a single vector with 96 elements. These daily-measurements vectors were concatenated to form a large vector with all the measurements available from the last eight years. In the cases where the measurements of a day were discarded due to corruption, we just skipped that day and concatenated the day before the corrupted data has appeared and the day after.

This data processing resulted in one single vector with the information of 2,880 days chronologically ordered. Thus, the simulations were performed with a data vector with 276,480 elements.

3.2 Results

The simulations are based on the data vector generated as described in Section 3.1, which is used to represent the readings of a sensor. The proposed scheme is applied to this data set and the fraction of the total samples that must be actually sent to the sink and the average reconstruction error (Eq. 1) are obtained. The smaller the fraction of samples sent is, the better is the proposed scheme efficiency. Furthermore, a small average reconstruction error means a better estimation of the sensed process. The simulation assumes the daily (96 samples) periodicity has already been defined. The identification of the period of the regular behavior of the process is independent of the parameters used to configure the scheme and only depends on the data set used.

The three parameters previously discussed are varied during the simulation in order to better understand their effects. In all simulations, the update frequency is one expected-behavior vector sent at each *update* days. Thus, higher values of *update* means lower update frequencies. The maximum tolerated sample error is equal to the parameter *configured_error* times the expected behavior of the specific hour. The α factor is bounded to 1.

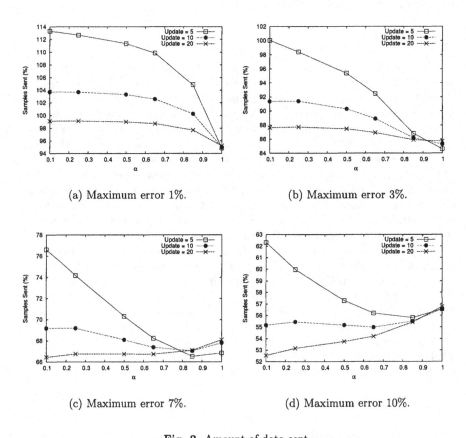

(a) Maximum error 1%.   (b) Maximum error 3%.

(c) Maximum error 7%.   (d) Maximum error 10%.

Fig. 2. Amount of data sent.

Fig. 2 shows the percentage of samples sent for different tolerated reconstruction errors. As we can see in Fig. 2(a), for very low tolerated errors, the scheme does not reduce much the percentage of samples sent. Moreover, it is possible to see that a bad tuning of the scheme can result in the transmission of more data than the original samples. Nevertheless, as the tolerated error is relaxed, the scheme can reduce significantly the percentage of samples sent. For a maximum tolerated error of 3% (Fig. 2(b)) it is possible to reduce the amount of data in 15%. A larger tolerated error, such as shown in Fig. 2(d), reduces the amount of data in almost 50%. It is worth noting that a large tolerated error does not necessarily mean a poor estimation, as we will show later while analyzing the average reconstruction error.

Analyzing Fig. 2, we notice that the configuration of the α and *update* parameters affects the results differently as the maximum tolerated error varies. For very small maximum tolerated errors (Figs. 2(a) and 2(b)), the scheme sends less samples when α is close to 1 and the parameter *update* is low. As we increase the maximum tolerated error, better results are achieved with a low α and a high *update*.

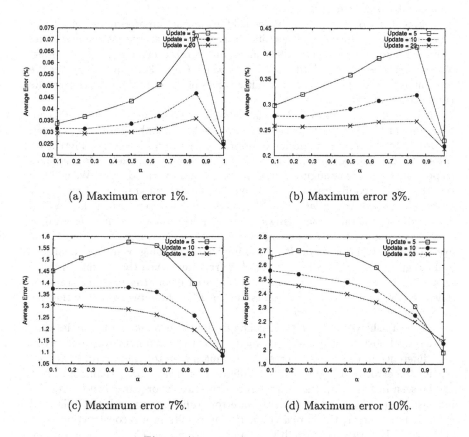

(a) Maximum error 1%.   (b) Maximum error 3%.

(c) Maximum error 7%.   (d) Maximum error 10%.

Fig. 3. Average reconstruction error.

Although a higher maximum error allows the transmission of less samples, this maximum error must be controlled in order to maintain the average reconstruction error satisfactory. Fig. 3 shows the average reconstruction error for different tolerated reconstruction errors. As can be seen, the average reconstruction error is significantly smaller than the maximum tolerated error. This means that we have a certain flexibility to define the maximum tolerated error for the scheme. Moreover, the average error presents some interesting behaviors. First of all, we see that for very small maximum tolerated errors, (Fig. 3(a)) the average error grows rapidly with the increase in α, until α reaches 1, when the average error falls sharply. It occurs because an α equals to 1 results in sending the exact readings of the update day as the expected-behavior vector for the next days. As the tolerated error grows, the increase of the average error according to α gets smoother (Fig. 3(b)) and in certain cases the error is reduced with the increase of α (Fig. 3(d)).

Fig. 3 also shows that, as it happened for the fraction of samples sent, the α and *update* configurations affects differently the average error as the maximum tolerated error grows. When the maximum tolerated error is low, the lowest average error is achieved with a higher *update* (Figs. 3(a) and 3(b)). As the maximum tolerated error grows, smaller values of *update* achieve better results (Figs. 2(c) and 2(d)).

The results shown in Figs. 2 and 3, highlight the importance of a correct configuration of the scheme in order to achieve the best possible results. Moreover, according to the metric we decide to optimize, we can achieve very different results. One possible configuration is to decide to always transmit as few samples as possible for every configuration of the maximum tolerated error. We will call this the *Greedy* configuration, and it could be implemented using α equals to 1 and a low *update* value, whenever the maximum tolerated error is low. When the maximum tolerated error grows we adopt a low α and a high *update* value. Another option, named *Proud* configuration, is to always try to minimize the average reconstruction error. It can be implemented using α always equal to 1 and assigning high values for the *update* parameter, when the maximum tolerated error is low. For higher maximum tolerated errors the *update* parameter must be low. Fig. 4 shows the results obtained for these two configurations as a function of the tolerated error.

Fig. 4(a) shows that for both configurations the number of samples sent decreases almost linearly with the increase in the maximum tolerated error. The difference in the results increase as the maximum tolerated error increases, but for the error range analyzed this difference is always lower than 10%. As it can be seen in Fig. 4(b), the average reconstruction error grows faster with the increase of the tolerated reconstruction error. When we use a larger tolerated reconstruction error, the *Proud* configuration results in a reconstruction error 20% lower than the error resulting from the use of the *Greedy* configuration, in the expence of sending a few more samples. This suggests that it may be interesting to balance the two metrics in the configuration of the field-estimation scheme.

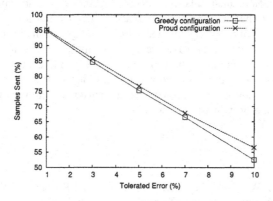

(a) Amount of samples sent.

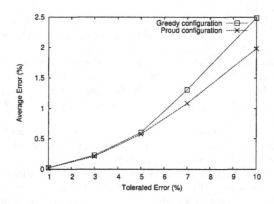

(b) Average Reconstruction Error.

Fig. 4. Results from the ideal configurations.

4 Conclusion

This paper introduces and analyzes an event-driven field-estimation scheme. The scheme exploits the fact that not all the collected samples result in useful information. Therefore, we reduce the number of samples sent to the sink and, as a consequence, the energy consumption in the network.

The field-estimation scheme is analyzed based on real-site-collected data from a meteorological station. We take two metrics into account while evaluating the scheme: the amount of data sent to the sink and the average reconstruction error. The results show that the configuration of the scheme severely impacts the results, suggesting an automated configuration procedure. Moreover, the scheme configuration must take into account the two metrics simultaneously. The results show that a significant increase in the estimation quality can be achieved in expense of a slightly smaller gain. A configuration aiming to optimize the average reconstruction error results in much smaller errors, achieving a gain a little smaller than the gain achieved by a Greedy configuration.

In the future, we intend to analyze the impact of the network losses on the results and to develop an adaptive configuration mechanism to ensure the achievement of the best possible results.

References

1. I. F. Akyildiz, W. Su, Y. Sankarasubramaniam, and E. Cayirci, "Wireless sensor networks: a survey," *Computer Networks*, vol. 38, pp. 393–422, 2002.
2. S. Tilak, N. B. Abu-Ghazaleh, and W. Heinzelman, "A taxonomy of wireless micro-sensor network models," *ACM Mobile Computing and Communications Review (MC2R)*, 2002.
3. A. Kumar, P. Ishwar, and K. Ramchandran, "On distributed sampling of smooth non-bandlimited fields," in *Information Processing In Sensor Networks - IPSN'04*, apr 2004, pp. 89–98.
4. G. P. Pottie and W. J. Kaiser, "Wireless integrated network sensors," *Communications of the ACM*, vol. 43, no. 5, pp. 51–58, may 2000.
5. R. Willett, A. Martin, and R. Nowak, "Backcasting: adaptive sampling for sensor networks," in *Information Processing In Sensor Networks - IPSN'04*, apr 2004, pp. 124 – 133.
6. M. Rahimi, R. Pon, W. J. Kaiser, G. S. Sukhatme, D. Estrin, and M. Sirivastava, "Adaptive sampling for environmental robotics," in *IEEE International Conference on Robotics & Automation*, apr 2004, pp. 3537–3544.
7. M. A. Batalin, M. Rahimi, Y.Yu, D.Liu, A.Kansal, G. Sukhatme, W. Kaiser, M.Hansen, G. J. Pottie, M. Srivastava, and D. Estrin, "Towards event-aware adaptive sampling using static and mobile nodes," Center for Embedded Networked Sensing - CENS, Tech. Rep. 38, 2004.
8. I. Lazaridis and S. Mehrotra, "Capturing sensor-generated time series with quality guarantees," in *International Conference on Data Engineering (ICDE'03)*, mar 2003.
9. H. Chen, J. Li, and P. Mohapatra, "Race: Time series compression with rate adaptivity and error bound for sensor networks," in *IEEE International Conference on Mobile Ad-hoc and Sensor Systems - MASS 2004*, oct 2004.
10. D. O. Cunha, R. P. Laufer, I. M. Moraes, M. D. D. Bicudo, P. B. Velloso, and O. C. M. B. Duarte, "A bio-inspired field estimation scheme for wireless sensor networks," *Annals of Telecommunications*, vol. 60, no. 7-8, 2005.
11. M. Weiser and J. S. Brown, "The coming age of calm technolgy," in *Beyond calculation: the next fifty years*. Copernicus, 1997, pp. 75 – 85.
12. Universidade de São Paulo, *Departamento de Ciências Exatas*, LCE - ESALQ - USP, 2005, http://www.lce.esalq.usp.br/indexn.html - visited in Feb. 2005.

Exploiting Web Technologies to Build Autonomic Wireless Sensor Networks

Flávia C. Delicato[2], Luci Pirmez[1], Paulo F. Pires[2], José Ferreira de Rezende[3]

[1]NCE – Federal University of Rio de Janeiro, Brazil
[2]DIMAp - Federal University of Rio Grande do Norte, Brazil
[3]GTA - Federal University of Rio de Janeiro, Brazil
{fdelicato, luci, paulopires }@nce.ufrj.br; rezende@gta.ufrj.br

Abstract. Most of the current wireless sensor networks are built for specific applications, with a tight coupling between them and the underlying communication protocols. We present a more flexible architectural approach for building WSNs, in which application-specific features are decoupled from the underlying communication infrastructure, although affecting the network behavior. We propose a framework based on Web technologies that provides a standard interface for accessing the network and configurable service components tailored to meet different application requirements, while optimizing the network scarce resources. Also, a set of ontologies is defined as part of the framework for representing shared knowledge of the WSN domain.

1 Introduction

Wireless sensor networks (WSNs) are distributed systems composed of hundred to thousands of low cost, battery-powered and reduced size devices, endowed of processing, sensing and wireless communication capabilities.

One major reason for the increasing interest in Wireless sensor networks (WSNs) in the last few years is their potential usage in a wide range of application areas such as health, military, habitat monitoring and security [1]. However, before WSNs can be widely employed, they must be cheaper, easier to use and more flexible than they are at present.

Currently existent software for WSNs is not flexible enough to meet the different demands of their potential applications. Most of existing WSNs require loading application code in sensor nodes before they can be deployed. Once the WSN becomes operational, applications can be only slightly modified to adapt their behavior to changes in the execution context. By context, we mean everything that can influence the behavior of an application [1]. We can distinguish three specific levels of awareness, in the context of WSNs: *device awareness, environment awareness* and *application awareness*. Device awareness refers to everything that lies on the physical device the application relies on, such as memory, battery, processing power and so on. Environment awareness refers to everything that is external to the physical device, such as bandwidth, network connectivity, location, neighboring nodes, and so on. Finally, application awareness refers to all

Please use the following format when citing this chapter:

Delicato, F.C., Pirmez, L., Pires, P.F., de Rezende, J.F., 2006, in IFIP International Federation for Information Processing, Volume 211, ed. Pujolle, G., Mobile and Wireless Communication Networks, (Boston: Springer), pp. 99–114.

application-specific information, such as QoS parameters, values of sensor-collected data, query and sensing task descriptions.

It is important to point out that the WSN execution context is extremely dynamic, since it mirrors the network and application states. WSN nodes can have their battery depleted, new nodes can be added in the network after the initial deployment, and both bandwidth and the quality of wireless links are likely to change a lot along a sensing task lifetime. Furthermore, the application interests may be truly dynamic, with query parameters and QoS requirements changing along the time.

Several works, such as [3], highlights the close relationship among application requirements and the WSN performance. Energy saving is a key issue in WSN environments, which dictates the network operational lifetime. Application-specific optimizations may increase the WSN overall performance, mainly regarding the energy consumption. At the same time, such optimizations assure that a minimum level of QoS is provided to applications. Each class of application has specific features and different QoS requirements and it is best served by a different network configuration. WSN configuration comprises the network logical topology and the data dissemination protocol, among other factors. To sum up, the careful choice of the WSN configuration may increase the efficiency from both the network and the application point of views. However, configuration decisions should not be left in charge of application developers, which should deal with a higher abstraction level. Therefore, applications should be able to interact with the WSN through a standard high-level programming interface (API). Through this API the clients can issue their queries and QoS parameters, dynamically monitor or modify the network behavior according to their variable requirements and receive the sensor-collected data.

Furthermore, most applications need to directly access the data generated and pre-processed by the WSN in order to use it as inputs for their internal analysis and processing tasks. Such kind of interaction characterizes an application-to-application interface. Web Services technologies [4] have being successfully adopted as a feasible solution for enabling such kind of application interoperability.

The pervasiveness and the wireless nature of sensor devices require network architectures to support *ad hoc* configuration. A key technology of true *ad hoc* networks is service discovery, functionality by which "services" (functions offered by nodes) can be described, advertised, and discovered by other devices or applications. All the current service discovery and capability description mechanisms are based on *ad hoc* representation schemes and rely on standardization. A crucial requirement for the future, widely accessed WSNs is interoperability under unpredictable conditions, i.e., networks which were not designed for specific, predefined purposes, should be able to be accessed by different applications, which dynamically discover their functionality and take advantage of it. The tasks involved in the dynamic utilization of WSN services involve service discovery and description. Service description may involve representing information about the sensing task and QoS parameters. Thus, an ontology language is useful to describe the characteristics of WSN devices, their sensing capabilities, and specific information of applications accessing the WSN.

We propose a framework based on Web technologies for designing WSNs. The framework has three main goals: (i) to establish a programming model for WSNs, aiming to standardize the design and the interoperability of applications and to increase the flexibility of network usage; (ii) to provide a standard interface for accessing the WSN, allowing both the retrieval of information about the execution context, and the submission of tasks and requirements to adjust the network behavior according to each application; and (iii) to supply components that offer functionalities needed by WSN applications from different domains.

The proposed programming model follows a service-based approach in which WSNs are service providers to client applications. The interface provided by the framework for accessing the network is implemented by a communication service based on Web services technologies. The set of network-supplied services is published and accessed through an XML-based language [5]. XML messages exchanged between the WSN and applications are formatted and packed through the SOAP protocol [6].

The functionalities provided by the framework are implemented as a set of configurable service components. These components are responsible for managing the network behavior such that requirements of different applications can be met, while the network resources are optimized. The communication service can be customized through extension mechanisms, allowing different communication protocols, devices and services to be seamlessly incorporated in the WSN architecture.

The proposed framework provides mechanisms to acquire, to reason about and to adapt the WSN behavior according to context information. Such capability allows sensor nodes to maintain consistent contextual knowledge and change their behavior according to it. Such knowledge is achieved through sharing context information among different entities of a WSN system, namely, sensor nodes, applications and infrastructure components. Sensors monitor and periodically send context information. Applications inspect the current context and eventually change previously stated execution policies. Framework service components must guarantee that defined QoS parameters are met, and that the current execution context is valid. To meet this goal the framework adopts a set of common ontologies to support the communication among the several entities that comprise the WSN domain.

The main benefits of the proposed framework can be assessed under two points of view: the application and the WSN. From the application point of view, the framework provides an abstraction of a generic WSN, which offers services for several application domains, with different requirements. Such services are accessed in a flexible way and through different high level programming languages (Java, C++, etc), according to the application developer choice. The utilization of the proposed framework allows building autonomic WSNs, customized according to specific application needs. At the same time, it leverages the development of custom and context-aware applications for WSN environment. Another important aspect is that, through the use of XML language and the SOAP protocol, both *de facto* Web standards, the proposed framework naturally provides interoperability between the WSN and the Internet.

From the network point of view, the framework services supply mechanisms to obtain the best match between network configuration and application requirements, as well as to inspect and dynamically adapt the network behavior according to changes in the execution environment. By using these services it is possible to reach high network efficiency in terms of energy consumption.

Although the framework provides several service components, the focus of this work is mainly in the communication service, which adopts Web technologies. Therefore, such component is described in details and evaluated. The remainder of this paper is divided as follows. Section 2 presents related works. Section 3 details the proposed framework. Section 4 describes the developed system prototype and Section 5 concludes the paper.

2 Related Work

Our work has features that distinguish it from other existent proposals for designing WSNs. First of all, it proposes a service-based approach for the WSN design, in which all interactions among applications and the underlying wireless network rely on a consumer-provider relationship. Such approach was inspired in the area of Web Services [4] and its major advantage is offering a flexible and generic programming model for WSNs. In contrast with the service-based approach, there are works that propose database approaches [7, 8] or event-based programming models [9] for designing WSNs.

The second particular feature of our work is the proposal of a high-level interface for accessing the network. This interface, instead of relying on proprietary formats or languages, such as [9], which adopts a proprietary procedural script language, provides a standard mechanism for representing data and formatting messages exchanged between applications and the network. The adoption of the ubiquitous standards XML and SOAP provides high portability and flexibility to WSN applications. The XML high degree of extensibility allows it to be adopted both as a query and as a tasking language. On the other hand, the adoption of proprietary languages hinders interoperability among applications and WSNs.

The third feature of our framework is that it provides configurable service components that allow dynamically configuring and customize the underlying network infrastructure and protocols. In spite of there being other works [2] that share such a goal, these works do not address the issue of representing and interpreting application requirements. Another relevant feature of our framework is the use of mechanisms for providing applications with context awareness. Such feature is also supplied by CARISMA [2], which, however, was designed for generic wireless networks, and does not address WSN specific requirements.

In Garnet [10], an architectural framework for WSNs is presented. Garnet focuses on problems regarding the management of data-streams in the context of WSNs. The mechanisms proposed in Garnet are complementary to our work, in the sense that they can be incorporated as service components in our framework.

Regarding the use of ontologies, a pioneer work defines an ontology for sensor nodes [11], which seeks to capture the most important sensor features to describe their functionalities and current state. Such work has similarities with ours in the sense that the contextual information is described by ontologies, with the goal of adapting the WSN behavior to different execution states. However, differently of our proposal, they do not employ ontologies neither for WSN service discovery nor for definition of execution policies by the application

3 Framework Description

This work proposes a framework based on Web technologies for designing WSNs. The framework supplies the basic underpinning for building flexible and configurable WSNs. Such framework comprises: (i) a service-based programming model for WSNs; (ii) a standard interface for accessing the network services; and (iii) a set of configurable service components to aid the application development and to control the network behavior during the execution of submitted sensing tasks.

The proposed framework can be described according to its logical and physical models. The logical model includes: (i) the description of the services provided by the framework to support the execution of WSN applications; (ii) the specification of logical components which supply such services; and (iii) the description of the interfaces of such components among each other, with applications and with the underlying network infrastructure. The framework physical model includes the detailed description of its components, according to the chosen implementation technologies. Although the framework provides several service components needed to the efficient operation of WSNs, this paper focuses on the communication service.

3.2 Logical Model

The basic service provided by WSNs is collecting environmental data and delivering it to applications. Such delivery depends on: (i) the discovery of the WSN capabilities; (ii) the request of data by applications and (ii) the way through which the communication among data producers (sensor nodes) and data consumers (applications) takes place. Our framework provides applications with an abstraction of such delivery service so that it can be configured according to different needs. This abstraction is supplied by the **communication service** that, among other functions, provides applications with a high level interface for accessing the WSN services. The discovery of the WSN sensing capabilities is accomplished through the **discovery service**. This service allows WSNs to advertise their capabilities and applications to advertise a high level description of their sensing requirements. Furthermore, the discovery service accomplishes a matching function between sensing capabilities and application requests in order to allow applications to find suitable WSNs.

One of the goals of our framework is to facilitate the task of application developers, by dealing with low-level issues regarding network infrastructure and protocols. With this intention in mind, the framework supplies a **configuration service**, detailed in [12], responsible for the choice and setting of network protocols, as well as a service for **active node selection** [13], responsible for the choice of sensor nodes that should be activated to accomplish a given sensing task. Once the framework takes these low level decisions, it should control the execution of the received sensing tasks, and manage the utilization of the network resources. In order to perform these tasks, **resource management** and **admission control services** are supplied. To deal with the highly dynamic execution context of WSNs, the framework also provides **inspection and adaptation services**. Furthermore, components of generic services are provided, which are useful for all WSNs.

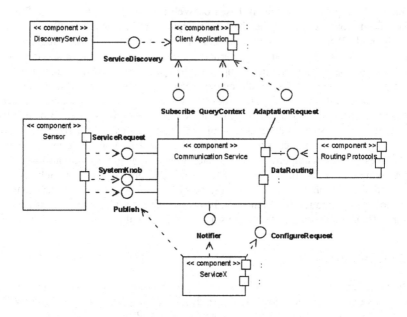

Figure 1: Logical Components and Interfaces

The functionalities of the framework services are provided by a set of components. Figure 1 depicts the main logical components and the interfaces among each other and with the external world (applications, sensor nodes and network protocols). The depicted interfaces represent units of service provision offered by their respective component. The main component is the communication service. All the other services are directly connected to the communication service, except the discovery service. Additional services can be seamlessly integrated into the system, provided that they are connected to the communication service through its interfaces. In the following paragraph, the functions of the main interfaces are summed up.

`ServiceDiscovery` **Interface** is used by applications to find out a WSN able to perform their sensing task. `Subscribe` **Interface** contains service primitives: (i) to allow the application to submit a query or task (`SubscribeInterest`); (ii) to notify the application about sensor published data, in the case of asynchronous queries (`ReceiveResults`); (iii) to allow the application to submit an execution policy, which consists of information on the WSN behavior while executing the requested task (`SubmitExecPolicy`); and (iv) to allow the application to submit QoS parameters to be met during the execution of the requested task

(SubmitQoSParameters). **QueryContext** **Interface** allows applications to inspect the WSN state. **AdaptationRequest Interface** is used by applications to request the activation of an adaptation policy in order to recover the network from a state of QoS violation. **Publish Interface** allows sensor nodes to advertise their capabilities (PublishConfiguration primitive) and to publish their collected data (PublishData), and to allow service components to publish results of their processing tasks (PublishResults primitive). **Notifier Interface** contains primitives to notify framework services about data or application subscription arrivals. **ConfigureRequest Interface** is used by a service component to indicate how a sensor node may request its execution. **DataRouting Interface** contains service primitives used for exchanging data between the framework and the underlying network routing protocols. **ServiceRequest Interface** is used by sensor nodes to request a framework service that requires an explicit request to be activated. **SystemKnobs Interface** allows the framework services to interact with hardware devices, such as processor, sensor, radio transmitters and receivers. It contains service primitives that allow modifying the current state of such devices, enabling a fine-grained control over the network operation.

3.2 Physical Model

The proposed framework makes use of Web Services technologies in the specification and implementation of its components. The adoption of a Web service-based approach was motivated by the fact that such an approach relies on protocols and languages largely used on the Web, thus facilitating the interoperability among the system and client applications. Most of the WSN client applications need gather the data generated and pre-processed by the network as input for their own analysis and processing software. Such interaction characterizes an application-to-application interface. Web Services architecture supplies a feasible solution to enable that kind of application interoperability.

The use of Web Services technologies in both the physical model and the framework implementation implies that framework services are exposed as Web Services. The logical interfaces presented in Section 3.1 are physically described through WSDL documents [14] and XML schemas [5]. Messages exchanged among the external and internal components (in other words, the service primitives) are implemented as SOAP or XML messages.

Regarding the physical constraints to be hold in the framework design, sinks are devices more robust than sensors and represent the network access point. Therefore, they are fully designed following the Web Services architecture. Thus, the implementation of the communication service in sink nodes is based on the SOAP protocol. To avoid the overhead imposed by SOAP, the implementation of the communication service inside sensors is based on lightweight XML messages, and formatted accordingly to specific schemas, which aim to generate XML messages as compact as possible. Optionally, in order to further reduce the communication overhead, the XML binary format, WBXML [15], can be used inside the network. The framework service components are implemented as software modules. These components are described in the next sections.

3.2.1 Communication Module

This module is responsible for the communication service implementation. It includes a SOAP proxy responsible for the interaction with client applications and XML drivers for communicating with the underlying network protocols and devices. SOAP proxies are programs that translate function calls in the application programming language to SOAP messages so as to invoke respective operations of the network services. Conversely, SOAP reply messages are converted to data and function calls in the application programming language. SOAP proxies use primitives of the **Subscribe, QueryContext** and **AdaptationRequest** logical interfaces, which are implemented as operations of the communication module and are described in the WSN WSDL document.

Similarly to SOAP proxies, drivers for different protocols consist of software modules that convert functions calls, according to the programming language of a given communication protocol, in operation calls defined according to the framework API, and vice-versa. In the same way, drivers convert XML messages generated by the framework components in proprietary data formats of the communication protocol, and vice-versa.

To provide the application requested QoS and to enable the adaptation of the network behavior according to execution contexts, the framework components should be able to directly interact with hardware devices, such as sensors and radio transmitters. This requirement is met by specifying an API that abstracts the behavior of the WSN configurable parameters (communication protocols and devices). This API consists in the implementation of the **SystemKnobs** logical interface. The device manufacturers enable low-level interactions with devices by supplying a service API. Drivers for the conversion between framework and devices APIs can be built from the supplied specifications.

The processing of a data message arriving in a WSN node, and its subsequent forwarding to the framework services, are performed by SOAP-based components in sink nodes and by XML-based components in sensor nodes. The communication module also contains an ontology database and a reasoning engine, which comprise the semantics components of the framework.

SOAP-based Components. The communication module in sink nodes is composed of a SOAP engine and a set of handlers. The SOAP engine is responsible for coordinating the SOAP messages flow through the several handlers and for guaranteeing that the semantics of SOAP protocol is respected. Handlers represent the logic of message processing and act as dispatchers for the several services supplied by the framework. Handlers intercept SOAP messages, parse the message-header fields indicating the services that are to be executed over the data packet, and dispatch the packet for the components that implement such services.

XML-based Components. To avoid the overhead of the SOAP protocol, XML messages exchanged inside the network are formatted according to a specifically designed schema. Such schema is a lighter SOAP-like specification that generates more compact messages than the original SOAP protocol. The XML-based communication module is the counterpart, in sensor nodes, of the SOAP-based communication module in sinks. It is composed of a message dispatcher, which is a lighter version of the SOAP engine, and a set of handlers, responsible for forwarding messages to the service components provided by sensor nodes.

Knowledge base. Corresponds to the ontology database. It contains the adopted ontology model, that is, the definitions of the classes and properties created for describing sensor features, execution contexts and policies, application queries and tasks. The full database is implemented only in sink nodes. Sensor nodes keep a sub-part of the ontology definitions needed for representing their own capabilities and information about execution contexts.

Reasoning engine. A software module responsible for reasoning with ontology knowledge, that is, static knowledge derived from the underlying ontology model. Its function is to decide whether WSN nodes can meet the requirements of a submitted application task.

3.2.2 Service Modules

The service interfaces offered by the framework to the external world (applications and other services) are described through WSDL documents. Therefore, a WSDL document defines the format of messages used to submit application interests and QoS requirements and to request inspection or adaptation of the network behavior (Figure 2). The framework also provides a WSDL document that describes the interfaces to be used by service developers to incorporate new services in the WSN architecture. Furthermore, XML schemas are provided which describe the interfaces to be used by network protocol developers. Primitives described in the logical interfaces correspond to definitions of service operations, which are invoked through SOAP or XML messages.

The external discovery module of the framework discovery service allows applications to find both the location of a potentially interesting WSN and the format of messages to interact with it. The use of SOAP and XML, both part of the Web Services architecture, makes UDDI [4] a natural choice as the discovery protocol to be used by applications.

Sink nodes implement a Web Service comprising all the functionalities offered by the WSN and they keep a repository containing the WSDL documents that describe the Web Service interfaces. To access a WSN, an application initially locates the WSN sink node through UDDI and then obtains the WSDL document to learn the message format to communicate with the network. Therefore, the external discovery module is composed of WSDL documents and of the necessary specifications for publishing the WSN Web Service in the UDDI registry.

The **configuration service** is implemented only in sink nodes, by the **decision module**. The **inspection and adaptation service** is implemented as two independent modules: (i) the **inspection module**, that allows the application to inspect the network behavior at runtime, supplying a representation of the current execution state; and (ii) the **monitoring and adaptation module**, responsible for monitoring the states of the network and application and for activating adaptation policies whenever it is necessary or requested by the application. The **monitoring and adaptation module** accesses the local ontology database and, similarly to the communication module, it contains a reasoning engine. This engine is responsible for reasoning with both ontology knowledge and contextual knowledge. Contextual knowledge is a dynamic knowledge that is inferred from situational information reported by sensor nodes. Once that information is available, the module verifies if the WSN execution context at every given moment represents a valid state. Otherwise, a predefined adaptation policy is triggered to repair the network state.

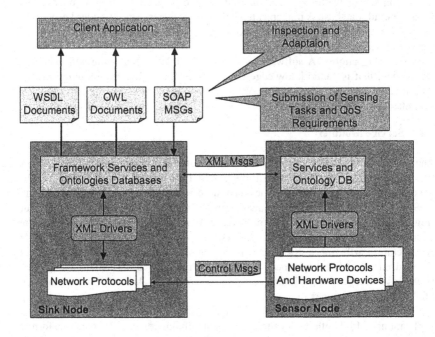

Figure 2: Communication among the framework components

The inspection module is implemented only in sink nodes and the monitoring and adaptation module is implemented both in sink and sensor nodes. The **resource and task management service** is also implemented as two independent modules: an **admission control module** and an **active node selection module**, both implemented only in sink nodes. Each generic service supplied by the framework is implemented as a separate module in the proposed system. Modules of generic services can be implemented and supplied by third parts. The use of XML-based APIs in the framework design allows services to be easily incorporated to the WSN system, provided that they implement the defined interfaces.

3.2.3 WSN Ontology

We detected three situations in which it would be worthwhile to add semantics in the context of accessing and using WSNs:

- To locate networks that potentially meet the interests of an application, given a high level description of the requested services. The goal here is to discover the address (URL) of the access point (sink) of such WSNs, through which applications are able to access and use the WSN services. In this case, the UDDI protocol, used for discovering WSNs, should be added with semantic capacities. Addressing such situation is out of the scope of our work.

- Once a specific WSN has been chosen, to determine if the sensing task requested by the application can be fully accomplished by such network, given the task detailed description, including QoS requirements.

- Once the task has been initiated, to share knowledge on the execution context, allowing (i) sensor nodes to send information about the network and the application current states; (ii) applications to monitor such state; and (ii) service components to verify if a given execution state is valid and the eventual need of triggering adaptation mechanisms in case of violation of QoS parameters.

We designed a WSN ontology to capture the most relevant features of sensors, execution context and application requirements for the purposes of service discovery and context monitoring (items 2 and 3 above). Therefore, we created classes and properties to describe concepts related to the descriptions of sensor node capabilities, application tasks and policies, and execution contexts. For purposes of service discovery, we defined: (i) three main classes for describing WSN features (*WSN*, *SensorNode* and *SensorField*); and (ii) four main classes for describing application requirements (*Task*, *Query*, *QoSParameters* and *SensorType*). For purposes of describing execution policies and contexts, and verifying if the current state fits in a valid policy, the main classes we created are: *ExecutionContext*, *ApplicationState*, *NetworkState*, *ExecutionPolicy* and *CurrentState*. The defined ontologies are concisely depicted in Figures 3 and 4. The framework reasoning engines have a set of rules that allows reasoning based on such ontologies.

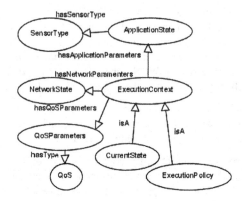

Figure 3: Main ontologies for execution policies and contexts

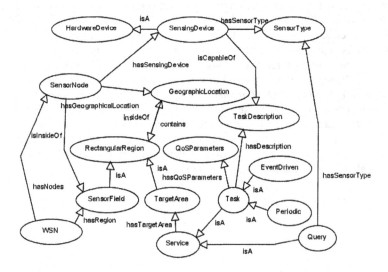

Figure 4: Main ontologies for tasks and WSN descriptions

The ontologies designed for the WSN domain were defined by using the OWL/RDF language [16]. The Web Ontology Language (OWL) is intended to provide a language to describe the classes and relations between them that are inherent in Web documents and applications. The OWL language can be used (i) to formalize a domain by defining classes and properties of those classes; (ii) to define individuals and assert properties about them, and (iii) to reason about these classes and individuals to the degree permitted by the formal semantics of the OWL language. We will not present the OWL files containing the complete description of ontologies, for lacking of space. The OWL-DL [16] version of the language was used for representing the ontologies stored on the sink node knowledge base and the OWL-Lite [16] version for ontologies on the sensor node database.

4 Framework Prototype

As a proof of concept for the proposed framework, a prototype was constructed which implements its main building blocks. The goals of building the prototype were to validate the high-level interaction among applications and the WSN, according to the proposed programming model, and to establish a basis for evaluating the system requirements in terms of memory and processing power. From the implemented prototype it is possible to infer the feasibility of developing WSN applications based on the proposed framework with the currently existent hardware for sensor nodes.

The prototype was implemented in Java programming language. Since the hardware device features and, hence, the software components to be deployed in each device largely differ between sink and sensor nodes, two development platforms were used to implement each type of node.

The implementation of the prototype was divided into two phases. The goal of the first phase consisted of modeling and implementing the communication module in the sink nodes. The implementation of such module allowed to validate the high level interaction among applications and the WSN and to check the calls of operations supplied by the network Web Service. The goal of the second phase was to analyze the computational load of the communication module in sensor nodes. In that phase, the adoption of messages in both XML and WBXML formats was evaluated, in order to compare their performance, in terms of network traffic and memory consumption. A simple generic service component was also implemented to evaluate the amount of memory spent by sensor devices to receive XML messages, process and forward such messages through the different handlers and deliver them to the module that implements the requested service. The implemented service was data aggregation. Since data aggregation is a basic operation, required by all classes of current WSN applications, our work leverages the aggregation function as a first class operation supplied as one of the framework service components.

The prototype of sink nodes was executed in a Pentium 4 1.8 GHZ with 1.5 GB of RAM and 40 GB HD. The WSN Web Service and the classes representing the functionalities needed for the sink node were implemented using Apache Axis platform for Web Services [17] and J2SE 1.4.2_01. The document describing the WSN services was written in WSDL language. The previously described operations SubscribeInterest, PublishConfiguration and PublishData were provided by the implemented Web Service. Operations are invoked through SOAP messages.

As it was previously described, applications access the WSN by using SOAP proxies. In the developed prototype, the client application was implemented in Java language. Therefore, the WSDL2Java tool [17] was used for generating the Java proxy for accessing the network. WSDL2Java tool is supplied along with the Axis package and it consists of a Java class which receives as input a WSDL document representing a Web Service and it generates method calls in Java corresponding to the invocation of the respective service operations.

In order to validate the communication between client applications and the WSN, an event-driven application was implemented as a Java application that emits queries for the network and receives the results. The application, after obtaining the URL of the sink node through UDDI, gets a reference for the WSN Web Service and invokes the operation of interest submission, representing an asynchronous query. Sensing data meeting the application interests are reported by sensors through the PublishData operation and delivered to the application through the ReceiveResults operation.

In order to evaluate the feasibility of implementing the proposed framework in sensor nodes, we emulated the hardware of WINS NG 2.0 [18] nodes, which are endowed of SH-4 167 MHz processors and have 32 MBytes of RAM. The framework components in sensor nodes were implemented by using the J2ME (Java Micro-edition) platform, with CLDC configuration (Connected Limited Device Configuration) and MIDP profile (Mobile Information Device Profile). CLDC configuration defines the base set of application programming interfaces and a virtual machine for resource-constrained devices often connected through a wireless network. MIDP profile was designed to mobile and cellular phones and it offers a set of basic functionalities needed for mobile applications.

The *Wireless Toolkit* [19] was used for building the sensor node prototype. The Wireless Toolkit is a toolbox for developing wireless applications that are based on J2ME Connected Limited Device Configuration and Mobile Information Device Profile, and it was designed to run on cell phones, personal digital assistants, and other small mobile devices. The toolkit includes the emulation environments, performance optimization and tuning features. The kxml package [20] was used for implementing the communication module in sensor nodes. Kxml provides an XML parser and an XML writer light enough to run in the J2ME platform. Besides the communication module, an aggregation service module was implemented, which offers methods for accomplishing MAX, MIN and AVERAGE functions. The size of the ".jar" file (Java deployment format) composed of all classes needed for a sensor node running the proposed framework is 90kBytes, including all libraries. Such size is perfectly compatible with the memory resources of our target sensor nodes.

Table 1: Measurements performed using XML and WBXML formats (in bytes)

Method/Operation	XML Format		WBXML Format	
	Memory	Network traffic	Memory	Network traffic
PubContent (send)	10748	139	8152	47
PubContent (reception/forward)	10344	139	5964	47
AdvInterest (recep/forw)	33216	178	21140	57
PubData (send)	13136	42	9396	24
PubData (recep/forw)	6136	42	4016	24

To deal with the XML verbosity, there are binary versions suitable for resource-constrained environments. One widely used binary format is WBXML [15]. The kxml package includes support to handle WBXML messages. We implemented

XML and WBXML formats, in order to compare their performances in terms of number of bytes transmitted in the network and memory consumption on devices.

Wireless Toolkit includes tools for monitoring: (i) the frequency of use and execution time for every application method; (ii) the usage of memory while the application runs; and (iii) network data transmitted and received by the application. Such tools were used to perform measurements with the prototype. The methods of the prototype code were grouped according to the corresponding working stage of the network. Table 1 shows the results obtained by the memory and network monitors. In the table, PubContent refers to the stage of internal service discovery, in which sensors exchange messages describing their capabilities. AdvInterest refers to the stage of task submission for the application. PubData refers to the stage of data sending for the sensors. Results represent the measurements of one single node, that is, its individual memory consumption and the network traffic generated by it, when accomplishing each one of the mentioned operations. The performed measurements shown that the adoption of WBXML format resulted in a decrease of around 30% in the memory consumption and around 70% in the network traffic, in comparison to the XML format. Therefore, WBXML represents a better choice for representing message exchanging inside the WSN. It is worthwhile mentioning that message sizes in the WBXML format is lower even then message sizes of well known WSN protocols that adopt proprietary binary formats [21].

5 Conclusions

The proposed framework has the goal of acting as the underpinning for developing a new, more flexible and easier to use architectural approach for WSNs. Such approach is suitable for building the envisioned autonomic WSNs of the near future. WSNs have historically been built with a strong coupling among applications and the underlying network infrastructure. Such architectural approach is justified by the need to achieve energy efficiency. However, not only are these solutions proprietary, but they generate rigid systems, with WSNs specifically designed to particular applications. This scenario is not desirable, considering the costs of the infrastructure deployment, the potentially long operational lifetime of the network and its capability of serving several classes of applications. Therefore, rather than being coupled to specific applications and often built by the same application development team, future WSNs should be designed with a flexible architecture, satisfying the demands of a broad range of applications from different groups of users.

Acknowledgements

This work was supported by the Brazilian Research Council, CNPq.

References

1. I. F. Akyildiz, W. Su, Y. Sankarasubramaniam, and E. Cayirci, Wireless sensor networks: a survey. *Computer Networks*, **38** (4):393–422 (2002).
2. L. Capra, W. Emmerich, C. Mascolo, Reflective Middleware Solutions for Context-Aware Applications in: Proceedings of the Reflection2001, Japan, pp. 126-133, 2001.
3. J. Heideman, F. Silva, and D. Estrin, Matching Data Dissemination Algorithms to Application Requirements. in: Proceedings of the the ACM SenSys, pp. 218-229, USA, Nov. 2003.
4. S. Graham, et al., *Building Web Services with Java: Making Sense of XML, SOAP, WSDL, and UDDI*. (Sams Publisher, 2002).
5. W3C Recommendation (February 4, 2004) "Extensible Markup Language (XML) 1.0 (Third Edition)"; http://www.w3.org/TR/REC-xml.
6. W3C Recommendation (June 4, 2003) "SOAP version 1.2."; http://www.w3.org/TR/soap12-part0/.
7. P. Bonnet, J. E. Gehrke, and P. Seshadri, Towards Sensor Database Systems. in: Proceedings of the 2nd International Conference on Mobile Data Management, Hong Kong, Jan. 2001.
8. Cougar Project (April 5, 2006); http://www.cs.cornell.edu/database/cougar/.
9. C. Shen, C. Srisathapornphat, C. Jaikaeo, Sensor Information Networking Architecture and Applications, *IEEE Personal Communications* v. 8, pp.52–59, Aug. 2001.
10. L. St. Ville, P. Dickman, Garnet: A Middleware Architecture for Distributing Data Streams Originating in Wireless Sensor Networks. in: Proceedings of the First International Workshop on Data Distribution for Real-Time Systems (DDRTS'03), Providence, Rhode Island, USA, May 2003, pp.235-240.
11. S. Avancha, C. Patel, and A. Joshi, Ontology-driven Adaptive Sensor Networks, in: Proceedings of the First Annual International Conference on Mobile and Ubiquitous Systems: Networking and Services (MobiQuitous'04), Boston, Massachusetts, August 2004, pp. 194-202.
12. F. Delicato, et al. Service Oriented Middleware for Wireless Sensor Networks (in Portuguese). Nucleo de Computação Eletrônica – Federal University of Rio de Janeiro Technical Report No.NCE04/04.
13. F. Delicato, et al. Application-Driven Node Management in Multihop Wireless Sensor Networks. in: Proceedings of the 4th IEEE International Conference on Networks (ICN 2005), Reunion Island, April 2005.
14. W3C Working Draft. Web services description language (WSDL) Version 2.0 Part 1: Core Language (March 27, 2006); http://www.w3.org/TR/wsdl12/.
15. W3C Note (June 24, 1999) "WAP Binary XML Content Format"; http://www.w3.org/TR/wbxml/.
16. W3C Recommendation. OWL Web Ontology Language (February 10, 2004); http://www.w3.org/TR/owl-guide/.
17. Apache Axis (April 5, 2006); http://ws.apache.org/axis/.
18. Sensoria WINS 3.0 Spec. (April 5, 2006); http://www.sensoria.com/products-wins30.htm.
19. J2ME Wireless Toolkit (April 5, 2006); http://java.sun.com/products/j2mewtoolkit/.
20. KXML Project (April 5, 2006); http://kxml.objectweb.org/.
21. C. Intanagonwiwat, R. Govindan, D. Estrin, Directed diffusion: a scalable and robust communication paradigm for sensor networks. in: Proceedings of the ACM/IEEE MobiCom 2000, USA, Aug. 2000.

Energy Efficiency Maximization for Wireless Sensor Networks *

Inwhee Joe

College of Information and Communications
Hanyang University
Seoul, Korea
iwjoe@hanyang.ac.kr

Abstract. Because of the remote nature and the size of sensor nodes, they rely on limited battery energy that cannot be replenished in many applications. Thus, low power consumption technology is a major issue in wireless sensor networks in order to prolong system lifetime. In this paper, we propose to maximize energy efficiency in wireless sensor networks using optimal packet length in terms of power management and channel coding. The use of power management cannot improve energy efficiency, but it saves a lot of energy because the transceiver is turned off while it is not used. Also, we evaluate optimal packet length without power management in such that the energy efficiency can be maximized. Finally, we show that the BCH code for channel coding can improve energy efficiency significantly compared to the convolutional code.

1 Introduction

A wireless sensor network has been recognized as an important technology in realizing ubiqutous computing. In an early stage, it is designed for an unmanned surveillance system, monitoring military tendency in terrain where access is difficult. Recently, a sensor network is used for remote sensing in a number of areas including intelligence traffic system, factory process control or environment control of intelligent building. The concept of sensing and wireless connection promises many new application areas. Sensor networks provide a new kind of capability that enables us to observe and interact with physical phenomenon in real time and in detail that was unobtainable before.

In the wireless sensor network, a large number of sensor nodes are deployed either inside the phenomenon or very close to it. Each node consists of sensing, data processing, and communication components. Sensor nodes are embedded with an onboard processor. When events of interest are detected by sensor nodes, they use their processing power to carry out simple computations and transmit only the required data to a remote base station instead of sending the raw data.

---

* This work was supported in part by grant No. IITA-2005-C1090-0501-0022 from the ITRC Support Program of the Ministry of Information and Communication, and in part by grant No. HY-2003-T from the Research Fund of Hanyang University.

Please use the following format when citing this chapter:

Joe, I., 2006, in IFIP International Federation for Information Processing, Volume 211, ed. Pujolle, G., Mobile and Wireless Communication Networks, (Boston: Springer), pp. 115–122.

The wireless sensor network is quite different from the traditional wireless networks [6]. It has a large number of sensor nodes and they are densely deployed. The distance between neighbor nodes is shorter compared to other wireless networks. The data rate and mobility in the wireless sensor network are low. Because of the remote nature and the size of the individual nodes, they rely on limited battery energy that cannot be replenished for most wireless sensor networks. In many cases, sensor nodes are placed in the field for years at a time without maintenance or human intervention of any kind. Thus, low power consumption technology is a major issue in wireless sensor networks in order to prolong system lifetime.

In this paper, we show that energy efficiency can be improved by optimal packet length at the data link layer. The optimal packet length is obtained in terms of energy efficiency. Also, we present that the use of power management for improving energy efficiency is not justified. Then, we show optimal packet length without power management. Power management is to turn off the transceiver when it is in the idle state. Finally, we evaluate that the BCH code for error control can improve energy efficiency significantly compared to the convolutional code.

The structure of this paper is as follow. In Section 2, we compute the probability of error as a function of neighbor distance between sensor nodes. In Section 3, we compare the optimal packet length with power management versus without it in terms of energy efficiency. In Section 4, we show that the BCH code can improve energy efficiency significantly compared to the convolutional code. Finally, we conclude this paper in Section 5.

2   Channel Estimation

In this section, we estimate the raw channel BER (Bit Error Rate) for typical wireless sensor networks. The probability of bit error (P_b) under a FSK modulated Rayleigh fading channel model for wireless sensor networks is defined as follows [7]:

$P_b = \frac{1}{2+\gamma}$ .... (1)

$\gamma : E_b/N_o$

$\gamma(dB) = 77 - 10\alpha \log(d)$ .... (2)

$\alpha : path\ loss\ exponent = 4.0$

where γ is the average received bit energy to noise ratio. According to the receiver implementation, γ depends on the neighbor distance d between sensor nodes. The path loss is the average propagation loss as a function of the distance d on the order of α.

We assume the RFM-TR1000 transceiver with -9dBm output power, 7.5dB noise figure and 6dB implementation losses. Fig. 1 presents the probability of bit error by Equation (1) according to the neighbor distance with path loss exponent $\alpha = 4$ in the worst case design. Normally, most sensor nodes are separated

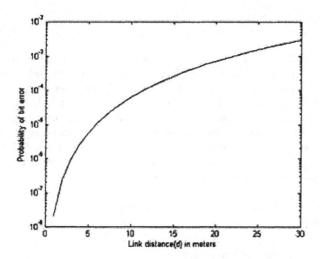

Fig. 1. Probability of bit error as a function of neighbor distance

from each other at a distance between 10 and 20m in wireless sensor networks. Therefore, the estimated channel BER lies in the range of 2×10^{-4} and 3×10^{-3} in this case.

3   Power Management and Optimal Packet Length

Due to the time-varying nature of the wireless channel, the throughput is very sensitive to the packet length. It is well known that the variable packet length with channel conditions can result in significant throughput improvement [4]. For example, if the wireless channel condition becomes worse, the smaller packet length is more desirable because the error rate is higher and the larger packets are likely to fail in transit. However, the variable packet length is not appropriate for wireless sensor networks due to the complexity. Even if the throughput is lower, we support the use of the fixed packet length for energy efficiency in wireless sensor networks, which is more important in this case. Moreover, we propose to use the optimal fixed packet length in terms of maximizing the energy efficiency.

Power management is to turn off the transceiver to reduce energy consumption when it is in the idle state. With the use of power management, it is possible to accomplish significant energy savings. However, since sensor nodes normally communicate using short packets, energy efficiency could be reduced instead due to the dominance of start-up energy. The energy efficiency equation is defined by [1]

$$\eta = E_{th} \cdot R \dotfill (3)$$
$\eta :$ *energy efficiency*

E_{th} : *energy throughput*
R : *reliability*

where the energy throughput E_{th} represents the ratio of energy consumed for actual data transmission to entire packet transmission, and the reliability R represents the successful packet reception rate. That is, the energy efficiency η can be obtained from the energy throughput multiplied by the reliability, which means how much energy is actually used for successful data transmission.

According to the use of power management, Equation (3) can be expressed in more concrete form. While Equation (4) represents energy efficiency as a function of packet length with power management, Equation (5) represents energy efficiency without power management as follows:

$$\eta = \frac{E_c l}{E_c(l+h)+E_s} \cdot (1 - PER).................................(4)$$
$$\eta = \frac{l}{l+h} \cdot (1 - PER)................................(5)$$

E_c : *communication energy consumption*
E_s : *start − up energy consumption*
l : *payload length*
h : *header length*
PER : *packet error rate*

We compare energy efficiency with power management versus without it in Figs. 2 and 3. Fig. 2 shows energy efficiency for the neighbor distance 10m, while Fig. 3 shows energy efficiency for the neighbor distance 20m. From these results, we can find out that the use of power management cannot improve energy efficiency. However, if power management is not used, it causes a lot of energy waste. In summary, even if power management cannot improve energy efficiency, it should be employed in order to minize the waste of energy.

It is apparent that if the packet length is too small, it suffers from an efficiency problem due to the larger overhead. On the other hand, if the packet length is too large, it experiences higher packet error rates especially for the wireless channel with high error rates. Since an error packet means a total loss of energy consumed for the packet transmission, it also suffers from an efficiency problem in this case. Therefore, there exists an optimal packet length in the sense of maximizing the energy efficiency. In particular, when energy efficiency is at peak, the optimal payload length is 280 bits for 10m of neighbor distance and it is 60 bits for 20m of neighbor distance, if power management is applied. Also, the maximum values of energy efficiency are measured by 0.88 and 0.62, respectively.

4   Channel Coding and Optimal Packet Length

Channel coding is one of typical approaches to increase link reliability in the design of wireless networks with poor channel conditions. Before it is applied to wireless sensor networks, we should check first if channel coding can improve

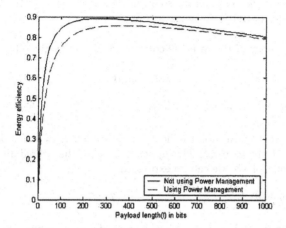

Fig. 2. Energy efficiency as a function of payload length for neighbor distance $d = 10m$ and $h = 16bits$

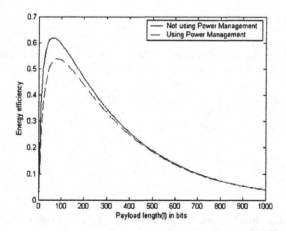

Fig. 3. Energy efficiency as a function of payload length for neighbor distance $d = 20m$ and $h = 16bits$

energy efficiency. In this section, energy efficiency is compared between the BCH code and convolutional code. Turbo and LDPC codes are not considered here, because their iterative decoding process consumes a lot of energy. It turns out that they are not appropriate for wireless sensor networks due to the very limited energy.

The energy efficiency of the rate-1/2 convolutional code is given by

$$\eta = \frac{E_c(\frac{n}{2}-h)}{E_c n + E_s + E_{dec}} \cdot (1 - \acute{P}_b)^n \dots\dots\dots\dots\dots\dots(6)$$

$\acute{P}_b$: *Probability of bit error for convolutional code*

where n is the packet length, h is the header length, and E_{dec} is the decoding energy consumed at the receiver. The upper bound on the probability of bit error for the convolutional code can be expressed by

$$\acute{P}_b < \frac{1}{k} \sum_{d=dfree}^{\infty} \beta d P(d) \dots\dots\dots\dots\dots\dots(7)$$

where d denotes the Hamming distance in the trellis diagram between some path and the all-zero path, d_{free} is the minimum free distance, β_d is the cofficient of the first derivative of the transfer function $T(N, D)$ with respect to N, and $P(d)$ is the first-event error probability.

For the BCH code, we first consider a binary BCH code with hard decision. The encoder adds τ parity bits to the l payload and h header bits. As a result, the packet length n equals to $l + h + \tau$. The energy efficiency of the BCH code with the t error correction capability is given by

$$\eta = \frac{E_c(n-h-\tau)}{E_c n + E_s + E_{dec}} \cdot \sum_{j=0}^{t} \binom{n}{j} P_b^j (1 - P_b)^{n-j} \dots.(8)$$

Equation (9) gives the decoding energy for a t error correction binary BCH code of length n, defined as

$$E_{dec} = (2nt + 2t^2)(E_{add} + E_{\mu lt}) \dots\dots\dots\dots\dots(9)$$
$$E_{add} = 3.3 * 10^{-5} m (mW/MHz)$$
$$E_{mult} = 3.7 * 10^{-5} m^3 (mW/MHz)$$
$$\tau = mt(\tau \leq mt)$$

τ : *number of parity bits*
t : *error correction capability*

where E_{add} and E_{mult} are the energy consumptions in the addition and multiplication under $GF(2^m)(m = |\log_2 n + 1|)$.

Fig. 4 shows energy efficiency for the convolutional code using Equation (6) versus the BCH code using Equation (8) each at the channel BER 10^{-3}. From these results, we observe that the use of channel coding can improve energy efficiency significantly. It is also shown that the energy efficiency of the convolu-

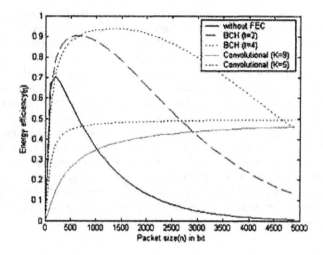

Fig. 4. Energy efficiency as a function of packet length for comparison of BCH versus Convolutional codes with $h = 16bits$

tional code is only half or so, compared to that of BCH code. The reason for the lower energy efficiency is that the convolutional code causes a larger overhead in that for each packet the half of it is data and the rest is redundancy. In other words, since more than half of the total energy is consumed for redundancy and control overhead, it leads to a substantial degradation in terms of energy efficiency. On the other hand, the BCH code introduces much less redundancy unlike the convolutional code.

Since high energy efficiency is required for wireless sensor networks, the use of the BCH code is a viable solution. As compared to the case without the use of channel coding, it would rather improve the energy efficiency. Also, we find out that the energy efficiency is reduced in case of the BCH code as the error correction capability t is increased. In particular, the optimal packet length is 700 bits and its energy efficiency is 0.90 for the error correction capability of 4, while the optimal packet length is 1400 bits and its energy efficiency is 0.93 for the error correction capability of 2. With the use of the BCH code, the energy efficiency can be increased up to 0.93 from 0.7, which is the maximum value of the case without the use of channel coding.

5   Conclusions

Because of the remote nature and the size of sensor nodes, they rely on limited battery energy that cannot be replenished in many applications. Thus, the energy efficiency is a critical factor in wireless sensor networks in order to prolong system lifetime.

122   Inwhee Joe

Due to the time-varying nature of the wireless channel, the throughput is very sensitive to the packet length. It is well known that the variable packet length with channel conditions can result in significant throughput improvement. However, the variable packet length is not appropriate for wireless sensor networks due to the complexity. Even if the throughput is lower, we support the use of the fixed packet length for energy efficiency in wireless sensor networks, which is a more important factor in this case. Moreover, we propose to use the optimal fixed packet length in terms of maximizing the energy efficiency.

In this paper, we have shown that energy efficiency can be maximized by optimal packet length in wireless sensor networks. The use of power management cannot improve energy efficiency, but it saves a lot of energy because the transceiver is turned off while it is not used. Also, we have found out that the BCH code can improve energy efficiency significantly compared to the convolutional code. From our test results, we have concluded that energy efficiency can be improved substantially through optimal packet length and channel coding.

References

1. Y. Sankarasubramaniam, I.F. Akyildiz and S.W. McLaughlin, "Packet Size Optimization and its Implications on Error Control for Sensor Networks," Proceedings of the 1st IEEE International Workshop on Sensor Network Protocols and Applications, May 2003.
2. E. Shih, B.H. Calhoun, S. Cho, and A.P. Chandrakasan, "Energy-Efficient Link Layer for Wireless Microsensor Networks," IEEE Computer Society Workshop on VLSI 2001, pp. 16-21, April 2001.
3. K. Sohrabi, J. Gao, V. Ailawadhi, and G.J. Pottie, "Protocols for Self-Organization of a Wireless Sensor Network," IEEE Personal Communications Magazine, pp. 16-27, October 2000.
4. I.F. Akyildiz and I. Joe, "A New ARQ Protocol for Wireless ATM Networks," Proceedings of IEEE International Conference on Communications ICC'98, pp. 1109-1113, June 1998.
5. G.J. Pottie and W.J. Kaiser, "Wireless Integrated Network Sensors," Communications of ACM, Vol. 43, No. 5, pp. 51-58, May 2000.
6. I.F. Akyildiz, W. Su, Y. Sankarasubramaniam, and E. Cayirci, "A Survey on Sensor Networks," IEEE Communications Magazine, pp. 102-114, August 2002.
7. T. Rappaport, "Wireless Communications: Principles and Practice," Prentice Hall, 2002.
8. I. Joe, "A Novel Adaptive Hybrid ARQ Scheme for Wireless ATM Networks," ACM-Baltzer Wireless Networks Journal, Vol. 6, No. 3, pp. 211-219, June 2000.

A Simple and Fair Proposal to Improve the Performance of the IEEE 802.11e Enhanced Coordination Function

Marta Barría[1], Pablo Sánchez[2] and Luciano Ahumada[3]

[1] Departamento de Computación, Universidad de Valparaíso,
Avenida Gran Bretaña 1091, Valparaíso, Chile.
[2] Departamento de Electrónica, Universidad Técnica Federico Santa María
Avenida España 1680, Valparaíso, Chile.
[3] Escuela de Ingeniería Informática, Universidad Diego Portales
Avenida Ejército 441, Santiago, Chile.

Abstract. A simple and fair proposal to improve the performance of the IEEE 802.11e standard is presented in this paper. Our proposal is accomplished by means of increasing the priority of those queues that have not been able to transmit during certain period of time, depending on the elapsed time waiting to transmit. Results show that this proposal improves the performance of wireless networks using IEEE 802.11e EDCF since low priority queues reduce their waiting time to access the channel and high priority queues are not degraded.

1 Introduction

Wireless Local Area Networks (WLAN) are gaining popularity at public hot spots, home and work. To provide an efficient and robust network in a wireless environment for a collection of mobile stations, the IEEE 802.11 working group has chosen the Carrier Sense Multiple Access with Collision Avoidance (CSMA/CA) protocol as the standard protocol [1]. This standard contains two access methods: the distributed coordination function (DCF) and point coordination function (PCF), with the former being specified as the fundamental method. Notice that they can only support best effort traffic [2].

With the widespread use of wireless services and the emerging requirements of real-time voice, audio and multimedia applications, Quality of Service (QoS) support becomes a key requirement. To address this challenge, the IEEE 802.11 Task Group E published the IEEE 802.11e draft [3], presenting the enhanced distributed coordination function (EDCF) and the hybrid coordination function (HCF) providing

Please use the following format when citing this chapter:

Barría, M., Sánchez, P., Ahumada, L., 2006, in IFIP International Federation for Information Processing, Volume 211, ed. Pujolle, G., Mobile and Wireless Communication Networks, (Boston: Springer), pp. 123–131.

differentiated services in terms of priority schemes to access the medium for different stations or traffic nature. The EDCF assures the best service for high priority traffic and minimum service for those of low priority. Although this mechanism improves the performance of a wireless real time traffic service, it may not be a fair scheme for those queues of medium or low priority since the EDCF parameters are not adapted to the network status and low or medium priority traffic may not be treated fairly since they could suffer starvation or extremely high latency.

In this work we present a novel method to improve the performance of the IEEE 802.11e EDCF, being fair with all traffic categories and simpler than other proposals [2]. Different changes to the IEEE 802.11e have been proposed. However, most of them only care about high priority queues, sacrificing ACs of low or medium priority. Thus, if the performance of those models is evaluated in terms of a fair scheme, they seem to be not appropriated enough. To achieve fairness, fair scheduling mechanisms have been proposed for WLANs. Among them, the Distributed Fair Scheduling (DFS) tries to adjust *backoff* intervals [6], Distributed Weighted Fair Queuing (DWFQ) [7] adjusts contention windows, and Distributed Deficit Round Robin (DDRR) [8] suggests the use of different inter-frame space (IFS) intervals through a mapping scheme to avoid possible collisions. Distributed Elastic Round Robin (DERR) [9] determines an allowance value according to users' requirements. Both DFS and DWFQ present poor performance in terms of the throughput and delay due to collisions although better fairness can be achieved. DDRR presents better performance in throughput and delay than DFS and DWFQ; however DERR not only improves performance in throughput and delay, but also exhibits better fairness if it is compared to DDRR [9].

We aim to establish a simple methodology by the estimation of simple parameters in each station, without the knowledge of the entire network or the state of the shared wireless medium. Our technique is based on considering that all stations are statistically similar, that is, traffic arrival to each priority queue is described by the same Poisson process. Therefore, looking for fairness at each station will create a fair network.

The rest of this article is presented as follows: in section 2 we describe the IEEE 802.11 DCF and 802.11e EDCF, section 3 contains the proposal, section 4 the performance evaluation and simulation results and finally in section 5 we present our conclusions.

2   Brief Description of IEEE 802.11 DCF and 802.11e EDCF

2.1   The IEEE 802.11 Distributed Coordination Function

The IEEE 802.11 standard [1] defines both the physical (PHY) and medium access control (MAC) layer protocols for WLANs. The IEEE 802.11 standard calls for three different PHY specifications: frequency hopping (FH) spread spectrum, direct sequence (DS) spread spectrum, and infrared (IR).

The basic data rate for the DS system is 1Mbits/s encoded with differential binary phase shift keying (DBPSK). Similarly, a 2Mbits/s rate is provided using differential quadrature phase shift keying (DQPSK) at the same chip rate. Higher rates of 5.5 and 11Mbits/s are also available using techniques combining quadrature phase shift keying and complementary code keying (CCK); all of these systems use 22 MHz channels. The IEEE 802.11 MAC layer specifications, common to all PHYs and data rates, coordinate the communication between stations and control the behavior of users who want to access the network.

According to IEEE 802.11 standard stations access the channel using a *basic access method*, or an optional *four-way handshaking access method* with an additional Request-To-Send/Clear-To-Send (RTS/CTS) message exchange. Under the basic access method, a station, when ready for a new data frame transmission, first senses the channel status. If the channel is found to be busy, the station defers its transmission and continues to sense the channel until it is idle. After the channel is idle for a specified period of time called the distributed interframe space (DIFS) period, the station defers its transmission and continues to sense the channel until it is idle. If the medium is sensed idle for a period greater than a DCF Interframe Space (DIFS), the station goes into a *backoff* procedure before it sends its frame. Upon the successful reception of a frame, the destination station returns an ACK frame after a Short Interframe Space (SIFS). If an ACK is not received within an ACK timeout interval, the station assumes that either the data frame or the ACK was lost and needs to retransmit its data frame by repeating the basic access procedure.

The *backoff* procedure shall be invoked by the station when the medium is sensed busy as indicated by either the physical or CSMA/CA algorithm. To begin the backoff procedure, the station shall set its *Backoff* Timer to a random *backoff* time. All *backoff* slots occur following a DIFS period during which the medium is determined to be idle for the duration of the DIFS period. Note that the time immediately after the DIFS period is slotted. The timeslot duration is at least the time required for a station to detect an idle channel plus the time required for switching from listening to transmitting mode. The *backoff* window is based on a random value uniformly distributed in the interval [CWmin; CWmax], where CWmin and CWmax represent the Contention Window parameters. The *backoff* timer is decreased by one for each idle slot, stopped if the channel is sensed busy, and then reactivated if the channel is idle again and remains idle for more than a DIFS time duration. When the *backoff* timer reaches zero, the data frame is transmitted.

A virtual carrier sense mechanism is also provided at the MAC layer. It uses the request-to-send (RTS) and clear-to-send (CTS) message exchange to make predictions of future traffic on the medium and updates the network allocation vector (NAV) available in stations. Communication is established when one of the wireless nodes sends a short RTS frame. The receiving station issues a CTS frame that echoes the sender's address. If the CTS frame is not received, it is assumed that a collision occurred and the RTS process starts over. The RTS/CTS scheme is designed to avoid the so-called Hidden Terminal problem [1], which occurs when mobile stations are unable to hear each other.

Typically, time-bounded applications such as Voice over IP (VoIP), or videoconferencing require specified bandwidth, low delay and jitter, but can tolerate some losses. The point is that in DCF, all the stations compete for the channel with the same priorities. There is no differentiation mechanism to guarantee bandwidth, packet delay and jitter for high-priority multimedia flows [2]. If this is added to channel fading [4], it results simple to understand that the DCF may not be the best scheme to support QoS oriented services.

2.2   The IEEE 802.11e Enhanced Distributed Coordination Function

The EDCF enhances the DCF. It provides distributed and differentiated channel access for frames with 8 different priorities. It is a part of a single coordination function, called the Hybrid Coordination Function (HCF), of the 802.11e MAC specifications. All the details of the HCF [3] are beyond the scope of this paper as we focus on the EDCF.

Data frames from the higher layers, with a specific priority value, arrive at the MAC layer. Then, each QoS data frame carries its priority value in the MAC frame header. An 802.11e station shall implement four access categories (ACs), mapping the arrived frames to a specific AC queue according to a predefined mapping table, as shown in Table 1. This is usually extracted from IEEE 802.1d bridge specification [5].

Table 1. AC Mapping Table

Priority	AC	Traffic Type
0	0	Best effort
1	0	Best effort
2	0	Best effort
3	1	Video Probe
4	2	Video
5	2	Video
6	3	Voice
7	3	Voice

The AC queues differ from each other on the specific value of the initial length of the contention window $CW[AC]_0$. This means that high priority traffic will be described in terms of a smaller *backoff* interval than the corresponding value for those of low priority.

Each AC in a station will sense the channel and it will start an independent *backoff* procedure after an arbitrary inter-frame space (AIFS) during which the medium is determined to be idle. The AIFS value may be different for each AC, i.e. AIFS[AC] may differ from each other. The minimum value of AIFS[AC] is DIFS. After an AIFS period, each *backoff* timer will take a random value in the interval $[1; CW[AC]_0+1]$.

The *backoff* timer of each AC is decreased by one for each idle slot, stopped if the channel is sensed busy, and then reactivated if the channel is idle again and remains idle for more than an AIFS time duration. When the *backoff* timer reaches zero, the data frame is transmitted.

When there is more than one AC finishing the *backoff* at the same time, the collision is handled in a virtual manner by a virtual collision handler. That is, the highest priority frame among the colliding frames receives a transmission opportunity (TXOP) and the others perform a *backoff* with increased CW values, whose size will be given by their previous value CW[AC] and a persistence factor (PF), according to:

$$CW[AC]_i = (CW[AC]_{i-1}+1) \cdot PF[AC] -1 \qquad i > 0 \qquad (1)$$

Therefore, the *backoff* timer will take a random value in the interval $[1; CW[AC]_i +1] = [1;(CW[AC]_{i-1}+1) \cdot PF[AC]]$. Notice that this procedure does not avoid colliding packets from different stations to access the shared physical medium.

3   The TBPS scheme

The EDCF is a non adaptive protocol, since the priority of each AC is static. Therefore, if the offered load is high, certain traffic classes may experience starvation because of an increasing number of virtual collisions, being an unfair scheme for those ACs of low or medium priority. If we also take into account collided packets from different stations, or a non-ideal wireless channel, the problem is even worst.

In this work we propose the use of a dynamic priority scheme for the AC queues, named Time Based Priority Scheme (TBPS). Our proposal is to update the ACs priorities depending on the waiting time to transmit a frame of each queue. Hence, if any AC queue has not been able to transmit a frame because of virtual collisions, i.e. the scheduler mechanism of the virtual collision handler, its priority is increased allowing it to transmit a frame in a number of retrievals not bigger than the number of working queues in that station. This change of priority implies that if a virtual collision occurs, the "virtually collided" AC with longer waiting time interval must use the AIFS and CW values of the queue with immediately higher priority.

This scheme establishes a hard transmission limit. After a successful transmission attempt, each AC must load their original values of CW and AIFS. Then, the QoS of each AC will be a function of its own initial contention window $CW[AC]_0$ and AIFS[AC] periods guaranteeing that a single AC will always be able to use the channel in a number of retrievals not bigger than the number of working queues in that station. Therefore, fairness is assured by means of a simple method that only requires the estimation of local parameters, being less complex than those that need a complete knowledge of the network.

4   Performance Evaluation and Simulation Results

We based our simulations design on the event-oriented software presented in [10]. Our simulations have a confidence interval of 95%. Simulated stations used three different AC queues: AC3 with high priority (HP), AC2 with medium priority (MP) and AC1 with low priority (LP). If a virtual collision occurs, the classic EDCF would let AC3 be the first station to transmit, and AC1 the last. Our dynamic proposal suggests that the order will depend on the elapsed time by each AC waiting to transmit a frame. This implies that if a virtual collision happens, the queue that has been waiting to transmit for a longer period of time must replace its CW[AC] and AIFS[AC] values taking those of the following queue with higher priority. For example, if AC3 is the queue being on hold for a longer period of time, it must replace its CW and AIFS values taking those of AC2. After a successful transmission attempt, each AC must load their original values of CW and AIFS.

Once the virtual collision handler of each station selects an AC queue to transmit, it may sense an idle or busy channel. If the channel is idle, data frames may collide with those of another station trying to transmit or start a successful transmission. During our simulations, we analyze the performance of this proposal in terms of the busy channel probability, defined as the probability that the shared wireless medium is not idle. We use a unique packet length for all ACs and stations. We normalize packet and CW lengths to the slot lengths defined by the PHY layer. The defaults settings are described in Table 2.

Table 2. Default settings to run the simulations

Parameter	AC3	AC2	AC1
Priority	HP	MP	LP
AIFS	4 slots	5 slots	6 slots
CWmin	8 slots	16 slots	32 slots
PF	2	2	2
Packet length	38 slots	38 slots	38 slots

We evaluate the network performance in terms of the latency and mean occupation of the network. Latency is defined as the time interval for a packet to come into their queue until it accesses the medium. The mean occupation of each AC is the ratio between the successfully used slots (without collisions) and the entire number of time slots.

4.1   Simulation Results

Figure 1 shows that if the busy channel probability is increased, the mean occupation of each AC is significantly decreased since the *backoff* is continuously interrupted and the probability of finding an idle channel for a period longer than AIFS is also diminished. Notice that AC3 always presents higher occupation, since it has higher priority. It can also be seen that the dynamic priority method improves the performance of AC2 and AC1 as compared to the static mechanism, without a significant change on the performance of AC3.

Figure 2 shows the latency results. It can be seen that the latency is reduced for low and medium priority queues AC2 and AC1, and AC3 does not present significant changes. This improvement makes the dynamic approach a better scheme if the offered load is high or if the network is saturated since QoS requirements may be achieved for all queues.

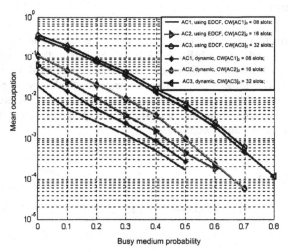

Fig. 1. Mean occupation in terms of the busy medium probability

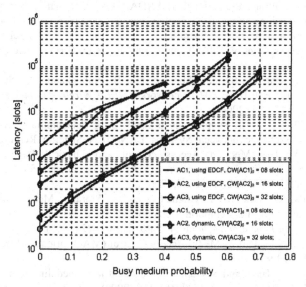

Fig. 2. Latency in terms of the busy medium probability

5 Conclusions

The main contribution of this article is the novel mechanism to handle virtual collisions as an upgrade of the IEEE 802.11e EDCF. This method is simpler than those already published since it only requires the estimation of local parameters, i.e. parameters from the same station. This dynamic methodology improves the performance of low priority queues, maintaining the performance of high priority ACs. Simulations results show that the use of this proposal makes significant improvements on latency and occupancy.

Acknowledgments

This project was partially supported by project DIPUV-48/2005 and project Semilla-UDP.

References

1. IEEE 802.11 WG, Reference number ISO/IEC 8802 -11:1999(E) IEEE Std. 802.11, 1999 edition. International STANDARD for Information Technology-Telecommunications and information exchange between Systems Local and Metropolitan area networks- Specifics requirements- Part 11: Wireless LAN Medium Access Control (MAC) and Physical Layer (PHY) Specifications, (1999).
2. Huang Zhu, Ming Li, Imrich Chlamtac, and B. Prabhakaran, "A Survey of Quality of Service in IEEE 802.11 networks", *IEEE Wireless Communications Magazine*. **11**(4) 4-14 (2004).
3. IEEE 802.11 WG, Draft Supplement to standard for Telecommunications and Information Exchange between Systems LAN/MAN Specific Requirements-Part 11: Wireless Medium Access control and Physical Layer (PHY) Specifications: Medium Access control (MAC) Enhancements for Quality of Services (QOS), IEEE 802.11e/ D2.0, (2001).
4. L. Ahumada, R. Feick, R. A. Valenzuela and C. Morales: Measurement and Characterization of the Temporal Behavior of Fixed Wireless Links. *IEEE Transactions on Vehicular Technology*. **54**(6) 1913-1922 (2005).
5. IEEE 802.1d-1998, Part 3: Media Access Control (MAC) bridges, ANSI/IEEE Std. 802.1D, (1998).
6. N. H. Vaidya, P. Bahl, and S. Gupta, "Distributed fair scheduling in a wireless LAN," in *Proc. ACM MobiCom '00*. 167-178 (2000).
7. Banchs and X. Perez, "Distributed weighted fair queuing in 802.11 wireless LAN," in *Proc. IEEE ICC '02*. 3121-3127 (2002).
8. W. Pattara-Atikom, S. Banerjee, and P. Krishnamurthy, "Starvation prevention and quality of service in wireless LANs," in *Proc. IEEE Wireless Personal Multimedia Communications* '02. 1078-1082 (2002).

9. Huei-Wen Ferng, Chung-Fan Lee, Jeng-Ji Huang, and Ge-Ming Chiu, "Designing a Fair Scheduling Mechanism for IEEE 802.11 Wireless LANs" *IEEE Communications Letters*, **9**(4) 301-3003 (2005).
10. S. Mangold, and S. Choi. "IEEE 802.11e Wireless LAN for Quality of Service". *European Wireless* (EW'02). 32-39 (2002).

A Comparative Analysis of Adaptive Middleware Architectures Based on Computational Reflection and Aspect Oriented Programming to Support Mobile Computing Applications

Celso Maciel da Costa[1], Marcelo da Silva Strzykalski , and Guy Bernard[2]

1   Pontifícia Universidade Católica do Rio Grande do Sul, Faculdade
de Informática, Av. Ipiranga, 6681, prédio 30,
bloco 4, Porto Alegre, Brazil celso@inf.pucrs.br,
WWW home page: http://www.inf.pucrs.br/~celso
2 Institut National des Télécommunications, Département Informatique
Rue Charles Fourier, 91000,
Evry, France
guy.bernard@int -evry.fr,
WWW home page: http://etna.int-evry.fr/~bernard

Abstract. Mobile computing applications are required to operate in environments in which the availability for resources and services may change significantly during system operation. As a result, mobile computing applications need to be capable of adapting to these changes to offer the best possible level of service to their users. However, traditional middleware is limited in its capability of adapting to environment changes and different users requirements. Computational Reflection and Aspect Oriented Programming paradigms have been used in the design and implementation of adaptive middleware architectures. In this paper, we propose two adaptive middleware architectures, one based on reflection and other based on aspects, which can be used to develop adaptive mobile applications. The reflection based architecture is compared to an aspect oriented based architecture from a quantitative perspective. The results suggest that middleware based on Aspect Oriented Programming can be used to build mobile adaptive applications that require less processor running time and more memory space than Computational Reflection while producing code that is easier to comprehend and modify.

1   Introduction

Recent advances in wireless networking technologies and the growing success of mobile computing devices are enabling new classes of applications that present new kinds of problems to designers. These applications have to be aware and adapt to variations in the system's environment such as fluctuating network bandwidth, low battery power, slow CPU speed and low memory [1].

In the past decade middleware technologies, which reside between the operating system and the application, have enhanced the design and the implementation of

Please use the following format when citing this chapter:

da Costa, C.M., da Silva Strzykalski, M., Bernard, G., 2006, in IFIP International Federation for Information Processing, Volume 211, ed. Pujolle, G., Mobile and Wireless Communication Networks, (Boston: Springer), pp. 133–148.

distributed systems. Middleware hides from the programmer the complicated details about networking communication, remote method invocation and naming providing an easy platform to build complex distributed systems. However, current generation of mainstream middleware has been designed for stationary distributed systems, being heavyweight, inflexible and monolithic [2]. It does not provide support for dealing with the new dynamic aspects in which mobile computing applications need to operate nowadays [3].

Mobile computing applications require a middleware that can be adapted to changes in their execution context and customized to fit in many kinds of devices. However, conventional middleware is limited in its capability of supporting adaptation. Adaptive middleware has evolved from conventional middleware to solve this problem. Such next middleware generation should be run time configurable and allow inspection and adaptation of the underlying software. Adaptive middleware provides two types of adaptation: static and dynamic. Static adaptation occurs during compiling or startup time, while dynamic adaptation occurs during application run time.

In order to support adaptation, adaptive middleware employs the following software engineering paradigms in addition to object-oriented programming: Computational Reflection [4] enables middleware to inspect and adapt itself at runtime. Component-based design [5] enables the decomposition of middleware functionality making easier to modify the middleware structure both statically and dynamically. Aspect-Oriented Programming [6] enables separation of middleware crosscutting concerns (such logging, security and transaction control) at development time and later at compile or run time, where these concerns can be selectively woven into application code. Software Design Patterns [7] enable reuse of best adaptive designs in adaptive middleware.

Separation of concerns is recognized as a fundamental mechanism for managing the complexity of software systems. Software Engineering methodologies capture functional and nonfunctional requirements of a software system that should be designed and implemented. Object oriented paradigm captures well functional requirements and core concerns (application domain). However, this paradigm has limitations to modularize crosscutting concerns. The aspect oriented paradigm proposes a new way for identifying, encapsulating and manipulating nonfunctional (system-level) concerns.

This paper presents adaptive middleware architectures based on reflection and aspects to support adaptation. Sections 2 and 3 introduce Computational Reflection and Aspect-Oriented Programming related concepts. Section 4 analyzes a set of requirements that future middleware platforms should incorporate in its architecture to supporting adaptive mobile applications. Section 5 discusses several adaptation techniques that can be employed in mobile computing applications to reduce energy consumption and to allow user interaction when disconnected from the remote system. Sections 6 and 7 present middleware architectures based on reflection and aspects to support adaptation. Section 8 describes two prototypes based on both paradigms, which were developed to validate the architectures proposed. Section 9 evaluates the performance of both prototypes. Section 10 briefly presents and compares our approach with related work and we outline conclusions and directions for future works in section 11.

A Comparative Analysis of Adaptive Middleware Architectures Based on   135
Computational Reflection and Aspect Oriented Programming to Support Mobile
Computing Applications

2   Computational Reflection

Smith [8] and Maes introduced reflective computing systems in the context of programming language community to support the design of more open and extensible languages. Such computing systems can be made to manipulate representations of itself in the same way as it manipulates representations of its application domain. This self-representation is constituted of both its state and behavior, and can be used to inspect and adapt the software system's internals.

More specifically, reflection refers to the capability of a system to reason about, and possibly, alter its own behavior [9]. It is the ability of a system to watch its computation and possibly change the way it is performed. A reflective system provides a representation of its own behavior, which can be used to inspection (i.e., the internal behavior of the system is exposed) and adaptation (i.e., the internal behavior of a system can be dynamically changed) and is causally connected to the underlying behavior it describes. Causally connected means that changes made to the self-representation are immediately mirrored in the underlying system's actual state and behavior and vice-versa, i.e., the manipulation of the internal representation structures directly affects the system observable external behavior.

A reflective system is logically structured in two or more levels, constituting a reflective tower. The first level is the base-level and describes the computations that the system is supposed to do. The second one is the meta-level and describes how to perform the previous computations. The entities working in the base-level are called base-entities, while the entities working in the other levels (meta-levels) are called meta-entities. Each level is causally connected to adjacent levels, i.e., entities working into a level have data structures reifying the activities and the structures of the entities working into the underlying level and their actions are reflected into such data structures.

3   Aspect Oriented Programming

Aspect Oriented Programming (AOP) is a new paradigm that focuses on the issue of handling crosscutting concerns. Crosscutting concerns are elements of software that can not be expressed in any functional unit of an object oriented programming language abstractions, such as a method or a class. The AOP approach proposes a solution to the crosscutting concerns problem by encapsulating these into a single unit called aspect. An aspect is a modular unit of crosscutting implementation and is designed to encapsulate state and behavior that affect multiple classes into reusable modules. An aspect oriented software system is composed by a set of classes that handle the localized concerns (functional requirements, or application functionality) and a set of aspects that handle the global concerns (nonfunctional requirements).

In general, aspect-oriented approaches are static - aspect code and functional modules (classes) are traditionally woven together at compile time. Static weaving produces well-formed and highly optimized woven code whose execution speed is comparable to the code without AOP. However, there are certain environments (mobile computing, for example) where we have to be able to change the global policies implemented through aspects dynamically, during runtime [10]. Dynamic weaving means that aspects can be added or removed at any time during runtime. Thus, this approach allows the integration between classes and aspects at runtime, resulting in a system that is more adaptable and extensible.

4   Adaptive Architecture Requirements

Efstratiou *et al.* [11] suggests that there are limitations of current approaches for supporting adaptive applications. Specifically, these approaches lack of support for enabling applications to adapt to numerous different attributes in an efficient and coordinated way. Thus, a new approach is required, which must provides a common space for the coordinated, system-wide interaction between adaptive applications and the complete set of attributes that could be used to trigger adaptation.

This new approach is based on a set of requirements that could be used to develop an appropriate architecture for supporting adaptive applications. The first key requirement of the architecture is to provide a common space for handling the adaptation attributes used by the system in which new attributes can be introduced as and when they become important. The second requirement is to be able to control adaptation behavior across all components involved in the interaction on a system-wide level. A further requirement is to support the notion of system-wide adaptation policies that should enable a system to operate differently given the current context and the requirements of the user. A final requirement arises from the fact that most mobile applications operate in a distributed environment, reason for what the adaptation mechanism need to coordinate all elements involved in the system distributed operation.

5   Adaptation Strategies

Future mobile environments will require software to dynamically adapt to rapid and significant fluctuations in the communication link quality, frequent network disconnections, device resource restrictions and power limitations. Such scenario implies in the fact that software will have to include adaptation techniques in its design and implementation.

Several adaptation techniques can be triggered in all levels of an adaptive application, from system level to user level. In the middleware level, three approaches can be identified [1 2]: middleware services can attempt to reduce application bandwidth requirements by using data compression techniques before transmission, data can be prefetched and cached during periods of bandwidth high availability in preparation to future bandwidth reduction or service disconnection and clients can be redirected to services available in the local context until network connectivity can be established. In addition, we can include in the middleware level some adaptation techniques to reduce energy consumption and allow users to continue working when in disconnected state.

5.1   Power Management

Since one of the main limitations of mobile computing devices is battery life, minimizing energy consumption is essential for maximizing the utility of these computing systems. Adaptive energy conservation algorithms can extend the battery life of portable computers by powering down devices when they are not needed. The disk drive, the wireless network interface, the display, and other elements of mobile computing devices can be turned off or placed in low power modes to conserve energy.

Many physical components are responsible for ongoing power consumption in a mobile device. The top three items are, in this order [13]: CPU, screen and disk. Due the fact that hardware technology in this area is still rapidly evolving, power

A Comparative Analysis of Adaptive Middleware Architectures Based on   137
Computational Reflection and Aspect Oriented Programming to Support Mobile
Computing Applications

management techniques to reduce display consumption are not explored in this section.

5.1.1   Processor

Power consumed by the CPU is related to the clock rate, the supply voltage and the capacitance of the devices being switched. The reduction in CPU power consumption as the clock rate decreases is a result of the switching characteristics of the logic gates in CMOS VLSI circuits. The power wasted by logic gates during switching is equal to the supply voltage squared divided by circuit's resistance. Because the switching resistance is commonly fixed, the wasted power is proportional to the square of the operating voltage. Besides, the total power required by CPU is proportional to $C\,V^2\,F$, where C is the total capacitance of the wires and transistor gates, V is the supply voltage and F is the clock frequency. While C can only be changed during the VLSI circuit design, newer devices are beginning to make possible to vary F and V during runtime, which allows achieving linear and quadratic savings in power.

Dynamic Voltage Scaling (DVS) has been a key technique in exploiting the characteristics above mentioned to reduce processors energy dissipation by lowering the supply voltage and operating frequency if it is expected a large amount of CPU idle time [14]. DVS tries to address the tradeoff between performance and battery life taking into account two important features of most current computing systems. First, the peak computing rate needed is much higher than the average throughput, so, high performance is only needed for a small fraction of the time, which allows lowering the operating frequency of the processor when full speed is not a requirement. Second, processors are based on CMOS logic. Such technology allows scaling the operating voltage of the processor along with its frequency. In this manner, by dynamically scaling both voltage and frequency of the processor based on computation load, DVS can provide the performance to meet peak computational demands, while on average, providing the reduced power consumption.

Weiser *et al.* [15] propose an approach that balances CPU usage between periodic bursts of high utilization and the remaining idle periods under the control of the operating system scheduling algorithms by predicting the upcoming workload requirements and adjusting the processor voltage and frequency accordingly. Three algorithms derivate from this approach: OPT, FUTURE and PAST. Each of these algorithms adjusts the CPU clock speed at the same time scheduling decisions are made by the operating system scheduler with the goal of decreasing time wasted in idle loops while retaining interactive response for the user. OPT is completely optimistic (and impractical) because it requires perfect future knowledge of the work to be done in an interval. FUTURE is similar to OPT, except by the fact it looks to the future only in a small window. Unlike OPT, it is practical because it only optimizes over short windows (it is assumed that all idle time in the next interval can be eliminated). PAST is a practical version of FUTURE that uses the recent past as a predictor of the future. Instead of looking a fixed window into the future, it looks a fixed window into the past, and assumes the next window will be like the previous one. Obviously, such approach depends on an effective way of predicting workload to save power by the adjustment of processor speed fast enough to accommodate the workload.

5.1.2   Disk

Spinning down the disk when it is not being used can save power. Such technique is possible by the fact that most mobile computers disk drives have a new mode of operation called SLEEP mode (in such mode, a drive can reduce its energy consumption to near zero by allowing the disk platter to spin down to a resting state). Most, if not all current mobile computers use a fixed threshold specified by the manufacturer to determine when to spin down the disk: if the disk has been idle for some predetermined amount of time, the disk is spun down. The disk is spun up again upon the next access. The fixed threshold is typically about many seconds or minutes to minimize the delay from on demand disk spin-ups.

Spinning a disk for just a few seconds without accessing it can consume more power than spinning it up again upon the next access since spinning the disk back up consumes a significant amount of energy. Therefore, spinning down the disk more aggressively reduce the power consumption of the disk in exchange for higher latency upon the first access after the disk has been spun down.

Douglis *et al.* [16] investigated two types of algorithms for spinning a disk up and down minimizing power consumption and response time: off-line, which can use future knowledge and on-line, which can use only past behavior. Off-line algorithms are useful only as a baseline for comparing different on-line algorithms. On the other hand, on-line algorithms are implementable. A perfect off-line algorithm can reduce disk power consumption by 35-50% when compared to the fixed threshold suggest by manufacturers. On the other hand, an on-line algorithm with a threshold of 10 seconds reduces energy consumption by about 40% compared to the 5minute threshold recommended by manufacturers.

5.2   Disconnected Operation

Wireless networks are very susceptible to suffering disconnections, so it is a very important aspect to keep in mind when designing architectures to support mobile computing. We can classify the disconnections in two main categories: forced disconnections (usually accidental and unavoidable, that takes place when the user enters in an out-of-coverage area) and voluntary disconnections (when the user decides to disconnect from the network to saving energy).

Forced disconnections as well as voluntary disconnections are frequent in a mobile computing environment. But, as can been seen in Coda File System project [17], the use of caching and server replication techniques can mitigate the undesirable effects of disconnections, which allows users to be able to continue working even in disconnected state. In this mode of operation, a client continues to have read and write access to data in its cache during temporary network outages, being the system responsible to propagating modifications and detecting conflicts when connectivity is restored. In addition, dis connected operation can extend battery life for avoiding wireless transmission and reception.

6   Reflective Middleware Architecture

Welling [18] asserts that adaptive techniques must be decoupled from basic application functionality due to the complexity of building adaptive applications for mobile computing. Such principle allows both applications and adaptive techniques be designed and implemented independent of each other.

In this direction, Zhang and Jacobsen [19] observe that middleware platforms architectures have been evolving exactly by the necessity of a software layer that decouples applications from the concern of handling the complexity related to distributed computing environments.

The architecture proposed in this section employs this principle of decoupling adaptation techniques (meta-level) from application basic functionality (base-level), as can be seen in figures 1 and 2.

A Comparative Analysis of Adaptive Middleware Architectures Based on   139
Computational Reflection and Aspect Oriented Programming to Support Mobile
Computing Applications

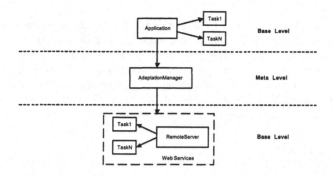

Fig. 1. Separation of concerns in the proposed reflective middleware architecture

The Adaptation Manager (AM) decides which adaptation strategies should be executed from data supplied by the inspection task of each resource managed by the same. Attention might be given to this module in the architecture. Because conflicts may arise during the execution of a specific adaptation strategy, this module must guarantee that such conflicts can be solved in a coordinate manner. The set of attributes (computational resources) to be managed by the AM must be extensible; by the way, new attributes can be added in the proposed architecture. The AM depends on two modules which responsibilities are complementary, described below.

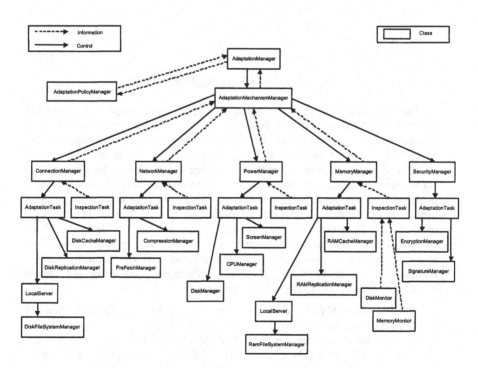

Fig. 2. The proposed reflective middleware architecture

The Adaptation Policy Manager loads the adaptation policies described in the application profile, which is defined by the application's user. The application profile (which describes the application nonfunctional behavior) is encoded using the

Extensible Markup Language (XML) due the fact such language supports a representation of information that is both easily handled by machines and readily understandable by humans. The application profile presented in figure 3, for example, inspect the battery resource each 10 seconds and spindown the hard disk and scale CPU frequency when the amount of energy available in the battery is below 10%. In addition, the Adaptation Policy Manager updates dynamically the adaptation policies using statistical learning methods.

```xml
<?xml version="1.0"?>
<ApplicationProfile>
<InspectionTasks>
<Task name="BatteryInspector">
<Frequency value="10"></Frequency>
</Task>
</InspectionTasks>
<AdaptationTasks>
<Task name="DiskManager">
<Resource name="Battery">10</Resource>
<Threshold value="10"></Frequency>
</Task>
<Task name="CpuManager">
<Resource name="Battery">10</Resource>
<Threshold value="10"></Frequency>
</Task>
</AdaptationTasks>
</ApplicationProfile>
```

Fig. 3. An example of the application profile

The Adaptation Mechanism Manager inspects and adapts the following attributes: connectivity, network bandwidth, energy and memory. The following modules manage such attributes: Connection Manager, Network Manager, Power Manager and Memory Manager. Besides, this module should guarantee the security of data exchanged between the application and the Remote Server. Such behavior is encapsulated in the Security Manager module. It should be noted that the attributes managed by this module can be extended dynamically by changes in the application profile. At the run time, the Adaptation Mechanism Manager checks the conditions of each adaptation rule described in the application profile to determine if an adaptation task should be performed. To execute this operation, the class AdaptationMechanismManager provides two methods that systematically iterates through each rule coded in the application profile to check conditions and load or unload adaptation tasks in accordance to these rules.

The Connection Manager monitors the connectivity between the application and the Remote Server. In case of disconnection, the data handled by the application are gotten from the Local Server module. The methods invoked toward the Remote Server are stored in the local cache and will be deferred to execute by the Replication Manager adaptation task when the Remote Server was in connected mode again.

The Network Manager monitors the network bandwidth. This module compresses the body message that will be sent to the Remote Server. Besides, this module pre-fetches messages that were posted in the Remote Server and were not replicated to the Local Server yet.

A Comparative Analysis of Adaptive Middleware Architectures Based on   141
Computational Reflection and Aspect Oriented Programming to Support Mobile
Computing Applications

The Power Manager monitors energy. If the amount of energy in a moment were below a boundary expressed in the application profile, the interface between the application and the user is text based. Besides, the hard disk can be put in spindown mode and the CPU frequency can be scaled to save battery power.

The Memory Manager monitors memory and disk space. If the amount of disk space in a moment were below a boundary exp ressed in the application profile, the messages posted in the Local Server as well as data from local cache will be stored in the RAM memory, not more in the hard disk. The deferred methods will be stored in RAM memory either.

The Security Manager module should guarantee the confidentiality (XML Encryption) and the integrity (XML Signature) of the XML messages exchanged by the application and the Remote Server.

7   Aspect Oriented Middleware Architecture

Following the separating of concerns principle of software engineering, the architecture proposed in this section employs the principle of separating global concerns (nonfunctional concerns) from local concerns (functional concerns or application domain concerns), as can be seen in figures 4 and 5.

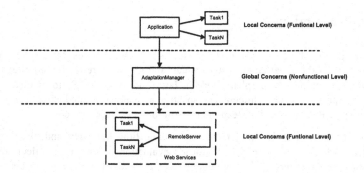

Fig. 4. Separation of concerns in the proposed aspect oriented middleware architecture

Aspects and classes in a modular structure compose the architecture. The Adaptation Manager is a class whose methods are intercepted by aspects (ConnectionManager, NetworkManager, PowerManager, MemoryManager and SecurityManager). Each aspect allows the addition and the removal of code used to manage computational resources in a dynamic way in accordance to the application profile defined by the application's user. It should be emphasized that each aspect in this architecture has the same responsibility owned by each class with the same name in the reflective middleware architecture presented in section 6.

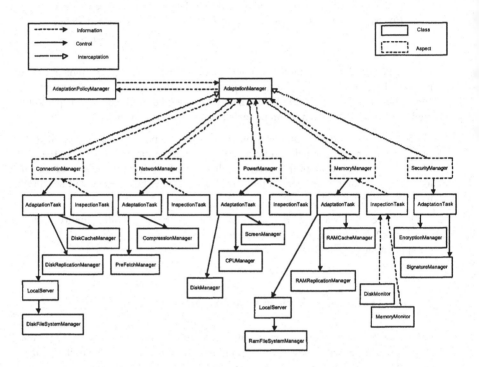

Fig. 5. The proposed aspect oriented middleware architecture

8   Implementation

A simplified mail server prototype based on Web Services technology was
implemented in the Java language to evaluate the proposed reflective architecture.
The same prototype was implemented in Java and Aspectj [20] to evaluate the
proposed aspect oriented architecture. Aspectj is an aspect-oriented extension to the
Java language that enables the clean modularization of crosscutting concerns.

Both prototypes only implement the Connection Manager and the Power
Manager modules. Therefore, the platform's evaluation performance reflects only
these attribute's measures. We have employed a collaborative relationship between
the operating system and the application by the middleware level in such prototypes,
each of one modifies its behavior to conserve energy to meet user-specified goals for
battery duration. In addition, our approach predicts future energy demand from
measurements of past usage.

The Power Manager measures energy consumption by using the ACPI subsystem
in Linux to get an accurate evaluation of the remaining capacity of the battery. The
Screen Manager changes the user interface from text to graphic mode and vice-versa
in accordance to the current energy level available. The CPU Manager implements
the PAST algorithm using the CPUFreq loadable kernel module framework [21],
which is a project for adding support for CPU frequency and voltage scaling to the
Linux kernel. The PAST algorithm calculates that the upcoming interval will be as
equally busy as the previous interval. The speed policy is as follow: if the prediction
is for a mostly-idle interval, PAST decreases speed; and if the prediction is for a
busy interval, PAST increases speed. To avoid excessive fluctuations in processor
speed (variable performance for the user), PAST will limit the amount in change of

A Comparative Analysis of Adaptive Middleware Architectures Based on   143
Computational Reflection and Aspect Oriented Programming to Support Mobile
Computing Applications

speed in a decision to a maximum of 20% of the maximum speed. The Disk Manager implements the on-line disk spindown algorithm by the use of noflushd [22], which is a Linux daemon hat monitors disk activity and spins down idle disks. It then blocks further writes to the disk to prevent it from spinning up again. Writes are cached and flushed to disk when the next read request triggers a spin-up.

The application environment is composed by a Local Server and by a Remote Server. The Remote Server was implemented with the use of the Axis server API [23]. It is a Java class that exposes public methods for invocation and is responsible by the following operations: create mailboxes, delete mailboxes, delete messages, list messages, read a message and send a message. The Remote Server encapsulates in its public interface the semantics of the main SMTP commands as exposed in the Simple Mail Transfer Protocol (RFC2821) as well as the semantic of the main IMAP client commands as exposed in the Internet Message Access Protocol (RFC3501). The Local Server is responsible by delete messages, list messages, read a message and send a message. It implements partly both specifications in the local system context and employs a queued remote procedure call based technique [24] that permits applications to continue to make non-blocking remote procedure calls even when the Remote Server is off-line enabling the system to operating in disconnected mode. In this case, requests and responses are exchanged upon network reconnection. The consistency between data replicated from Remote Server to Local Server is based in some clustering principles employed in mobile databases context [25]. Clustering maintains two copies of every object: a strict version, which is globally consistent, and a weak version, which can be globally inconsistent, but must be locally consistent. Weak versions are transformed in strict by the Replication Manager, which compares the version number of both weak and strict objects to decide which is the mo re recent.

The proposed system operates as follows. At the mail's client first request the mailbox data is copied from the Remote Server to the Local Server. The read operations are always local and in this case the disconnections from the Remote Server are not important. The write operations are executed simultaneously in the Remote Server and Local Server. The mail client is a Java class that implements the user interface and employs Axis client API to call the services exposed by the Remote Server. The class that implements the AM, which allows the adaptation techniques to take place, intercepts all the calls sent by the client.

9   Evaluation

In this section, it is made a comparative analysis between computational reflection and aspect oriented programming in the context of adaptive middleware to support mobile computing applications.

We try to prove that aspect-oriented paradigm can be used to develop adaptive mobile applications that require only a small overhead in terms of running time as well as memory footprint, using less computational resources than reflection. It should be emphasized that the following measures are the mean value gotten after 5000 executions for each operation below in an AMD K6-2 500 MHz machine with 184 Mb of memory running a Fedora Core Linux 2.0 kernel 2.6.19.

Table 1. Running time to response a service request

Implementation	Create a mailbox	Delete a mailbox	Delete a message
Reflection-based	3027.33 ms	2268.50 ms	2658.50 ms
Aspect-based	2817.66 ms	2205.50 ms	2118.37 ms

Table 2. Running time to response a service request (continuation)

Implementation	List messages	Read a message	Send a message
Reflection-based	370.33 ms	76.66 ms	3279.50 ms
Aspect-based	323.25 ms	93.12 ms	2732.27 ms

The collected results presented in tables 1 and 2 suggest that aspects can be used to develop mobile adaptive applications that require only a small overhead in terms of running time when compared to reflection. The write operations (create a mailbox, delete a mailbox, delete a message and send a message) require less time than reflection. Almost read operations require less time, with exception of the read a message operation.

Table 3. Code size

Implementation	Code size (disk)	Code size (memory)	Number of classes
Reflection-based	149507 bytes	2066232 bytes	64
Aspect-based	150359 bytes	2329536 bytes	62 +2 aspects

From table 3, it can be verified that aspect-based code size in disk is 0,5 % bigger than reflective-based code. Besides, aspect- based code size in memory is 11,30 % bigger than reflection- based. Thus, the reflection-based implementation requires less memory resources than the aspect-based. The number of decomposition's units (classes and aspects) in both implementations is practically the same, 64 units.

10 Related Work

The middleware community has already investigated the principle of reflection during the past years, mainly to achieve flexibility and dynamic reconfigurability of the Object Request Broker (ORB) of CORBA. Examples include OpenCorba [26], DynamicTAO [27] and OpenORB [28]. OpenCorba is a CORBA compliant ORB that uses reflection to expose and modify some internal characteristics of CORBA. OpenCorba is implemented in NeoClasstalk, a reflective language based on Smalltalk. OpenCorba allows the dynamic modification of a remote invocation mechanism though a proxy class, which is its major reflective aspect. DynamicTAO is a reflective CORBA ORB written in C++ which extends TAO [29] to support runtime configuration already at the startup time of the ORB engine and non-CORBA applications OpenORB is a reflective middleware that has been implemented using Python and was designed to target configurable and dynamically reconfigurable platforms for applications that require dynamic requirements support.

A Comparative Analysis of Adaptive Middleware Architectures Based on   145
Computational Reflection and Aspect Oriented Programming to Support Mobile
Computing Applications

However, such platforms were based on standard middleware implementations and are therefore targeted to a wired distributed environment.

FlexiNet [30] is another CORBA compliant ORB implemented in Java that uses reflection to provide dynamic adaptation. Nevertheless, FlexiNet only supports static configuration of communication protocols stack layers at compile time.

OpenCOM [31] is a reflective middleware based on a component framework built atop a subset of Microsoft's COM, which can be specialized to application domains such as multimedia, real-time systems and mobile computing. However, OpenCOM only runs at Microsoft platforms. On the other hand, mobile devices such smart phones and personal digital assistants (PDA) is already coming with the Java Virtual Machine installed by default, which justifies our approach. Moreover, the Java language allows the development of applications that run in heterogeneous operating systems and machine architectures.

RECOM [32], like FlexiNet, has a reflective structure based on the Java platform that supports different transformations on a remote method invocation. RECOM supports dynamic configuration of the binding between the client and the server, such as inserting into the communication protocol stack some reflective layers of high level features which meet the needs of some nonfunctional properties required by adaptive middleware platforms. However, such platform only supports dynamic adaptation of the remote invocation mechanism (cache the results on client side and redirect the invocation to an alternative server when the initial server is down). Differently, our reflective architecture is extensible; thus, new attributes (computational resources) can be added and removed from the same and be managed in a coordinate manner.

CARISMA [33] is an adaptive middleware platform implemented in Java that employs reflection and metadata to enable context-aware interactions between mobile applications. In such platform, the middleware can be seen by applications as a dynamically customizable service provider, where the customization takes place by means of application profiles. Each application profile defines associations between the services that the middleware delivers, the policies that can be applied to deliver the services and context configurations that must hold in order for a policy to be applied. Our abstraction of application profiles is based on this work.

The middleware community to achieve the same objectives targeted by the reflection paradigm has recently investigated the aspect-oriented approach. Yang *et al.* [34] proposes a systematic approach implemented in AspectJ (a compile-time Java based aspect-oriented programming language) for preparing an existing program for adaptation and defining dynamic adaptations. Such work is based on two insights: make programs adapt-ready implies on recognizing that the concerns that tend to warrant dynamic adaptation are crosscutting in nature, and encapsulate the logic for adapting the run time behavior of a program into an adaptation kernel, that is an engine for firing adaptation rules each of which comprises a condition under which an adaptation should occur and an action that indicates the appropriate adaptive response. Aspects are used to weave calls (traps) to the adaptation kernel into the application program. During run time, the adaptation kernel checks the condition of each adaptation rule to determine if an adaptation should be performed and executes the corresponding actions if the condition is satisfied. Two modules compose the adaptation kernel: the adaptation manager, which monitors the conditions for the rules and loads code to add new behavior to the application program and the rule base component, which adds new adaptation rules (condition-actions pairs) to the adaptation kernel. Our aspect oriented middleware architecture is semantically equivalent to this architecture. However, our architecture employs aspects only to define pointcuts for adaptation, using reflective techniques to achieve dynamic adaptation.

11 Conclusion

Because conventional middleware technologies do not provide appropriate support for handling the dynamic aspects of mobile applications, the next generation of applications will require a middleware platform that can be adapted to changes in the environment and customized to several computational devices.

Computational Reflection allows the creation of a middleware architecture that is flexible, adaptable and customizable. Aspect Oriented Programming allows the creation of a middleware architecture that is adaptable, modular and easier to modify. Such assertions were validated by the experimental evaluation of both paradigms. From the experimental evaluation results we can suggest that aspect oriented middleware platforms require more memory resources while reflection based platforms require more processor time to run.

About future work, we have to solve the problems below mentioned. The Adaptation Policy Manager does not have yet a module to resolve conflicts that can occur between the application policies. In addition, the statistical learning methods employed by this component to updating policies dynamically have to be designed and implemented, the remaining architecture s components (Network, Memory and Security Managers) have to be implemented and we have to investigate methods and techniques to employ dynamic weaving in our prototype.

12 References

1. Capra, L., Emmerich, W., Mascolo, C. Exploiting Reflection and Metadata to build Mobile Computing Middleware. In: Proceedings of Workshop on Middleware for Mobile Computing. Heidelberg, Germany, November 2001.

2. Capra, L., Blair, G. S., Mascolo, C., Emmerich, W., Grace, P. Exploiting Reflection in M obile Computing M iddleware.   ACM SIGMOBILE Mobile Computing and Communications Review, Vol. 6, No. 6, pp 34-44, 2002.

3. Kon, F., Gordon, B., Costa, F., Campbell, R. H. The Case for Reflective Middleware, CACM, Vol. 45, No. 6, pp 33-38, 2002.

4. Maes, P. Concepts and Experiments in Computational Reflection. In: Proceedings of the ACM Conference on Object-Oriented Languages, December 1987.

5. Szyperski, C. Component Software: Beyond Object-Oriented Programming. Addison-Wesley, 1999.

6. Kiczales, G., Lamping, J., Mendhekar, A., Maeda C., Lopes, C. V., Loingtier, J. M., Irwin, J. Aspect-Oriented Programming. In: Proceedings of European Conference on Object-Oriented Programming, Springer-Verlag LNCS 1241, June 1997.

7. Schmidt, D., Stal, M., Rohnert, H., Buschmann, F. Pattern-Oriented Software Architecture, Volume 2, John Willey, 2001.

8. Smith, B. C. Reflection and Semantics in a Procedural Language. PhD thesis, MIT Laboratory of Computer Science, 1982, MIT Technical Report 272.

9. Sizhong, Y., Jinde, L. RECOM: A Reflective Architecture of Middleware. In: Proceedings of the 3rd International Conference on Metalevel Architectures and Separation of Crosscutting Concerns, Kyoto, Japan, September 2001.

10. Gilani, W., Spinczyk, O. A Family of Aspect Dynamic Weavers. In: Proceedings of the 2004 Dynamic Asp ects Workshop, Lancaster, England, March 2004.

A Comparative Analysis of Adaptive Middleware Architectures Based on   147
Computational Reflection and Aspect Oriented Programming to Support Mobile
Computing Applications

11. Efstratiou, C., Cheverst, K., Davies, N., Friday, A. Architectural Requirements for the Effective Support of Adaptive Mobile Applications. In: Proceedings of 2nd International Conference in Mobile Data Management. Hong Kong, Springer, Vol. Lecture Notes in Computer Science Volume 1987, pp. 15-26, January 2001.

12. Friday, A., Davies, N., Blair, G. S., Cheverst, K. W. J. Developing Adaptive Applications: The MOST Experience. Journal of Integrated Computer-Aided Engineering, Volume 6, Number 2, 1999, pp143-157.

13. Welch, G.F. A Survey of Power Management Techniques in Mobile Computing Operating Systems. Operating Systems Review, Volume 29, Number 4, October 1995.

14. Pillai, P., Shin, K. G. Real-Time Dynamic Voltage Scaling for Low-Power Embedded Operating Systems. In: Proceedings of the Eighteenth ACM Symposium on Operating systems principles, Alberta, Canada, October 2001.

15. Weiser, M., Welch, B., Demers, A., Shenker, S. Scheduling for Reduced CPU Energy. In: Proceedings of Symposium on Operating Systems Design and Implementation, November 1994.

16. Douglis, F., Krishnan, P., Marsh, B. Thwarting the Power-Hungry Disk. In: Proceedings of Winter USENIX Conference, California, 1994, pp. 292–306.

17. Satyanarayanan, M., Kistler, J. J., Mummert, L. B., Ebling, M. R., Kumar, P., Lu, Qi. Experience with Disconnected Operation in Mobile Computing Environment. In: Proceedings of the 1993 USENIX Symposium on Mobile and Location-Independent Computing, Cambridge, MA, August 1993.

18. Welling, G.S. Designing Adaptive Environmental-Aware Applications for Mobile Computing. PhD thesis, Rutgers University, New Brunswick, July 1999.

19. Zhang, C., Jacobsen, H. Aspectizing Middleware Platforms. Technical Report, Computer Systems Research Group, CSRG-466, University of Toronto, Canada, January 2003.

20. Aspectj. (December 20, 2005); http://eclipse.org/aspectj/.

21. CPUFreq. (December 15, 2005); http://www.linux.org.uk/listinfo/cpufreq.

22. Noflushd. (November 13, 2005); http://sourceforge.net/projects/noflushd.

23. Apache Software Foundation. (January 12, 2005); Axis: A framework for constructing SOAP processors. http://ws.apache.org/axis.

24. Joseph, A., deLespinasse, A., Tauber, J., Gifford, D., and Kaashoek, M. Rover: A Toolkit for Mobile Information Access. In: Proceedings of the Fifteenth ACM Symposium on Operating Systems Principles, December 1995.

25. Pitoura, E., Bhargava, B. Maintaining Consistency of Data in Distributed Environments. In: Proceedings of Fifteenth International Conference on Distributed Computing Systems, Vancouver, Canada, May 1995.

26. T. Ledoux. OpenCorba: A Reflective Open Broker. Lecture Notes in Computer Science, vol. 1616, 1999.

27. Kon, F., Román, M., Liu, P., Mao, J., Yamane, T., Magalhaes, L. C., R., Campbell, H. Monitoring, Security and Dynamic Configuration with the DynamicTAO Reflective ORB. In: Proceedings of the IFIP/ACM International Conference on Distributed Systems Platforms, New York, April 2000.

28. Blair, G. S., Coulson, G., Robin, P., Papathornas M. Architecture for Next Generation Middleware. In: Proceedings of the IFIP International Conference on Distributed Systems Platforms and Open Distributed Processing, the Lake District, England, September 1998.

29. Douglas, C. S., Cleeland, C. Applying Patterns to Develop Extensible ORB Middleware. IEEE Communications Magazine Special Issue on Design Patterns, 37(4), 54-63, May 1999.

30. R. Hayton, ANSA Team. FlexiNet Architecture. Architecture Report, Citrix Systems (Cambridge) Limited, February 1999.

31. Clarke, M., Blair, G., Coulson, G., Parlavantzas, N. An Efficient Component Model for the Construction of Adaptive Middleware. In: Proceedings of Middleware 2001, Heidelberg, Germany, November 2001.

32. Sizhong, Y., Jinde, L. RECOM: A Reflective Architecture of Middleware. In: Proceedings of the 3rd International Conference on Metalevel Architectures and Separation of Crosscutting Concerns, Kyoto, Japan, September 2001.

33. Capra, L., Emmerich, W., Mascolo, C. CARISMA: Context-Aware Reflective Middleware System for Mobile Applications. IEEE Transactions on Software Engineering, 29(10):929-945, 2003.

34. Yang, Z., Cheng, B. H, C., Stirewalt, R. E. K., Sowell, J., Sadjadi, S. M., McKinley, P. K. An Aspect Oriented Approach to Dynamic Adaptation. In: Proceedings of ACM SIGSOFT Workshop on Self-healing Systems, Charleston, South Caroline, November 2002.

ISPCell: An Interactive Image-Based Streaming Protocol for Wireless Cellular Networks*

Azzedine Boukerche, Richard Werner Nelem Pazzi, and Tingxue Huang

SITE - University of Ottawa, Canada
PARADISE Research Laboratory
{boukerch, rwerner, thuang}@site.uottawa.ca

Abstract. Remote interaction with immersive 3D environments with acceptable level of quality of experience has become a challenging and interesting research topic. Due to the high data volume required to provide a rich experience to the user, robust and efficient wireless transport protocols have yet to be developed. On the other hand, cellular network technology has been widely deployed and is growing fast. The provision of remote interactive 3D environments over wireless cellular networks has several interesting applications, and it imposes some unsolved issues. Node mobility creates unstable bandwidth, which is a problem when providing smooth interaction to users. Although PDAs and cell phones are low resource devices, which makes it prohibitive to load and render entire virtual environments, they can still render images with relative ease. Based on this idea, this paper proposes a streaming system which relies on an image-based rendering approach, and is composed of several modules: a packetization scheme for images, an image-based rendering approach based on view morphing and its corresponding RTP payload format, and finally a bandwidth feedback mechanism and rate control. This paper illustrates some of the problems faced in this area, and provides a first step towards their solutions. We discuss our algorithms and present a set of simulation experiments to evaluate the performance of the proposed schemes.

Key words: Interactive Streaming Protocol, Wireless Cellular Networks, Real-Time Protocol, Remote Virtual Environments, 3D Scenes, Low-Bandwidth Networks, Image-based Rendering, View Morphing

1 Introduction

For decades computer graphics technologies were trying to match virtual environments as closely as possible to real environments. The interaction with virtual environments has received a great deal of attention in recent years, which

---

* This work is partially sponsored by Grants from NSERC Canada Research Chair Program, Canada Foundation for Innovation and OIT/Distinguished Researcher Award.

Please use the following format when citing this chapter:

Boukerche, A., Pazzi, R.W.N., Huang, T., 2006, in IFIP International Federation for Information Processing, Volume 211, ed. Pujolle, G., Mobile and Wireless Communication Networks, (Boston: Springer), pp. 149–160.

includes video gaming, military simulations, medicine, architecture, product development and visualization, monitoring, virtual tours, and so on. The next step into the interactive virtual environment field was to enable users to remotely interact with the system, mainly to support collaborative interaction between systems and users. There has been a lot of interest and research on remote virtual environments issues lately, such as high quality graphical representations of the environments, system scalability, and low lag, just to mention a few. With the new development of wireless communication and mobile computing, an exciting research field has emerged, which enables users to interact with virtual environments using mobile devices, such as cell phones, PDAs, etc. Although, such thin devices have very low storage and processing power, thereby limiting the graphic rendering quality within these mobile devices. The dynamic nature of the bandwidth is another problem one has to face when providing remote interactive environments over wireless cellular networks. This issue, combined with the large amount of data required to be transmitted in order to load the environment on the thin device and later on to update the changes on the virtual environment, pose significant challenges in terms of network traffic, delay and storage.

In this paper, we propose an interactive streaming protocol (ISPCell) that enables users to interact with a remote virtual environment using their mobile devices. As opposed to the traditional geometry based rendering mechanism, this work focus on using an image-based rendering (IBR) technique on the client, which we refer to as view morphing [1], and requires low processing, as it renders novel views based on a collection of sample images. IBR algorithms are based on the plenoptic function [2]. View morphing is the simplest IBR algorithm as it relies on some geometric information about the scene, whereas lumigraph [3] and lightfield [4] use implicit or no geometry at all, which requires more processing.

IBR has some advantages over geometry-based rendering as it does not depend on the scene complexity, but on the image resolution, which fits perfectly to mobile devices. A client/server architecture is proposed and, basically, pictures are taken from the real world or from computer generated environments and stored on the server. The image acquisition is based on view morphing requirements, which needs some parameters such as depth information and position of the camera to render novel views. As the user navigates through the virtual environment, new views have to be displayed. The mobile device sends updates of the user position to the server. The server decides what images should be sent, based on the position of the user in the virtual environment. To improve the frame rate, a virtual user path prediction algorithm is proposed, allowing the server to pre-fetch some images to the client when enough bandwidth is available. The bandwidth feedback mechanism and rate control are designed to optimize the pre-fetching scheme, as its goal is to avoid starvation of images at the client side.

The interactive streaming protocol (ISPCell) is designed over the Real-Time Protocol (RTP) [5], which provides end-to-end delivery services for data with real-time constraints, for instance, audio and video. According to the RTP specification, a new RTP payload format has to be defined for each different media type. Also, because the Real-Time Streaming Protocol (RTSP) [6] is intended for continuous media, a new streaming protocol had to be specified, which deals with interaction and random media access.

This paper is organized as follows: Section 2 gives an overview of the related work found on the literature. Section 3 presents the project architecture and its modules. The algorithms are described in Section 4. An extensive set of simulation experiments were performed and the results are shown and discussed in Section 5. Finally, conclusions and future work are provided in Section 6.

2 Related Work

This section reviews 3D rendering mechanisms that have been developed for mobile devices, followed by a discussion of related image-based rendering techniques.

2.1 Traditional Geometric Rendering on Thin Devices

Most of the work on 3D rendering on mobile devices has been done over the OpenGL ES API [7], and are limited to the mobile device hardware performance. Thus, the rendering quality is still poor, or in a very low level of detail. The Mobile 3D Graphics API (M3G), defined in Java Specification Request (JSR 184) [8], is another industry effort to create a standard 3D API for Java-enabled thin devices. A solution to visualize more complex 3D scenes on mobile devices is possible through Image-Based Rendering (IBR), which is discussed in the next section.

2.2 Image-Based Rendering

Mobile devices have lower processing power and memory than a personal computer. These constraints make it difficult to present complex 3D scenes on such thin devices. This is where IBR mechanisms take place. As IBR works with images, the rendering cost depends only on the display resolution, while the traditional geometry rendering cost depends on the polygon count of the scene. Therefore, IBR is appropriate for mobile devices.

The IBR methods are categorized based on the geometry information they require to render novel views. Some image-based rendering technics do not require geometric information. Lightfield [4] renders a new view by interpolating a set of samples. The problem with IBR methods that do not rely on geometric information is the huge storage and the acquisition mechanisms. Due to the huge amount of data required to be transmitted when rendering a large environment, a combination of image-based and geometry rendering should be employed.

This project is based on View Morphing [1], which is able to render any novel image by morphing two or more reference images. The basic principle is depicted in Figure 1. Images I_0 and I_1 are acquired at points C_0 and C_1 respectively with focal length f_0 and f_1. The novel image I_n, with focal length f_n, at point C_n, is rendered by the interpolation of images I_0 and I_1. There is also an image cache on the client in order to reuse a previously received image, significantly improving the system performance and reducing the network traffic.

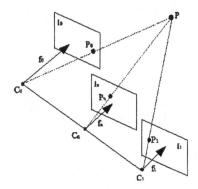

Fig. 1. View morphing with parallel views.

2.3 Remote Visualization of 3D Scenes

As discussed before, the visualization of complex 3D scenes on mobile devices can be improved by IBR . This subsection discusses some research works relevant to the solution proposed in this paper.

QuickTime VR [9] is the most popular image-based rendering system. But it is limited to panoramic scenarios, and the client device has to download the entire environment in order to start the navigation. ISPCell offers a higher level of freedom, as a user can walk through the environment, and there is no need to download the whole environment, as it is being constructed as the user visits different areas.

A client-server approach to image-based rendering on mobile terminals, similar to ISPCell, is presented in [10]. In this approach, the client send the user's position update messages to the server, which runs a 3D environment to take the necessary pictures and sends back to the client. The disadvantages of this work compared to ISPCell are that there is no pre-fetching mechanism, nor rate control, to make better use of the bandwidth, compromising the smooth interaction. Its main contribution in on the virtual camera placement algorithm.

Another work similar to ISPCell is discussed in [11]. This work relies on image-based rendering to enhance 3D graphics on mobile devices. The description of the client-server framework is very simple and, again, there is no mention of a pre-fetching, path prediction, or rate control mechanisms.

The next section introduces the project architecture and each of its modules.

3 The Proposed ISPCell Architecture

In this section, we shall discuss the main architecture of our ISPCell model, and its main components, which include: a modified JPEG codestream, the new RTP payload format for view morphing, the ISPCell streaming protocol, the bandwidth feedback mechanism, the rate control scheme, and the path prediction and pre-fetching algorithms.

3.1 Modified JPEG Codestream

A new JPEG codestream scheme was specified due to the error-proneness wireless channels. Figure 2 shows the new JPEG codestream. A packetization item is an atomic component of the new JPEG codestream, for instance a main header, a layer header, or a pixel block. Before being sent to the network layer, the image codestream is split into packetization items and encapsulated in RTP packets. The main issue behind this packetization scheme is to avoid that errors in one packet affect other packets, by keeping the packetization items independent from each other.

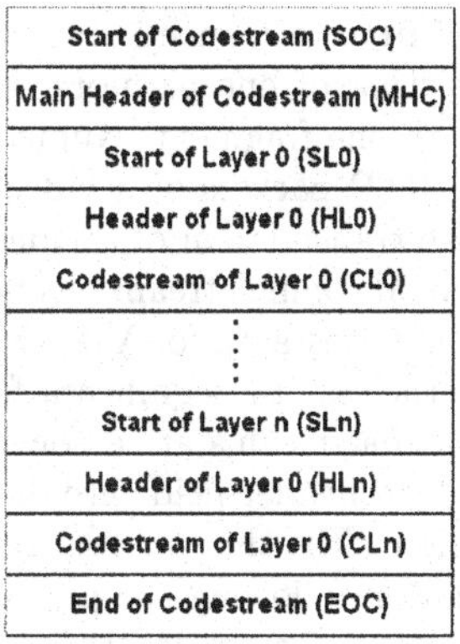

Start of Codestream (SOC)
Main Header of Codestream (MHC)
Start of Layer 0 (SL0)
Header of Layer 0 (HL0)
Codestream of Layer 0 (CL0)
$\vdots$
Start of Layer n (SLn)
Header of Layer 0 (HLn)
Codestream of Layer 0 (CLn)
End of Codestream (EOC)

Fig. 2. Structure of the new JPEG codestream

3.2 A New RTP Payload Format

The RTP protocol carries payloads of real-time applications, such as interactive navigation through virtual environments. For the streaming of any multimedia compressed data over wired or wireless networks, new payload formats over RTP are required, such as H.26x over RTP [12, 13] and G.7xx over RTP [14, 15]. Therefore, a new payload format for view morphing over RTP was specified, as

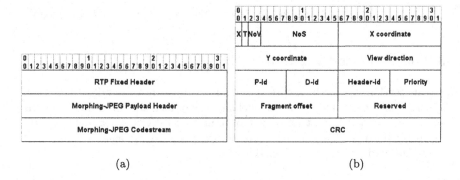

(a)   (b)

Fig. 3. (a) Structure of a RTP packet for View Morphing. (b) View Morphing payload header.

well as a new packet header for view morphing, as depicted in Figure 3(a) and Figure 3(b) respectively.

The RTP fixed header fields are the same as those of other RTP application payloads. Only the following fields are exceptions, and are specific to the View Morphing algorithm:

- **Payload Type**: according to the RTP standard, this field specifies the format of the RTP payload and determines its interpretation by the application [14].

- **Number of Video Unit**: the transmission stream is constructed from a series of video units consisting of one or more images. In general, a video unit is divided into more than one fragment. Number of Video Unit (NVU) is a random value given to all RTP packets of a video unit. This field helps the receiver identify the complete transmission of a video unit.

- **Timestamp**: The View Morphing stream has no strict sampling instance. Unlike other media types, the timestamp for View Morphing does not indicate the sampling instance. Nevertheless, it is significant for calculating synchronization and jitter when other media streams are associated with View Morphing.

The View Morphing payload header fields are described bellow:

- Payload header extension (**X**): this bit flag is activated when there are some supplementary information following the payload header.

- Twin images (**T**): this bit is set to inform the renderer to process two images, otherwise the rendering algorithm can render the image directly.

- Number of images in a video unit (**NoV**): informs whether the packet contains zero, one or two images.

- Number of an image in the streaming (**NoS**): works as a sequence number to make sure all image fragments were received at the client.

- Viewpoint (**X,Y**): coordinates of the viewpoint.

- View direction (**VD**): angle that indicates the view direction.

- Viewpoint and view direction identification (**P-id and D-id**): these fields help identify the viewpoint and view direction when data is corrupted or lost.

- Codestream header identification (**header-id**): helps recovering the main header when data is corrupted.

- Priority of image layers (**Priority**): Morphing-JPEG supports layered compression. The server can send quality layers separately, so the lower the layer, the higher the priority.

- Fragment **offset**: to reassemble the codestream.

- **Reserved**: field reserved for future use.

- **CRC**: detects whether the payload header is corrupted or not, which part is corrupted and tries to correct some bits.

3.3 The Interactive Streaming Protocol Algorithm

Basically, the construction of an RTP packet begins with the assignment of the payload type field for the Morphing-JPEG. If the current packet is the first fragment of a video unit or it is the whole video unit, then check if this is the first packet for that session. If it is the first packet, the field NVU and timestamp in the RTP header receive a random value, that will be the first value of a sequence number. If this is not the first packet, NVU is incremented by one. All other fields are set according to the specification. For instance, the field X is set to 1 if there is an optional payload following the payload header; the field NoV is set according to the images the client will have to process, for instance, it will be set to 00 to instruct the client to process the first image on that video unit, 10 for the second, and 11 for the last one.

The algorithm for the client is just a parser for the server codestream. It first checks if the payload type field is set to Morphing-JPEG, and then checks the NVU field to see if it is different from the last one. If it is different, instructs the application layer to render the image at that moment. Then the algorithm gets the timestamp to calculate the synchronization and jitter. If the field X is set to 1, it will locate the optional payload header, parse the codestream and send it to the application. For the CRC scheme, the algorithm verifies if the viewpoint and direction are correct. If they are correct, the algorithm proceeds checking the priority and the remaining fields. If not, the algorithm gets the approximate values for viewpoint and direction from P-id and D-id, and runs the CRC on them. The final step is to check the offset field. If the offset is equal to the last offset plus the length of the packetization data, then it just appends the packetization data to the previous one. If that is not the case, the algorithm waits for a short timeout period. If the delayed packet does not arrive, it informs the server that an RTP packet was lost, which will adjust the parameters related to the feedback mechanism according to the reports of RTCP.

3.4 A Bandwidth Feedback Mechanism

The conventional RTP provides periodic feedback on the quality of data distribution through the RTP Control Protocol (RTCP). The RTCP is intended for wired network infrastructures, in which the available bandwidth changes smoothly. Therefore, the periodic transmission of control packets is enough to control the adaptive encodings and the speed of data distribution. However, wireless network bandwidth changes dramatically. The periodic feedback mechanism can not accurately and promptly reflect the situation of a wireless channel. The immediate feedback mechanism described in this paper involves sending ACKs for every received RTP packet. By keeping track of these ACKs, the server can establish the network status. The ACKs are kept as small as possible with only its type, a sequence number for ordering, and a timestamp. The timestamp is used to approximate the round trip time (RTT) of each RTP packet. Missing acknowledgments are interpreted as dropped RTP packets. Following is the description of the algorithm.

When the server receives an ACK, it will parse the RTP packet and extract the sequence number and timestamp. Then, the server adds the sequence number to a list of successfully transmitted packets. The server then calculates the RTT and adds it to the list of recently transmitted packets. For each recently transmitted packet, if the sequence number does not exist in the list of successfully transmitted packets, and if the RTT of the previous packet minus the RTT of the next packet is greater than an acceptable variation value, then the number of packets lost is incremented by one. If the number of packets lost is greater than 0, then the network status is set to congested. Otherwise, if the RTT of the last received packet minus the RTT of the first received packet is greater than a threshold, then the status is congested. If the RTT of the first received packet minus the RTT of the last received packet is greater than a threshold, then the status is unloaded. Otherwise the network status is constant.

3.5 The Rate Control Algorithm

The rate control mechanism is used by the server to make a better use of the available bandwidth. It is based on the reports from the feedback mechanism. If the network status is congested, the rate is decreased. If the status is unloaded, the rate is increased, and if the status is constant, the rate is left unchanged. The increment value is crucial for the performance of ISPCell. It only makes sense if it can stream an extra image, and not only an extra packet or so. Upon receiving a request, the server will determine the network status. If the network is unloaded, the rate is increased by an amount corresponding to one image. If the network is congested, the rate is decreased by an amount corresponding to one image.

3.6 Virtual User Path Prediction and Pre-Fetching Schemes

The path prediction mechanism is based on previous and recent virtual user's movement in the environment. There are two navigation modes: linear or rotational. For instance, if the user is moving along a straight line, and based on previous movements, the path prediction mechanism will probably infer that the user will continue on the same path. In the case of rotation in the virtual environment, the path prediction will get the nearby positions based on a threshold angle.

Based on the path prediction mechanism, the server will pre-fetch some images to the client device. The pre-fetching algorithm takes advantage of available bandwidth to send images in advance to the client, saving some requests and network traffic, improving the frame rate on the client.

4 Simulation Experiments

ISPCell was implemented and simulated on the NS-2 [16] network simulator. The cellular network scenarios consisted of several base stations, a streaming server, and mobile nodes ranging from 10 to 100, moving at 5m/s to 20m/s, in an area of 1500x1500 m^2. An image set composed of a thousand images was built on the server. Also, a request generator was implemented on the client, which requests those images from the server. In order to evaluate the performance of the proposed interactive streaming system, the following metrics were used: packet loss length, packet loss duration, packet burst length, packet burst duration, packet rate and packet delay. To evaluate our ISPCell path prediction scheme, we have chosen the following performance metrics: average number of images in the cache versus the number of requests.

4.1 Results and Analysis

Examining the results from Figure 4, one can notice the adaptability of the rate control mechanism reacting to the reports from the feedback mechanism. When one client was connected to the server, the amount of images in the clients cache is to 309 for only 150 requests. The control mechanism was aware of the available bandwidth, and was quick to utilize it by sending additional pre-fetched images. If the pre-fetching was not implemented, the number of images at the clients would not go over 150 (ratio of 1 image per request). Having such a large number of images for a little number of request helps making the streaming run more smoothly. When considering fifteen clients connected to the server, the bandwidth dropped. Again, the rate control mechanism was able to adjust to the new scenario and reduce the streaming rate. For the same number of requests (150), the server only managed to stream 176 images; almost half when the compared to one connected client.

Packet loss length indicates the average number of lost packets. The packet loss duration represents a period during which the average number of packets are lost. With a higher traffic, more packets are lost. However, depending on how the packetization item is grouped and if an appropriate packet length is applied, the packet loss length will be reduced. The packet burst length and the packet burst duration represent the burst performance of the RTP. A burst is a period during which a high rate of packets is lost.

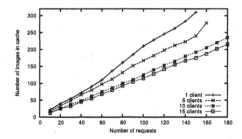

Fig. 4. Performance of the pre-fetching mechanism.

The number of handoff increases along with the traffic load. Therefore, *packet loss length* and *packet loss duration* also increases, as can be seen in Fig. 5(a) and Fig. 5(b) respectively. It can also be noticed that the speed of mobile hosts does not heavily affect the *loss length* and *the loss duration*.

The *packet burst length* and *packet burst duration* represent the streaming feature of an error-prone communication channel. During the burst period, RTP packets can not reach the destination. The burst is mainly caused by the handoff. Fig. 5(c) and Fig. 5(d) show the burst performance of the ISPCell. These two metrics do not depend on the node speed but on the node density. Both *packet burst length* and *packet burst duration* increase based on the fact that hand-offs are successfully completed with more difficulty, as the number of nodes increases.

The *packet rate* metric depends on several factors including the sender's transmission speed, the network communication bandwidth and the packetization scheme. As depicted in Fig. 5(e), the packet rate decreases as the number of nodes increases, due to the extra traffic.

As shown in Figure 5(f), the packet delay stays around a stable value of 110 milliseconds and is not affected by the traffic and the node speed, which is good for the kind of application presented in this paper. Interaction requires fast protocols to maintain a smooth frame rate for a reasonable user quality of experience.

5 Conclusions and Future Work

Remote interaction in high quality virtual environments on mobile devices have promising applications. However, due to the large amount of 3D data to be transmitted, the drastic changes in bandwidth, as well as the error-prone wireless channel, streaming 3D data through wireless cellular networks represents one of the most challenging problem that one has to deal with. In this paper, we have proposed a new RTP protocol for view morphing rendering over wireless last-hop scenarios, which we refer to as ISPCell, and that consists of the new RTP header structure, the packetization scheme, and the immediate feedback mechanism.

We have described our proposed ISPCell protocol, and we have presented
a set of simulation experiments to evaluate its performance using ns-2. Our
results indicate that ISPCell exhibits a good performance using several realistic
scenarios. In the future, we plan to investigate further the performance of our
scheme using a probabilistic virtual path prediction, which we believe has the
potential to improve the system's performance.

References

1. S. M. Seitz and C. M. Dyer. View morphing. In Computer Graphics Proceedings, Annual Conference Series, pages 2130, Proc. SIGGRAPH96 (New Orleans), August 1996. ACM SIGGRAPH.
2. E. H. Adelson and J. Bergen. The plenoptic function and the elements of early vision. In Computational Models of Visual Processing, pages 320. MIT Press, Cambridge, MA, 1991.
3. S. J. Gortler, R. Grzeszczuk, R. Szeliski, and M. F. Cohen. The lumigraph. In Computer Graphics Proceedings, Annual Conference Series, pages 4354, Proc. SIGGRAPH96 (New Orleans), August 1996. ACM SIGGRAPH.
4. M. Levoy and P. Hanrahan. Light field rendering. In Computer Graphics Proceedings, Annual Conference Series, pages 3142, Proc. SIGGRAPH96 (New Orleans), August 1996. ACM SIGGRAPH.
5. H. Schulzrinne, S. Casner, R. Frederick, and V. Jacobson. Rtp: A transport protocol for real-time applications. Standards Track, Network Working Group, January 1996.
6. H. Schulzrinne, A. Rao, R. Lanphier, M. Westerlund, and A. Narasimhan. Real time streaming protocol (rtsp). Inernet Draft, Internet Engineering Task Force, February 2004.
7. OpenGL Embedded System. http://www.khronos.org/opengles/ 2006
8. Java Specification Request 184 (2005) - Mobile 3D Graphics API for J2ME http://www.jcp.org/en/jsr/detail?id=184
9. S. E. Chen. QuickTimeVR an image-based approach to virtual environment navigation. Computer Graphics (SIGGRAPH95), pages 2938, August 1995.
10. G. Thomas, G. Point, and K. Bouatouch. A client-server approach to image-based rendering on mobile terminals. Technical Report, ISSN 0249-6399, France, January 2005.
11. CHANG C., GER S.: Enhancing 3d graphics on mobile devices by image-based rendering. In Proc. 3rd IEEE Pacific-Rim Conference on Multimedia(2002).
12. T. Turletti and C. Huitema. Rfc2032: Rtp payload format for h.261 video streams. Stardards Track, Network Working Group, Octorber 1996.
13. C. Zhu. Rfc2190: Rtp payload format for h.263 video streams. Standards Track, Network Working Group, September 1997.
14. H. Schulzrinne and S. Petrack. Rfc2833: Rtp payload for dtmf digits, telephony tones and telephony signals. Standards Track, Network Working Group, May 2000.
15. R. Zopf. Rfc3389: Real-time transport protocol (rtp) payload for comfort noise (cn). Standards Track, Network Working Group, September 2002.
16. The Network Simulator. http://www.isi.edu/nsnam/ns/

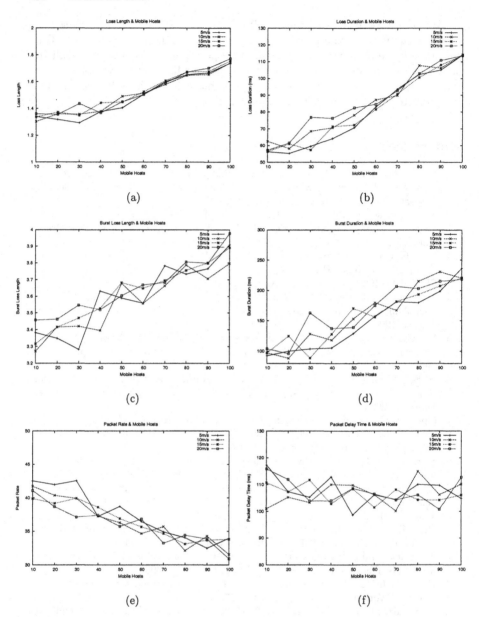

Fig. 5. (a) Packet loss length. (b) Packet loss duration. (c) Burst length. (d) Burst duration. (e) Packet rate. (f) Packet delay.

THE GENERIC CONTEXT SHARING PROTOCOL GCSP
Application to signaling in a cross-network and multi-provider environment

Rony Chahine[1] and Claude Rigault[2]

1 Département informatique et réseaux,
ENST, 46 rue Barrault, 75 013 Paris, France,
Corebridge, 3 rue Saint Philippe du Roule, 75 008 Paris
rony.chahine@enst.fr
2 Département informatique et réseaux,
ENST, 46 rue Barrault, 75 013 Paris, France
GET-Télécom Paris ; LTCI-UMR 5141 CNRS
claude.rigault@enst.fr

Abstract. This paper proposes a new signaling paradigm and a new signaling protocol called the Generic Context Sharing Protocol (GCSP) for the construction of a global control plane over present and future communication networks. After identifying the special nature of the control plane software involved in the setup of a conversational service instance it examines the various mechanisms for information sharing which leads to our new proposal. We show that this new data-based protocol is better suited to control plane requirements than the present day's command-oriented signaling mechanisms. We indicate the basic principles of the protocol and we give a brief description of the generic context. We show the place of this proposal in the present day research efforts and we mention a practical implementation case.

Keywords- Control plane, Signaling, Association, Generic Context, Data based communication, Cooperating Computing, Signaling Protocol.

Please use the following format when citing this chapter:

Chahine, R., Rigault, C., 2006, in IFIP International Federation for Information Processing, Volume 211, ed. Pujolle, G., Mobile and Wireless Communication Networks, (Boston: Springer), pp. 161–174.

1   Introduction: From the special nature of control plane software to new signaling mechanisms

In present and future communication networks, a control plane is required when services use a conversational communication paradigm. By "conversational communication paradigm" we mean that a communication environment is established before users start to exchange media and remains established till an explicit release is issued. This communication environment is persistent, and thus state-full, during the whole communication session. Services based on the conversational paradigm require dedicated functions to set-up modify and release the communication environment. We call these dedicated functions "Control Functions" [1], and we define the "control plane" as the set of all processes that execute control functions. The emblematic service using the conversational paradigm is the Plain Old Telephony Service (POTS) where resources are reserved in all participating switches and are freed when one of the participants hangs-up.

In the part 2 of this paper, we analyze the special nature of the software that executes network and service control activities. We characterize this special nature as "Cooperative Computing", and we examine the requirements of this type of computing. The requirement of interest for this paper is "Information Sharing" by means of signaling.

In the part 3 of this paper, we consider the different approaches to the problem of signaling between partner entities in the cooperative computing situation of the control plane and we come to the conclusion that the current "command based" mechanism is not the most efficient approach to the signaling problem and we show that in a cooperative situation a "data based" approach is more efficient. We therefore propose a "data based" mechanism for signaling leading to a paradigm shift in signaling methods. This proposal is in line with current control plane research efforts. It complements the NSIS [2] IETF work as a contribution to the NSIS Signaling Layer in the signaling protocols for conversational services and its relation to other works will be detailed in the paper. If we come to use a "data based" mechanism for signaling, it becomes necessary to standardize the Call Instance Data or the content of the dynamic session memories in each partner that we call "Local Contexts".

In the part 4 of this paper, we propose a generic data structure, called the Generic Context, shared by control entities in the same manner as management entities share information in Management Information Bases (MIB) [3] and we give an overview of this generic data structure.

In the part 5 we describe the basic principles of a new signaling protocol called Generic Context Sharing Protocol GCSP, based on the "data based" mechanism for signaling.

In the part 6 we show the place that this signaling protocol could occupy in the scope of present day research in the control plane and signaling area.

Finally in the part 7 we give an implementation example in GCSP in the case of a Computer Telephony Integration application

2   The special nature of control plane software

Control plane software is a very complicated and costly task. The origin of this problem may indeed be traced to the cooperative nature of control plane software. To understand this point we should underline that computer science may be divided into 3 main branches: centralized computing, distributed computing and cooperative computing. In *Centralized Computing*, a mainframe masters all the processes in a company. All peripherals are intelligence-less slaves executing orders from a single Master computer. In *Distributed Computing* many smaller computers, work together, specializing on given tasks and providing some activity independence. This new computing organization requires communication between the computers. The general solution developed by computer science for distributed computing is the "Client-Server" architecture, based on the "request and answer" communication paradigm. However, the client server architecture does not depart fundamentally from the former centralized. The client is mostly concerned by customization and interface problems and the essential service data and service logic are located in the central server position.

A radically new solution to the distribution of intelligence on many computers would be a new kind of computer science called *"Cooperative computing"*. In this scheme there is no central position, all the computers are equal and no one is in a *permanent* position to give orders to the others. While many different efforts are taking place towards the development of a theoretical solution for cooperative computing, (grid computing, peer to peer processing, agents...), no generally accepted theory has been yet proposed. However some examples of working cooperative applications have been successfully developed. The main one, for our concern, is the "call control" application of telephone switches. Indeed control functions work in a cooperative manner. In the telephone network all switches are equal, there is no centralized platform controlling the setup of a call or its release. Each switch works on a peer-to-peer basis to achieve a global service. It is this special cooperative nature of control activities, and of the lack of a theoretical base for this new type of computing, which leads "Call control applications" to be developed as very complicated ad hoc solutions.

However we may identify some key subjects for research in cooperative computing that are fundamental to control plane software:

- *Cooperative computing requires information sharing between partners*. In the control plane, this Information sharing is called "signaling". It derives that Signaling research is not merely a research problem for telephony; it is a fundamental cooperative computing research problem.

- *Cooperative computing requires the setup of Associations between the partners:* each process involved in a service session has pointers to his partner processes. All pointers, put together, form an association tree that gives a global view of the service session.

- *Cooperative computing requires policies for the distribution of decision authorities.* As there is no central control point, all entities are equal. The difficulty is to decide which entity should take a decision at a given time.

- Cooperative computing requires behavior models for the partners. A partner should be aware of the effects of his actions in the other partners. Each partner should have a behavior model of the partners with whom he cooperates. In telephony such behavior models are referred to as "call models".

- Trust and security. Authentication and ciphering are required in order to have a safe communication between two cooperating partners.

This list of research problems is certainly not exhaustive, but is sufficient to understand the complexity of control plane activities. The rest of this paper concentrates on the signaling problem.

3   Global Control plane requirement and candidate signaling mechanisms

3.1   The requirement for a global control plane

A service may be designed as a composition of various service components hosted by different service providers. For example in a bank call center, Bob has a user interface on his PC which allows him to search customers profile and to call them directly from his PC. The *Profile-lookup* component and the *call* component are provided by two different service providers and are integrated together to build a richer service with a single user interface. We call this a "multi-provider service". Let's assume further that when a customer calls Bob on his fixed office phone, Bob receives a screen popup on his PC with the customer profile. If Bob is away from his office, he may want to have the calling customer profile displayed on his PDA and take the call from his mobile phone. The service that was available in the bank private network is now extended across several networks. We call it a "cross-network" service. Today, signaling paths are missing both for multi-provider and cross-network services. Partial solutions do exist: web services or other types of middleware achieve some multi-provider services, but they do not apply to heterogeneous networks. Cross-network services require signaling gateways to do the translation from a signaling protocol to another. Cross-network services are considered in [4-7] for a limited set of services and in a more general, but very centralized manner by [8]. The requirements of multi-provider and cross-network services are very difficult to satisfy with existing control plane concepts. We therefore propose enhanced mechanisms that would achieve cross-network compatibility and extend a same "global" control plane over different networks and different component providers to achieve an easier service implementation.

3.2   Candidate signaling methods

During a service instance, control processes store their Call Instance Data (CID) in a temporary memory page that we call a *local context*. This memory page is released when the service instance is terminated. All the partners of a same service instance share the information in their local contexts by means of signaling. The various mechanisms for sharing information have been classified [9] into three different categories: "data based mechanism", "command based mechanism" and "object oriented mechanism".

In the *command based* mechanism local context data are private and therefore modified indirectly by an incoming command. A control process does not have the rights to read or modify directly a remote context; it uses instead a predefined set of commands. When a process receives a command it performs the necessary actions and modifies its local context.

On the contrary, in the *data based* mechanism, also called variable oriented approach, cooperating processes in a same service session can read each other CIDs or local context and thus modify them directly. To make this possible, local context should have a specific data structure that all processes can understand. A solution is to organize local context attributes following a tree structure, like a SNMP MIB, or an object oriented structure like the OSI MIB [10]. We will later show that it is preferable in a cooperative computing environment to use simple commands like Get and Set to read or modify instance data of a remote process instead of using a wide set of commands. Of course security is a requirement of such a mechanism: local contexts can be read only by trusted remote processes. The rights of a process to read and modify instance data in remote contexts should be set according to trust and security policies.

Finally in the *object-oriented* mechanism, processes communicate by invoking remote objects located on various machines using the client/server architecture. Examples of this mechanism are web services [11], CORBA [12] and RMI [13]. This object-oriented mechanism works well for "distributed computing" but may not be efficient for "cooperative computing" because the intelligence is centralized in the server.

3.3   Advantages of the data based mechanism

A multi-provider and cross-network service is designed by the association of heterogeneous components from different service providers. Since new heterogeneous components will continue to hit the market, future control protocols and signaling mechanisms should be carefully designed to allow these new components to cooperate with existing ones, and to allow the initiation of the operational phase before the design of all control application has been concluded. It has been shown in [9] chapter 1 that the data based mechanism is well suited for the design of such protocols and that it will allow building a more generic interface between heterogeneous components and will provide an easier service implementation and easier cooperation between network and service providers. Such a data based mechanism has been used by management protocols like SNMP, ILMI, CMIP and NetConf [14]. However, because of the unequal management functionality distribution these protocols are implemented in a centralized architecture and it is shown in [9] chapter 9 that in a centralized configuration this *Variable Oriented* approach (data based mechanism) may be inefficient with respect to bandwidth, CPU, time and memory. Indeed the management station has to multiply in an excessive way the Get/Set comments on the various agents of the star architecture and many authors now favor a command based approach for centralized management.

Up to now, the command based mechanisms have been the only method used in signaling. Signaling protocols like SIP [15] or ISUP [16] are all based on the command based mechanism. However in the cooperative computing situation of the control plane, a single point only addresses a few entities and does not suffer from the above inconvenient of data based mechanisms for centralized architectures. This would favor the simpler and more general data based approach.

Also, in a cooperative computing environment, processes have a behavior model and a current state. Signaling information will vary with the current state of the destination process, even if the requested service is the same. Such behavior is also known by context-sensitivity as described in [17, 18], it enables a software system to adaptively take different actions in different contexts. For example if the bank call center administrator sends a fire alarm to the phone of all the employee, depending on the phone current state, the system will send a text message and a beep sound to idle phones and a voice message to off hook phones. Data based mechanism is better suited for "context-sensitivity" in control plane applications because it allows to read, with a Get request, the current state of the remote partner process and adjust to this current state by sending adapted information.

We conclude from these arguments that a command based mechanism is the advisable choice for centralized computing applications while a data based approach is a better choice for a cooperative computing application: In non centralized control plane applications data based communication is not a handicap, it offers a generic and simple interface making multi-provider and cross-network services as well as context-sensitive services easy to implement.

We therefore propose a new signaling paradigm; more adapted to the cooperative computing nature of the control plane relying on a data based mechanism. For this purpose, we define a generic data structure: the "generic context" or "GC", for the Call Instance Data of the cooperating processes and a new signaling protocol, the "*Generic Context Sharing Protocol*" (GCSP), where signaling is achieved by reading or modifying data instances in remote contexts with Get/Set/Notify commands under trust and security restrictions.

4   Generic Context overview

The generic context GC is the data structure given to CIDs in all the contexts of the participating processes. It is similar to an SNMP MIB. As a detailed description of the generic context would be too long to develop here and would justify a complete paper, we only give a small outline, preferring to focus on GCSP mechanisms in part 5.

We use the SIMPSON [19] model to organize the GC. The SIMPSON model (Signaling Model for Programmable Services over Networks) gives a structure to service and control plane sub-functions. It takes in account multi-provider services as it includes client sub-services, provider (integrator) sub-services and component sub-services. All local contexts involved in a same session have the same Generic Context data structure. A Generic Context is opened at session initiation and erased at session termination; it persists only during the service session. The data structure schema of the Generic Context is designed according to an object-oriented approach, as done in the Common Information Model (CIM) [20]. Two control applications that use GCSP communicate by a data based mechanism and there is no remote method invocation as in object oriented communication. Data may be exchanged via Get/Set/Notify commands as in SNMP [21]. Structure and relationships between data in a generic context are described using an object-oriented approach. While the SNMP MIB has a hierarchical tree view of all managed objects; the simplicity of a MIB prohibits defining more complex data and expressing relations between data elements. The Generic Context offers a richer syntax for representing control information and control objects relationships. It has an object-oriented approach to allow a greater flexibility in its design. The operations and notifications may be described at a high level of abstraction which makes standardization easier and errors less likely [22, 23]. In comparison, MIBs do not allow the same degree of reusability since they do not support inheritance and lead to the addition of duplicated schema entries as models grow up to support more vendors and more device/application types.

The Generic Context maintains at the application level a persistent communication between partner processes. For this, a process holds in its Generic Context an association, or pointer, which binds it to a partner process with which it has working relations. This association allows processes to mutually address each other; a process can send requests and notifications at any time to a partner process during a service session. Security is taken into account in the Generic Context design. A dedicated trust and security object in the Generic Context handles the authentication, access rights and ciphering issues

5   Generic Context Sharing Protocol mechanisms

5.1   Protocol overview

GCSP triggers remote operations using Get/Set commands. Instead of sending a command to make a remote process execute an action, we modify a CID in the remote Generic Context with a Set command. When the remote process detects the change, it executes the action. A prior GET may be done to know the current value but *it is not mandatory*. The prior GET may be useful for performing context-sensitive actions. For example, rather than sending a Make Call (a, b) command to a remote entity, a GET downloads the concerned part of the Generic Context of that entity, we set the "Make Call" attribute to "true", "calling" to "a" and "called" to "b", then upload the object to the remote context with a SET. Upon detection of the change the remote entity makes the call. A direct Set with the necessary attributes would have also made the call.

With GCSP a process can read the current state of a partner and its behavior model before taking a further action and thus can predict its future state. To respect the performance requirement of signaling GCSP should be the least verbose and should allow the use of signaling transactions. Several modifications may be done on a context before uploading it. This is equivalent to transactions in MEGACO [24] and TCAP [25] which are essential to the protocol performances [26]. Renowned mechanisms may be used to increase performance. As in an SNMP MIB, GCs objects names can be replaced by numbers to reduce the size of GCSP messages. Study [9] shows that data based mechanism allows to initiate the operational phase of services before the design of all control applications has been concluded because it is easier to enrich the protocol stack. GCSP can also be encrypted with an SSL layer if it runs on TCP. The encapsulation of objects in a Generic Context guaranties the integrity of an object and protects from unauthorized access [22, 23].

5.2   GCSP mechanisms

GCSP is a text based protocol like HTTP [27] and SIP. A GCSP frame consists of a header and a body as shown in figure 1. GCSP is an application level protocol which uses UDP as SIP does [28] or could also use the NSIS transport layer. TCP can be used to support SSL encryption and firewall traversal. Reliability is assured by timers in the GCSP protocol stack that handles messages retransmission.

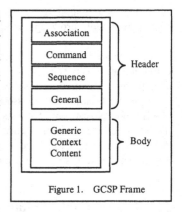

Figure 1.   GCSP Frame

5.3   Protocol frame

5.3.1   Header
Header lines provide information about the request or the response, or about the objects sent in the message body. Header lines are in the usual text format, which is one line per header, of the form "header-name: value", ending with CRLF. It is the same format used for email and news postings, defined in RFC 822, section 3. We give hereafter an outline of the different sections of the header.

5.3.1.1   Association
Two GCs of partner processes are bound together with an association. A GCSP association is bidirectional; both processes can address mutually each other. The association section in GCSP header consists of the source (From) and

From: chahine@enst.fr 400854585532112
To: rigault@enst.fr
Source-Context: 102
Destination-Context: 53

Figure 2.   Association section lines in a GCSP frame

destination (To) addresses (private and/or public), and the source and destination contexts IDs. Many addresses can be sent in the "From" and "To" fields. This association is similar to a TCP socket. However GCSP makes the association at the application level which allows to implement services independently from the transport protocol.

In figure 2 we give an example of association between two communicating processes. The "From" field indicates the source addresses, a public address (chahine@enst.fr) and a private address (400854585532112), while the "To" field indicates the destination address. Source-Context and Destination-Context are references of the source and the targeted GC. A context reference is unique within a single machine like a TCP port.

5.3.1.2   *Commands*

The command header describes the invoked command. A response is expected with a response code as in Http. Some commands have to indicate the full path of the target object in the remote GC. GCSP commands are as follow:

Get. A control process can query data in a remote Generic Context using a Get command. It must indicate the full path of the targeted part, for example the Generic Call Control part of the remote GC: Get Context.GenericCallControl lock GCSP/1.0 A *lock* keyword is mandatory if the control process wants to modify the remote context. This prevents other control processes of modifying the context before the initial control process, which made the Get command, uploads it. The lock keyword is not mandatory for read-only Get command. Following a Get command, a response is expected. The response indicates its status response. If it is 200 OK, the body of the response contains the queried Generic Context data: GCSP/1.0 200 OK

Set. A control process can upload a part of a remote Generic Context with a Set command. It must indicate the full path of the targeted part of the GC. The message body contains the Generic Context data that should be modified. The remote Generic Context is unlocked after a Set command or a time out: Set Context.GenericCallControl GCSP/1.0

Notify. GCSP is a state-full protocol. Control processes may send notifications with a Notify command. Subscription to notification is done via a Set command. For example a Detection Point DP is armed by a Set and when a filter criterion matches, a notification is sent to the concerned partner. The Notify header line indicates the object raising the notification and the message body contains the notification data. For example the notification below is sent to an application server after a filter criteria match. The GCSP body contains data relative to the Filter Criteria object which is the script ID to execute and the filter criterion priority: Notify Context. AccessComponent.UserProfile.FilterCriteria GCSP/1.0

Open-Context. To start a process in a remote entity, an Open-Context command is sent with the Association section filled except for the Destination-Context line. A new remote process is started which opens a context and answers back with a 200 OK response and put the Source-Context in the Destination-Context line and fills the Source-Context with the reference of the new Generic Context that has been created.

Close-Context. A communication is ended with a Close-Context command. Contexts involved are closed and freed from memory. After a process receives a Close-Context command, it answers back with a 200 OK (if the Generic Context is closed) with an embedded Close-Context command to notify the remote process that there is no more data to be send.

Describe. The skeleton of the Generic Context with its fundamental objects will be described in another paper. However to provide extensions the describe command may be used to discover the structure of a new object in a remote GC.

Lookup. Control processes that implement GCSP may communicate with other control processes using different signaling protocols via signaling mediators. A signaling mediator is a gateway that translates GCSP to another signaling protocol. GCSP may cooperate to locate the adequate mediator for a given signaling protocol.

5.3.1.3   Other headers

A sequence number tracks how many messages have been exchanged in a communication between two GCSP applications or also indicate a transaction number if any:

Sequence <sequence_number> <transaction_number>

A General header section is present in all GCSP frames. The header lines include: Content-Type, Content-Encoding, Content-Length, Date, Expiration

5.3.2   Body

A GCSP message may have a body of data sent after the header lines. If so, there may be header lines to describe the body such as: Content-Type and Content-Length. When a Get command is sent to a peer process, it usually responds by 200 OK in a header line and the queried object in the message body. Because SDP [29] does not take in account the description of an object that encapsulates another object and because the number of SDP attributes is limited to the alphabet size we use a new description language shown in the example below. In this example the objects in the figure 3 are represented as follow in the GCSP message:

```
<HEADER LINE_1>
<HEADER LINE_n>

<BLANK LINE>

#s: <Object_1>CRLF
attr_1: <value> CRLF
attr_2: <value> CRLF
attr_n: <value> CRLF
#s: <Object_2> CRLF
attr_1: <value> CRLF
attr_2: <value> CRLF
attr_n: <value> CRLF
#e: <Object_2> CRLF
#e: <Object_1> CRLF
```

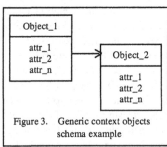

Figure 3.   Generic context objects schema example

6   Related work

Data based mechanisms have been used by management protocols like SNMP, IMLI and NetConf. They are specifically designed for the centralized architecture of management and have features that do not make them usable in control applications. For example, the request ID of the SNMP header which makes an association between two entities: the NMS and the agent. This is not what is required in control softwares where associations are made between 2 or more control processes involved in a same service session. Other protocols like NetConf are hard to consider in control software for efficiency reasons since they use an XML syntax for the content body, encapsulated in RPC messages and transferred by BEEP [30], SSH or SSL over TCP. While TCP is a reliable transport protocol for management, it is a handicap for control software because of its three way handshaking at the beginning that increases the call setup delay. Also some implementation of TCP can have delays of 6 and 24 seconds in the retransmission of the initial SYN packet. These reasons made SIP go on UDP and not TCP [28] and keep TCP for firewall traversal transport-layer security protocol such as TLS [31].

The NSIS working group at the IETF has defined a set of requirements, a scenario for future signaling protocols [32], and a framework divided into a transport layer and a signaling layer [2]. The transport layer is a robust layer that will assure the transport of application signaling in a similar manner as the SS7 network does with ISUP, MAP and INAP. While most of the work on NSIS Transport Layer is accomplished, there is still a lot to be done on the signaling applications layer. GCSP could be a candidate for the NSIS Signaling Layer Protocol for Cooperative Processes.

As we will see in part 7, GCSP provides a simpler approach to the design of signaling mediators. Today's mechanisms to accomplish multi-provider services, like web services CORBA and RMI, require that the different service components should all be on the Internet network. With the help of GCSP signaling mediators, service components may be located on different networks.

7   Validation

We have integrated the GCSP protocol to the Corebridge CTI (Computer Telephony Integration) applications suite. They consist of a server connected to a company PBX through the PBX CTI link (SIP, TAPI, CSTA or proprietary) and a set of CTI applications. A CTI application (phone bar), among many features, allows searching customers' profiles in a database, and initiating and handling phone calls. To initiate a call, the phone bar sends a command to the Corebridge server which forwards it to the PBX. To take in account the case where PBXs are implemented as SIP proxies, we have developed a GCSP/SIP signaling mediator. This mediator receives GCSP commands from the phone bar and sends SIP commands to the SIP proxy. Reversely, it receives SIP commands from the SIP proxy and sends GCSP commands to the phone bar. This generic architecture allowed us to support a wide range of PBXs with less cost of development efforts.

8   Conclusion

In this paper, we have underlined the cooperative computing nature of the control plane software and we have reached the conclusion that "data based signaling mechanisms" are better suited than "command based signaling mechanisms" to this cooperative nature of the control plane. Thus we have provided a brief description of the Generic Context that structures the common shared contexts and we have given a detailed description of the new GCSP signaling protocol used to share and modify GCs data in the control plane. Currently we are working on a SIP/GCSP signaling mediator, future publications will give more details on this work and the design of signaling mediators to interface with the various current signaling protocols and detailed descriptions of the Generic Context.

List of acronyms

BEEP: Block Extensible Exchange Protocol
CID: Call Instance Data
CIM: Common Information Model
CMIP: Common Management Information Protocol
CORBA: Common Object Request Broker Architecture
CSTA: Computer Supported Telephony Applications
GC: Generic Context
GCSP: Generic Context Sharing Protocol
ILMI: Interim Local Management Interface
ISUP: ISDN User Part (SS7)
MIB: Management Information Base
MEGACO: MEdia GAteway COntrol protocol
NETCONF: Network Configuration
NMS: Network Management Station
NSIS: Next Step In Signaling
POTS: Plain Old Telephone Service
RMI: Remote Method Invocation
SDP: Session Description Protocol
SIMPSON: Signaling Model for Programmable Services Over Networks
SIP: Session Initiation Protocol
SNMP: Simple Network Management Protocol
SSD: Service Support Data
TAPI: Telephony Application Programming Interface
TCAP: Transaction Capability Application Part (SS7)

References

1. C. Rigault, R. Chahine, Cooperative computing in the control plane; application to NGN services and control, IFIP MAN 2005

2. IETF RFC 4080, Next Steps in Signaling (NSIS): Framework, June 2005

3. RFC 1213, Management Information Base for Network Management of TCP/IP-based internets:MIB-II, March 1991

4. Vijay K. Gurbani and Xian-He Sun, Senior Member, IEEE, Terminating Telephony Services on the Internet

5. IETF RFC 3910: The SPIRITS (Services in PSTN requesting Internet Services) Protocol, October 2004

6. IETF RFC 2458: Toward the PSTN/Internet Inter-Networking - Pre-PINT Implementations, November 1998

7. IETF RFC 2848: The PINT Service Protocol: Extensions to SIP and SDP for IP Access to Telephone Call Services, June 2000

8. Parlay : http://www.parlay.org

9. Aiko Pars, PHD Thesis: Network Management Architectures

10. ISO documents 9595, 9596 and ITU.700, X.711

11. W3C, Web Services Description Language (WSDL) 1.1, 15 march 2001, http://www.w3.org/TR/wsdl

12. CORBA, www.corba.org

13. William Grosso, Java RMI, O'Reilly, first Edition October 2001

14. IETF draft: http://www.ietf.org/internet-drafts/draft-ietf-netconf-prot-12.txt

15. IETF RFC 3261, Session Initiation Protocol (SIP), June 2002

16. ITU-T Recommendation Q.764, Signalling system No. 7 – ISDN user part signalling procedures, 12/1999

17. B. Schilit, N. Adams, and R. Want, Context-Aware Computing Applications, Proc. IEEE Workshop Mobile Computing Systems and Applications, pp. 85-90, 1994.

18. A.K. Dey, Understanding and Using Context, J. Personal and Ubiquitous Computing, vol. 5, no. 1, pp. 4-7, Feb. 2001

19. Astronefs, Network and Telecommunication Global Service Convergence: White paper, http://www.infres.enst.fr/~rigault/white-paper.pdf

20. Common Information Model (CIM) Standards: http://www.dmtf.org/standards/cim/

21. IETF RFC 1157, Simple Network Management Protocol (SNMP), May 1990

22. S.M. Keller: System Management Information Modelling, IEEE Communications Magazine, page 38-44, May 1993

23. W. Stallings: SNMP, SNMPv2 and CMIP – The Practical Guide to Network Management Standards, Addison Wesley

24. IETF RFC 3015, Megaco Protocol Version 1.0, Novembre 2000

25. TCAP ITU-T Q.771_Q775, TCAP: Transaction Capabilities Application Part

26. Philippe Martins, Architecture de contrôle et middleware pour les réseaux de prochaines générations et évaluation de performances, PHD thesis, ENST Paris, April 2000

27. IETF RFC 2616, Hypertext Transfer Protocol -- HTTP/1.1, June 1999

28. H. Schulzrinne, J. Rosenberg, Signaling for Internet Telephony, February 2, 1998

29. IETF RFC 2327, SDP: Session Description Protocol, April 1998

30. IETF RFC 3080, Block Extensible Exchange Protocol, March 2001

31. IETF RFC 2246, The TLS Protocol Version 1.0, January 1999

32. IETF RFC 3726, Requirements for Signaling Protocols, April 2004

ASMA : Towards Adaptive Secured Multipath in MANETs

Vincent Toubiana and Houda Labiod
Ecole Nationale Supérieure des Télécommunication (ENST)
LTCI-UMR 5141 CNRS
GET/ENST/INFRES Department
46 rue Barrault – 75634 Paris Cedex 13 – France
Email : labiod@enst.fr, toubiana@enst.fr

Abstract. As they are used to create open communities, Mobile Ad hoc NETworks (MANETs) are not favourable environments to establish trust, which is necessary to provide security. Multipath routing mechanisms within infrastructureless networks environment seems appropriate and useful to enhance security protection. In fact, the level of trust can be increased so as many of potential security attacks are detected, revealed and stopped. Nevertheless an excessive control overhead is always generated. In this paper, we propose a global framework that integrates a set of concepts and mechanisms aiming at enhancing security in highly dynamic decentralized ad hoc networks. Our solution focuses on authentication, routing securing, trust management with reliable estimation of trust. A large panoply of attacks are prevented using our various mechanisms.

1   Introduction

Ad hoc networks rely on peer to peer architecture and collaboration between nodes to provide connectivity. Typically routing protocols proposed for these networks assume that every node collaborates and no node try to disturb the network. However, as this technology evolves rapidly and will be soon intensively deployed, threats have to be considered because ad hoc networks can be easily attacked by hackers and spammers. Furthermore being totally distributed, highly connected, open and implicit, MANETs can be used to spread virus. Remembering the Bluetooth virus appeared at the athletic games in Helsinki, it shows clearly that users are not aware of potential threat. Now imagine how fast the virus could spread in an ad hoc network and what could be the damage. Many attacks have already been considered for ad hoc networks and we can expect that a lot of specific attacks for future applications will be discovered whenever these new networks will be used. As these

Please use the following format when citing this chapter:

Toubiana, V., Laboid, H., 2006, in IFIP International Federation for Information Processing, Volume 211, ed. Pujolle, G., Mobile and Wireless Communication Networks, (Boston: Springer), pp. 175–185.

networks provide no authentication and so no traceability, hackers could act easily without being detected. Actually, in wireless networks users must refer to peers to route and transmit packets, hence they have to establish trust relationship to operate in a secure context. To define trust, we refer to the definition of D. Gambetta in [1] : " ...*trust (or, symmetrically, distrust) is a particular level of the subjective probability with which an agent assesses that another agent or group of agents will perform a particular action, both before he can monitor such action (or independently of his capacity ever to be able to monitor it) and in a context in which it affects his own action*".

To get feedback for the first time about a node, we distinguish two cases, 1) if we already know an agent we could use this agent to get feedback about the submitted action 2) we do not know an agent, so we could submit action which does not need an explicit feedback (i.e. : trying to reach a node that does not exist). Once we obtain a feedback about nodes, we can refer to them to estimate trust about other nodes, hence we refer to their reputation, which is defined by [1] as the *"perception that an agent creates through past actions about intentions and norms"*. This relation concerns only one agent and is defined as an aggregation of information collected by nodes on past interactions.

Based on these key concepts, we propose a global framework in order to meet security requirements through different functions such as authentication, efficient and low-cost multipath routing and trust management. Trust estimation is performed by close nodes and can be computed for either a node or a path, to maintain up-to-date trust information and to prevent gathering useless information. This paper is organized as follows. Section II gives a review on the security mechanisms proposed for ad hoc networks including trust management, authentication and routing protocols. Section III provides a description of our proposed framework. Section IV analyzes the robustness of our framework against some famous attacks. Finally, section V provides concluding remarks and highlights our future work.

2   Related Work

Security in MANETs is a critical research topic ; an intense research activity is undertaken. One of the major challenges of ad hoc networks is the authentication of the nodes as we may have to authenticate unknown nodes. Authentication can simply be provided by using a trusted third party common to all the nodes of the network. If nodes have different certification authorities, we have to build a PKI (Public Key Infrastructure). In a centralized mode, we use a unique authority of certification which is totally trusted, however if the authority is far this can create a high latency to get a certificate and the network comprises a single point of failure. To distribute the authority, one solution consists of using threshold cryptography[2] . Gathering at least "t" signatures of different certifications authorities is necessary to generate a certificate, hence the system is more distributed and robust to attackers, but this creates the problem to find the trusted entity and how to fix the threshold value to provide efficient security and low delay. To provide authentication and trust we can use the "Small World Theory" as proposed in PGP[3], however such model may generate a high overhead due to certification operations and in practice the size of the connected graph of trust remains small compared to the size of the whole network [4]. So, the probability to get the wanted certificate through a chain is very low. One solution to create more certification links may be to use the mechanism of [5] to distribute certificates in the network, however it is mainly based on the existence of an on-line certification authority ; once the authority is off-line nodes can not know really who to trust. Authentication can also be based on the identity mechanisms; this is the principle of encryption based identity. One of them is proposed in SUCV (Statistically Unique and Cryptographically Verifiable) [6], but the principal threat for this scheme is that anyone can create its own identity and so there is no way to know if an identity is legitimate or not. Consequently, this authentication is highly vulnerable to Sybil attacks [7]. And even if the problem of binding identity and key is solved, authentication is not a problem anymore ; identification becomes the real key challenge. A hybrid solution has been proposed as the composite key management [8] protocol which uses the trusted certification authority and PGP-like chain to provide short chain of trust in the network. However this solution does not clearly define which node takes part of the certificate chaining and this may create a high overhead as all the certification chain may remain long.

Once they are authenticated, nodes use secured routing protocols to communicate. These protocols often rely on powerful cryptography algorithms. ARIADNE[9] provides end-to-end security for both routing and forwarding ; however it relies on TESLA and symmetric cryptography. The mechanism of key distribution is not clearly defined in the protocol. ARAN[10] uses asymmetric cryptography for hop-by-hop encryption, but such mechanism assumes that the source trusts every node in the route because if there is at least one untrusted node, the whole route is untrusted. Recently some proposal use multipath routing [11] such as SecMR (Secure Multipath Routing) and the Secure MultiPath Protocol. Both provide security through redundancy : SecMR uses list in the routing packet to prevent node from being in two paths and Secure MultiPath Protocol uses information added to the RREQ (Route REQuest) by intermediate nodes to select the paths. As they do not refer to a pre-established trust, they have to use totally distinct paths resulting in high overload of the network and resource consumption ; these solutions are not scalable.

Obviously, security in ad hoc networks is a young research domain, no standard has been adopted yet, many issues have to be addressed and more studies are needed. Authentication and routing are tightly bound and creates a deadlock situation. However, only SUCV clearly define both and others suppose that there is a bootstrapping phase which avoids the problem. Moreover, most of the proposed solutions are not adaptive and so highly vulnerable to especially Denial of Service (DoS) attacks. In this paper, we propose a complete framework named Adaptive Secure Multipath for Ad hoc Networks(ASMA) which deals with necessary functions to resolve the critical security issues. We propose an approach which can be seen as a suitable candidate to make a balance between security requirements and system flexibility in the case of highly dynamic ad hoc networks. As it is based on a dynamic trust, this framework provides security without requiring a bootstrapping phase.

3   ASMA

This section gives an overview of the framework.

3.1   Definition

Without loss of generality, we define our functions in the [0;1] interval. Doing so, we can use probability and fuzzy logic theory [12].

a) Trust. Our aim is to use a trust model which is coherent and computable. Then we refer to the definition of [1] to propose the trust function : $Trust(A,B,F,C)$ is the trust that node A has in an agent B to perform an action F in a context C. Most of the definitions consider the agent B as a single node but we adopt a more general concept, as we use multipath routing, we consider that agent B is either a node or a path. As an attacker could act honestly as long as it knows we have a feedback and become malicious when it knows it is not observed. So a node should not be able to know if we have a feedback and this is an important part of the context which relies on multipath capabilities. Other parameters of the context include density of the network. We suppose that the trust function is continue for F and C, so we could estimate the trust of a node for a particular value (F,C) knowing the trust of the same node for (F',C'). Trust is composed of two values, the measured trust ($Mtru_i$ and the reputation trust (Rep). The trust is a weighted average of these two values :   with a in [0;1]. $Mtrust$ is computed as the number of successful actions divided by the number of submitted actions. It is clear that the number of actions submitted is an integer but the number of successful actions may be a float as some actions may not totally succeed or failed (for example recommendation). This definition requires considering only action on which we received a feedback. In order to be more flexible to recent changes, we can give a higher weight to recent actions.

b) Risk. We define risk of an action as the minimum of trust that we can accept to perform this action. Risk depends on the function, the user and the context of the action. Risk is defined by the function : $R(A,F,C')$; C' can be different of the context define for trust. Since A has all the knowledge to estimate the risk, we do not require the function to be continue for F and C'. Risk must be higher than 0,5. We settle that A trust B, and so that B is trusted by A, for the function F in the context C if : $Trust(A,B,F,C) > R(A,F,C')$.

c) Knowledge. In our mechanisms we use only asymmetric cryptography and certificate to bind entity to key. The certification management is symmetric and will be explained for centralized and distributed networks. Here we define the "knowledge relation" as follow : *node A knows a node B if A and B have exchanged there certificates*. This relation is symmetric as in [5]: if A knows B then B knows A. The relation is not extended to be transitive because if a node forges many identities it could use this transitivity to know the entire network. We also define $K(X)$ as the set of nodes which know X.

d) Reputation. Parameters of both trust and reputation are the same, however as reputation may be an aggregation of values, it can take less arguments. So we define the global reputation of node B for a function F as :

$$Rep(B,F) = \frac{1}{card(Net)} \sum_{A \in Net} \sum_{C \in S} Trust \frac{(A,B,F,C)}{card(S)}$$

. Where *Net* represents the set of nodes in the network and S the set of all the contexts. When we use recommendation from an other node, we use the trust we allow to the node which sign the recommendation. So the perceived reputation is the product of the recommendation and the trust we have in the recommender for recommendations. For node A the reputation of B for action F in context C is defined as :

$$Rep(A,B,F,C) = \frac{1}{card(Known(A))} \sum_{B \in Known(A)} Trust(A,D,Rec,C) \times Trust(B,D,F,C);$$

C' is the common context between D and A. From this value we can sum the reputation on different contexts to get an aggregate reputation.

3.2 Different Procedures of the Framework

We focus our work on on-demand routing approach. We based our routing protocol on DSR (Dynamic Source Routing) and just few packet extensions are needed to propagate "trust information". When a node wants to establish a communication, it first applies Multipath Key Management to get the certificate of the destination, then it executes the Multipath Adaptive Routing Protocol to find the route it will use. Finally, it uses the forwarding mechanism to send packets.

The Multipath Key Management : This solution is derived from composite key management which provides certificate chaining using graph of trust [8]. However this mechanism creates a high load due to the certificates chain when the destination is far (more than two hops). But in our solutions we assume that some known nodes get the certificate that we are looking for, then they can sign it and send it to us. So instead of starting a chain from the source to the destination, we create a chain from the destination to the first node which knows the source. Known nodes receiving the request may reply if they know the destination too. We also improve the reliability of the received certificates using multipath : in case we receive multiple responses, we use Dempster-Shafer [12] theory to compute the trust associated to the certificate. As nodes move and because we establish communication with different nodes, the set of nodes known by a node will be distributed among the network and the probability is low for two nodes to get the same set of known nodes.

Multipath Adaptive Routing protocol : Multipath routing provides redundancy and robustness, but implies drawbacks like increased load of the network and resource consumption which may be used to generate DoS. However when a node just arrives in the network, it knows no node and so can not have security requirement, hence multipath is a good solution to establish trust relations. Consequently we use adaptive multipath routing to allow new nodes to use multipath routing so they have good requirement on security. Hence nodes store feedback of different paths and then establish trust relation with other nodes in the network. Once the node has established trust relation, it decreases the number of paths it uses to get higher priority and slower delay. When we trust some intermediate nodes, we do not have to use totally disjoint paths, as this may not be possible, and may generates high load. It is enough to have just disjointed paths between trusted nodes. To   prevent excessive flood of request, node monitor the number of RREQ they forward. When an intermediate node forwards too many RREQ, it stops to forward RREQ unless they are signed by a trusted node, thus preventing DoS. We define the macro graph $MG(S,D)$ as the oriented graph connecting S to D which vertexes are nodes in $K(S)$ and an edge is the set of paths between two vertexes. The weight of an edge is the trust associated to it by its input vertex. If an edge contains multiple paths, nodes use Dempster-Shafer theory to compute the weight. Similarly to reactive approach, the route request phase remains the same. Modifications concern reply phase and forwarding.

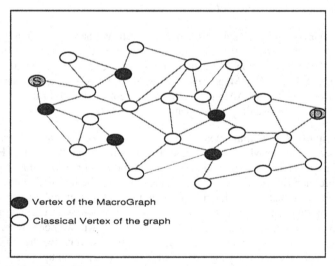

Fig. 1. Example of MacroGraph

Multipath response flooding : Before sending a RREQ, the source S estimates the risk R it can accept for the transaction knowing the context of the action. Then it sends the RREQ which includes R, a special byte to notify that the RREP (Route REPly) has to use multiple paths and add a list of nodes that can not be neighbor in the macro graph and a list of nodes that can not be on the macro graph, then it signs and broadcast the RREQ. Intermediate nodes known by the destination D append a signature of the packet in an extended destination list (this provide integrity of the route). Intermediate nodes in $K(S)$ and not blacklisted indicate that they forward the RREQ in the extended source list. Receiving the RREQ packet, D checks signatures of known nodes. If it has up-to-date information about nodes in the extended source list, it appends them in a reputation extension packet. Then it waits for a random timer $t1$ in $\left[\dfrac{R \times T \times HopCount}{2} ; R \times T \times HopCount \right]$ where T is adapted to the network and HopCount is the average number of hop records in RREQ. Once $t1$ expired, it signs RREP and sends it through all paths which have propagated the RREQ. Intermediate nodes do the same using a timer $t2$ in $[0 ; R \times T \times HopCount]$ and just nodes in $K(S)$ sign the RREP. Intermediate nodes in $K(S)$ check the RREP to find other nodes in $K(S)$, then they remove from the RREP all nodes which are not in $K(S)$ and just indicate the trust allowed to path to their neighbor in $MG(S,D)$. This prevent useless overhead as other nodes are not concerned by these nodes and allow trusted nodes to manage paths between them without referring to S. If a node is connected to nodes in $K(S)$ through many paths (the exact value depend on the density of the network) and is not the direct neighbor, it acts as a known node and requests an exchange of certificates with S.

We propose an extension to limit the multipath flooding. If S already knows a lot of nodes, it does not have to ask for flooding RREP and so can reach lower delay reducing the number of paths it uses. The source proceeds as previously but does not indicate that the RREQ must be flooded. Thus instead of sending the RREP by all the routes it received a RREQ, intermediate nodes always use the shortest path (or the trustiest, the metric can be defined by the user).

Forwarding adaptation : Upon receiving the packet, the source computes $MG(S,D)$ to achieve the required trust level (which may be higher than R but must correspond to the value returned by known nodes). Thanks to the concept of dynamic trust, for non critical packets, the source could select nodes which have been malicious and may now act honestly, offering them a chance to be trusted again. Then S sends a packet describing $MG(S,D)$ using the list of vertexes and edges. Every node in $MG(S,D)$ use the information it collected during the routing phase to achieve the security requirements of S. An advantage of such mechanism is that if a node changes often its identity, it will not know a lot of nodes and so can not require trust.

For the following packets, S does not have to include the list of trusted nodes, but just the list of edges and their weights, thus we reduce considerably the size of the header. As every trusted node knows the required weight for the edge, it can adapt the transmission of packets. During communications S gets feedback about paths and nodes, it can adapt the number of paths it uses to reach the destination. As this is done dynamically, the source can easily adapt security and/or QoS requirement. When a node does not receive packet for a long time, it simply removes the recorded path corresponding to the route. Updating trust is a problem when two different nodes declare that the other one is malicious and that we have neither feedback nor reputation to know which one is the liar. Thus we may try to obtain reputation about one of the nodes and so trust the one which has the best reputation. If there is no way to get feedback by different paths (and so to solve the problem), we can not know which node is lying, so these two nodes can not be neighbor on the macro graph anymore. For next RREQ, we add their names in the neighbor blacklist (two nodes in the list can not be neighbor). Afterwards if feedback is obtained about one of them, trust adaptation is applied as previously described. To get feedback, source requires that trusted nodes send cumulative acknowledgment. We also can use end-to-end acknowledgment to get a global feedback, then the destination signs the feedback and sends it by a trusted path. In case of link breakage detection, node signs the RERR (Route ERRor). If the upstream trusted node does not know the signature, it tries to recover it through another path. Otherwise, it sends the error to the source and signs it.

3.3   Operations

The framework ASMA goes through several steps :
- Initialization of nodes,
- Exchange of certificates before a communication,
- Route and trust establishment,
- Forwarding and route adaptation.

To illustrate the operation of ASMA, we give two different scenarios associated to the centralized and the distributed modes.

Centralized Mode : We suppose that a Certification Authority (CA) is present in the visited network. It can be either centralized or distributed among some nodes.
We distinguish four steps :
A) The node S broadcasts a Certification Request (CReq) which contains a sequence number and its public key (PK). Only nodes between S and the CA forward it.
B) The responding CA replies by sending a certificate of the public key. It adds a list of nodes' certificates which have forwarded the CReq and then sends it by the same path it received it. When a node forwards this packet, if its certificate is in the list, it stores the certificate of the requester and considers it as known.
C) In the case of reception of the same certificate, the source records it. Otherwise it considers the certificate with the best reputation. In both cases it associates to the certificate an "unknown value".
D) When interacting with an authenticated peer, the node asks for confirmation the CA's certificate. If it is confirmed, it associates to all the corresponding certificates the trust of the confirming peer. Otherwise, the node has to send the real certificate of the CA and to sign it with its own key (for non repudiation); it must have received it from what it claims to be the real authority. The source then asks other nodes to confirm the certificate. Then it will associate the certificate with the trust corresponding to the node that established the certificate.

Distributed Mode : A node connecting for the first time to the network broadcasts its PK. A forwarding node records the key and generates a certificate with probability *P(Cert,Path)* which depends on the number of distinct certificates already recorded and the number of path by which the node received the key. When it records a PK, the node signs it and sends it as a certificate. It then sends its own PK to be signed and returned by the requesting node. In that case, unless there is at least one trusted path, a malicious node could use a Man in The Middle attack to get certificates. As previously, the node associates the "unknown value" to this certificate. Later, during a communication with a node, we can get its certificates with trust value higher than an associated threshold.

4   Analyzing Robustness Against Attacks

This gives a good overview of the capabilities of the protocol to resist to attacks. For every attack, we consider that at least one path from the destination to the source is trustful, even if this is a strong requirement, it is necessary and there can not be network communication without this assumption.

4.1   Passive Attacks

Traffic Analyzes : Multipath routing approach make it very difficult for an attacker to guess where is the expected destination of packet and what are the critical paths. This still possible, but this kind of threat is not dangerous in domestic networks and is treated in military networks.
Information Leak : The information leak depends on the captured packet. If the first packet is captured then the information leak is critical, but if it concerns another packet, the leak is small as the header just contains source and destination information. We plan to reduce this leak using address substitution in future work.

4.2   Active Attacks

Wormhole Attack : If a wormhole exists between two nodes, the feedback about these nodes will remove the route from the macro-graph.
Byzantine Attack : If the Byzantine node is a trusted node we must refer to another path of the macro graph to prevent the attack. If the attack is performed by an untrusted node, there is a high probability of detection by a trusted node and the impact of the attack is low because the packet is routed by another path.
Resource consumption : If a node uses different identities during flooding its packet will be dropped. However a node could consume resource on a path, pretending forwarding traffic. For example the node may use two identities and pretends forwarding packets from the first identity to the second one using a loop. Nodes on the loop are not supposed to know neither the source nor the destination, hence they have no reason to not forwarding. To prevent this attack, intermediate nodes could

ask for the source's certificate when they suspect this attack. If nodes can forge identities, there is no other solution than to limit the number of forwarded packets for nodes that we do not know.

Spoofing : Although forging identities is penalizing because using identities reduces the number of nodes known by a single identity, it can not be totally prevented. In distributed networks, a node can generate as many IP addresses that it wants, but in a centralized mode, this situation depends on the capacity of the server to check the identity of the node requesting for an IP address.

Denial Of Service : Using many identities, nodes can flood the node with RREQ thus generate DoS as some legitimates RREQ are dropped. However nodes which are trusted by a lot of nodes are not concerned by this attack as their RREQ are not dropped.

Routing Attack : If all routing attacks can not be prevented, at least their impacts are drastically reduced as they have to impact all the paths to achieve their goal. *Source route modification* can only be performed by nodes on paths between trusted nodes and will be detected by trusted nodes. *Rushing attack* is not efficient in multipath routing because nodes do not only consider the first arrived RREQ. *Packet replication* is prevented thanks to the use of sequence numbers and signatures by the source. As we use DSR as base routing protocol, we can use its improvement on cache utilization. However the best way to secure DSR is to disable cache optimizations or to use it only if the packet is signed by a trusted node.

5   Conclusion

In this paper we give the main guidelines for designing a new framework to deal with security in MANETs. This framework called ASMA provides authentication and security routing using trust dynamic relations and based on multipath communication. We adopt an appropriate trust model suitable to our multipath reactive routing approach. Since dynamic trust is supported, no bootstrapping phase is needed. ASMA combines efficiently key management, routing and forwarding operations to securely transmit data packets through the network. Moreover, an other strength of our solution is that it can be used either in a centralized or a distributed mode. An analysis of the robustness of ASMA is illustrated by considering a large number of passive and active known attacks. For future work, we intend to complete and to evaluate the cited mechanisms.

Acknowledgement

This work was carried out through a France Telecom R&D Research Program. We would like to thank Laurent Reynaud for his helpful and very interesting comments.

6 References

1. D. Gambetta, "Can we trust trust?", Trust, Making and Breaking Cooperative Relations. basil Blackwell (1990) p. 213-237

2. J. Kong, P. Zerfos, H. Luo, S. LU and L. Zhang. "Providing robust and ubiquitous security support for mobile ad-hoc networks", in Proc. of the 9th IEEE International Conference on Network Protocols, 2001

3. P. Zimmermann. "The official PGP user's guide". MIT Press 1995

4. S. Capku, L. Buttyan, and J.-P Hubaux. "Small worlds in security systems: an analysis of the pgp certificate graph", in Proc. of the 2002 workshop on New security paradigms, 28-35, 2002

5. T. Li, Z. Wan , F. Bao , K. Ren, R. H. Deng, K. Kim, "Highly reliable trust establishment scheme in ad hoc networks",Computer Networks 45 (2004) : 687699

6. G. Montenegro and C. Castelluccia. "Statistically Unique and Cryptographically Verifiable (SUCV) Identifiers and Addresses". in Proc. of the Network and Distributed System Security Symposium (NDSS'02), 2002

7. J.R. Douceur," The Sybil Attack", in Proc. of the 1st International Workshop on Peer-to-Peer Systems, 2002

8. S. Yi, R. Kravets, "Composite Key Management For Ad Hoc Networks", in Proc. of the 1st Annual International Conference on Mobile and Ubiquitous Systems: Networking and Services (MobiQuitous'04), 2004

9. Y.-C. Hu, A. Perrig, and D. B. Johnson. "Ariadne : A secure on-demand routing protocol for ad hoc networks". In MOBICOM, 2002.

10. K. Sanzgiri, D. LaFlamme, B. Dahill, B. Neil Levine, C. Shields, E. M. Belding-Royer, "Authenticated Routing for Ad Hoc Networks,IEEE Journal on Selected Areas in Communications, vol. 23", no. 3, march 2005

11. R. Mavropodi, P. Kotzanikolaou, C. Douligeris, "Performance Analysis of Secure Multipath Routing Protocols for Mobile Ad Hoc Networks", in Springer WWIC 2005, p.269-278, 2005

12. T. M. Chen, V. Venkataramanan, "Dempster-Shafer Theory for Intrusion Detection in Ad Hoc Networks", IEEE Internet Computing Volume: 9 Issue: 6 Date: Nov.-Dec. 2005

Wireless Ad Hoc Networks on Underserved Communities: An Efficient Solution for Interactive Digital TV

Miguel Elias M. Campista, Igor M. Moraes, Pedro Miguel Esposito,
Aurelio Amodei Jr., Daniel de O. Cunha, Luís Henrique M. K. Costa,
and Otto Carlos M. B. Duarte*

Grupo de Teleinformática e Automação
Universidade Federal do Rio de Janeiro

Summary. The Brazilian government intends to use the Digital TV technology as a vehicle of digital inclusion on underserved communities. The wireless ad hoc network is a low-cost, scalable and easy solution to implement the return channel. This work analyzes the performance of an ad hoc return channel using the wireless IEEE 802.11 technology in different Brazilian geographical scenarios. The results show that a high connectivity is achieved when more than 20% of the nodes are turned on, regardless of the position of the gateway. The influence of the number of hops and the number of transmitting nodes is also analyzed. A minimum throughput of 2 Mbps can be reached for increasing number of hops in the forwarding chain for a one-node transmission. Besides, when the number of transmitting nodes increases, the aggregated throughput can achieve 3.5 Mbps. The results show that the ad hoc network is a promising solution for the return channel of the interactive Digital TV.

1 Introduction

More than 90% of the Brazilian residences have a TV set, but less than 10% have Internet access [1]. The terrestrial digital TV can offer a huge number of new functionalities. The digital TV improves the quality reception of audio and video streams, provides new services such as e-government and Internet access, and can further integrate underserved people to the digital world. New services are possible due to the adoption of an interactive channel, also called a return channel. This channel allows TV spectators to interact by sending data back to the TV station.

Our proposal is to use an ad hoc community network to build a shared return channel. Hence, every TV set top box is a node of the community network and all the traffic is forwarded to a gateway that forwards the traffic to the TV station using a broadband ISP. The main advantages of this proposal are: the ad hoc community network does not require a telecommunication infrastructure, multihop communications can reach long distances, the Internet access cost is shared by all the nodes of the network, and the other Internet services can

---

* Supported by CNPq, CAPES, FAPERJ, FINEP, UOL, FUJB, and FUNTTEL.

Please use the following format when citing this chapter:

Campista, M.E.M., Moraes, I.M., Esposito, P.M., Amodei Jr., A., de O. Cunha, D., Costa, L.H.M.K., Duarte, O.C.M.B., 2006, in IFIP International Federation for Information Processing, Volume 211, ed. Pujolle, G., Mobile and Wireless Communication Networks, (Boston: Springer), pp. 187–198.

be provided without additional costs. It is important to analyze the network connectivity and capacity.

The capacity of ad hoc networks is subject of many works. Hsu et al. [2] evaluate the performance of an ad hoc network using different routing protocols. Parameters like number of nodes and hops are analyzed. They examine through simulations the performance of large ad hoc networks. Although there is a high number of nodes, more than a thousand, the density is kept low and only one scenario is used. In [3], Hsu et al. perform a similar analysis varying the network traffic and adding mobility to the nodes. Both works show that the results are highly influenced by the network topology. Nevertheless, scenarios with mobility present better results for reactive routing protocols. Armenia et al. [4] develop a testbed for VoIP transmissions with the source node a few hops away from the destination. The delay of the voice flows is lower with OLSR than with AODV. This is due to the absence of route discovery procedures in OLSR. Borgia [5] finds that the recovery time is lower in OLSR than in AODV. Villela and Duarte [6] analyze the impact of multiple hops in an ad hoc network. They propose, the use of alternative paths to improve the network throughput in addition to the shortest path chosen by the routing protocol.

Most performance evaluation works consider homogeneous ad hoc networks. Our analysis is specific because all traffic is forwarded to and from a specific node, the gateway, which becomes the bottleneck. Another singularity is the activity period of a node. As it is associated to the TV set, we can expect that some nodes will be offline during the day. The connectivity is analyzed to know how many nodes must be on to guarantee a minimum "infrastructure" to provide access to all the network users. Network capacity is addressed analyzing the saturation throughput and the impact of multiple hops. Furthermore, the efficiency of different routing protocols is analyzed for each scenario.

This work is organized as follows. Section 2 introduces the return channel. Section 3 describes the Brazilian reference scenarios. The simulation parameters and the results are shown in Section 4. Finally, Section 5 concludes this work and presents some future directions.

2 The Ad Hoc Return Channel

In an ad hoc return channel, a forwarding node is the access terminal of each user, which runs a routing protocol and forwards data for its neighbors. The gateway is the interconnecting point with the TV station network. Every node must be able to communicate with the gateway, directly or through multiple hops. The signal of the TV station is usually sent using diffusion and the interactivity information goes through the return channel. The access terminals allow network connectivity forwarding data packets to and from the gateway. In this work, a node and an access terminal are synonymous.

An ad hoc return channel must have a minimum connectivity to provide communications between the terminals and the gateway. This connectivity is influenced by factors such as number of access terminals in a region, their transmission range, and the interval of time that they are on. The number of access terminals refers to the population density of a region. It is expected that most residences have, at least, one access terminal. This is already true for the analogical TV in Brazil [1]. Another key aspect to connectivity is the interval of time, which the terminals are on. Depending on the habits of the customers, during high audience TV programming, a lot of terminals are expected to be working. On the other hand, during low audience TV programming, only a few will be cooperating. Concerning per-node throughput, the IEEE 802.11 standard uses CSMA/CA to access the medium. With CSMA/CA, nodes inside the same transmission range contend for the medium. Therefore, increasing the number of transmitting nodes means a lower throughput per node. The transmission range also affects the throughput. Using lower transmission rates, the SNR tolerated is lower and consequently the transmission range increases. Additionally, antennas can be applied to increase the transmission ranges.

3 Reference Scenarios

Brazil is a continental size country and, consequently, has different regions with several demographic, geographic and social characteristics. To represent this diversity we consider five reference scenarios:

1. high-populated urban region with residences in mountains,
2. high-populated urban region with horizontal residences,
3. high-populated urban region with vertical residences,
4. medium or low-populated urban region with horizontal residences,
5. very low-populated rural region with large dimensions.

The parameters of the five reference scenarios are based on real data obtained from the Brazilian Institute of Geography and Statistics [7]. In Scenario 1, the data are from the Rocinha slum. Representing Scenario 2, the area of Ramos was chosen due to its high density of houses. Scenario 3 represents Copacabana, which is a dense area, composed by buildings. Representing Scenario 4, Parque Anchieta is a low-populated residential area. Scenario 5 refers to Paty do Alferes City which is located in the rural region of the Rio de Janeiro State. The parameters used in each scenario are shown in Table 1.

As in Brazil 90% of residences have at least one TV set [1], the number of nodes in the network is assumed to be the number of residences in the area. In Scenario 3, we suppose that there are 10 floors in each building, each floor is 3 m high, and every building is composed by one residence/floor.

The position of the nodes inside the simulation area depends on the scenario. A two-dimensional grid represents the urban regions composed by horizontal residences. This kind of grid suits these regions because they approximately follow a regular geographical distribution of residences. In the slum scenario, the two-dimensional grid also fits well because, although the distribution is not so regular, the residences are very close to each other. A three-dimensional grid

Table 1. Reference scenarios parameters.

Scenario	1	2	3	4	5
Neighborhood/City	Rocinha	Ramos	Copacabana	P. Anchieta	P. do Alferes
Total area (km^2)	1.4	2.8	4.1	3.9	319
Residential area (km^2)	1.4	1.5	2.5	2.2	-
Amount of residences	17000	11819	61000	7778	6813
Density (res./km^2)	12142	8117	24797	3487	21
Beta (β)	3.9	3.9	3.9	3.9	3.0
Nodes disposition	grid	grid	grid 3D	grid	random

is used for the urban scenario composed by vertical residences, or buildings. Each floor in the buildings is represented by a two-dimensional grid in the XY plane. Finally, in the rural region, the nodes are randomly located. Due to its low density, antenna deployment is considered to improve the connectivity.

4 Simulation Results

The transmission power, the signal attenuation, and the reception sensibility are taken into account to evaluate the transmission and the interference ranges for the different data rates of the 802.11 ad hoc network. We assumed a transmission power of 18 dBm, or 63.1 mW [8]. The path-loss model is used to compute the channel attenuation and, consequently, the transmission range of all the scenarios. We consider the propagation loss parameter $\beta = 3.9$ [9] for all urban scenarios and $\beta = 3.0$ for the rural scenario due to its lower density of residences. Thus, the interference range is equal to 74 m for Scenarios 1 to 4 and equal to 269 m for Scenario 5, which is also calculated with the path-loss model. The Internet gateway is always positioned at the center of each scenario or at one of its vertices. The results obtained have a confidence interval of 95%.

4.1 Connectivity Analysis

The connectivity analysis is of utmost importance because the collaborative communications provided by an ad hoc network must consider that the terminals may not be turned on all the time. The different scenarios use real values for residential area and density. Therefore, there may be from 7,000 to 61,000 terminals. Hence, a specific simulator written in C was implemented to analyze the connectivity. The simulator implements the Dijkstra algorithm to calculate the shortest path to the gateway and computes the percentile of connected nodes as well as the average number of hops to the gateway. A terminal is connected when it has at least one path to the gateway. We use physical transmission rates from 1 to 54 Mbps.

The connectivity is evaluated as a function of the percentage of nodes on that are randomly chosen for each simulation run. In Figures 1(a) and 1(b),

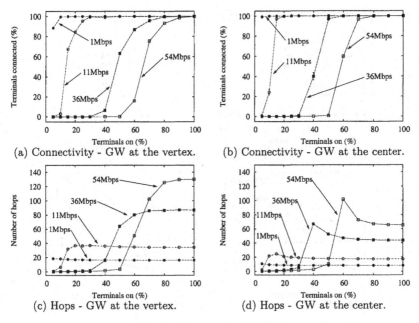

(a) Connectivity - GW at the vertex. (b) Connectivity - GW at the center.

(c) Hops - GW at the vertex. (d) Hops - GW at the center.

Fig. 1. Scenario 1 - Rocinha.

high network connectivity is achieved in Scenario 1 at the four simulated transmission rates. Nevertheless, when the gateway is positioned at the center of the scenario, high connectivity can be reached with a smaller percentage of nodes on. At 11 Mbps, when the gateway is in the center of the scenario, only 20% of the nodes need to be on to achieve high connectivity. With the gateway at one vertice, high connectivity only happens when 30% of the nodes are on. Figures 1(c) and 1(d) show that the average number of hops increases with the number of nodes on. In the beginning, only a few nodes are connected. Thus, there is a higher probability for the nodes near the gateway to be connected than for the nodes further from the gateway. As the further nodes get connected, the average number of hops increases. This is true until the network gets fully connected. After that, the average number of hops decreases because, as new nodes get into the network, new and smaller routes to the gateway are found.

The results of Scenarios 2 and 4 are similar to Scenario 1, therefore they were omitted. In Scenario 3, Figures 2(a) and 2(b) show that, independently of the percentage of terminals on, the network connectivity is near zero for 36 and 54 Mbps. This is due to a smaller number of neighbors. Despite being the more populated scenario, the average density for each XY plane is smaller than in Scenarios 1 and 2. The average density is 2500 residences/floor, assuming a 10-floor building. This density is almost five times smaller than in Scenario 1.

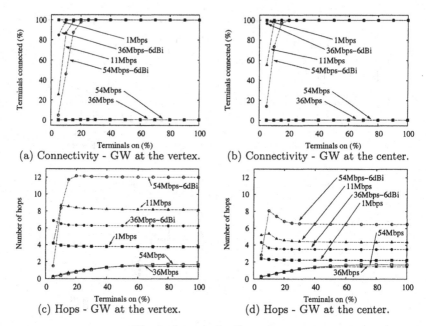

Fig. 2. Scenario 3 - Copacabana.

Nevertheless, antennas can be used to assure high connectivity at higher transmission rates in Scenario 3. Figures 2(a) and 2(b) plot the results obtained with 6 dBi antennas. The average number of hops for Scenario 3 is depicted in Figures 2(c) and 2(d). It is observed that the variation of the average number of hops is small increasing the percentage of nodes on and the transmission rates. Since high network connectivity can be achieved with a small number of nodes on, adding more to the network does not affect the average number of hops. Besides, the average number of hops in Scenario 3 is smaller than seen in Scenario 1. As high connectivity is reached at smaller rates, the transmission range is higher and the average number of hops to the gateway gets lower.

In Scenario 5, Figures 3(a) and 3(b) show that it is impossible to achieve high network connectivity with the specified values of the IEEE 802.11 standard without antenna. Only at 1 Mbps we can reach connectivity. Using the gateway at the center or at the vertex of the scenario, the deployment of an antenna with a gain of 6 dBi provides connectivity for more than 95% of the nodes with at least 60% of the nodes on. As in Scenario 3, the average number of hops is also smaller than in Scenario 1. This is due to the great distances between neighbor nodes, which is a characteristic of rural regions.

The results show the benefits of the gateway located at the center of the simulated area. Independent of the scenario, for distinct transmission rates,

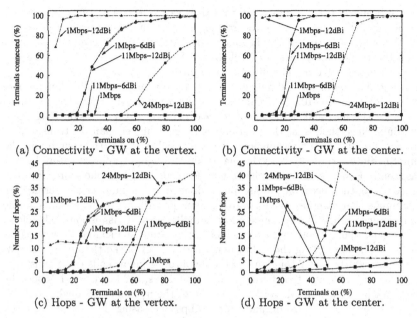

Fig. 3. Scenario 5 - Paty do Alferes.

high connectivity can be achieved with a small percent of nodes on. Besides, the average number of hops is smaller when the gateway is at the center.

4.2 Capacity Analysis

The capacity analysis evaluates the impact of the number of hops over the throughput of a one-node transmission and the network aggregated throughput when increasing the number of transmitting terminals. We developed an IEEE 802.11g module for ns-2 version 2.28 [10]. We used a lower number of terminals due to the limitations of ns-2, but we kept the density of nodes used in Section 3.

The transmission rates used in each scenario are chosen depending on the results of the connectivity analysis, Section 4.1. We use the highest transmission rate that offers 100% of connectivity when all nodes are on. The gateway is located in one of the vertices. The terminals send 1500 data packets using CBR/UDP, there is neither packet segmentation nor deployment of RTS/CTS mechanism. Where IEEE 802.11g can be deployed, the use of short slot time is assumed.

Forwarding Chain In this simulation set the impact of the number of hops over the throughput is shown. The number of terminals in the network and the data rates are varied. The data rate is varied from 56 kbps to 54 Mbps.

In Scenario 1, the number of terminals is varied from 4 to 196. The gateway is positioned at one vertex of the grid and the transmitting terminal is located at the opposite vertex of the diagonal. The distance among terminals is 9.09 m and the transmission rate is 54 Mbps. At this rate, the transmission range is approximately 12.6 m. The interference range is 74 m.

The maximum throughput of IEEE 802.11g is about 29 Mbps for an one-node transmission [10]. In Scenario 1, for 4 terminals, the route has two hops because the diagonal path cannot be reached due to transmission range constraints. Nevertheless, as the interference range is higher than the transmission range, simultaneous transmissions are not possible. Thus, the source and the intermediate terminals share the maximum throughput approximately by two as seen in Figure 4(a). While the added terminals are inside the source interference range, the maximum throughput is divided by the number of intermediate terminals that compose the forwarding chain [6]. Adding terminals outside the interference range of the source allows simultaneous transmissions. Therefore, increasing the network with terminals further from the source allows spatial reuse in the forwarding chain. In Figure 4(a), it is observed that when the spatial reuse starts, the throughput of the forwarding chain tends to be constant.

Figure 4(a) shows that for data rates of 56 kbps, 512 kbps, and 1 Mbps, the network is not saturated. On the other hand, the maximum throughput of the forwarding chain is constant and near 2 Mbps. Increasing the distance between the source and the gateway, the user may still get a reasonable throughput.

The results obtained for Scenarios 2 and 4 are similar to the results of Scenario 1. Therefore, they were omitted.

Scenario 3 simulates a region composed by buildings. Thus, in this scenario, the nodes are in a three-dimensional grid as detailed in Section 3. The gateway and the source terminal are located at the opposite vertices of the diagonal of the cube. To keep density, the nodes are 20 m away in the XY plane. The maximum possible data rate is 11 Mbps to maintain connectivity, as depicted in Figure 2. At this rate, the transmission range is 32 m. As mentioned before, the interference range is 74 m.

The maximum throughput obtained with only one source-destination pair is about 7 Mbps. This is the 10-node throughput seen in Figure 4(b). With 10 nodes, there is a one-hop transmission because the source-destination pair is 30 m away in the same building. This justifies the maximum throughput of 7 Mbps since there is only one node contending for the medium. From 40 nodes on, more hops are necessary and, consequently, the throughput decreases. As in Scenario 1, the throughput goes down while the added nodes are inside the interference range of the source. When the added nodes are located out of the interference range of the source, the throughput tends to a constant due to spatial reuse. In Scenario 3, this throughput is about 1.2 Mbps.

It is worth noting that in Scenarios 1 the throughput of the forwarding chain gets constant about 2 Mbps considering a physical transmission rate of 54 Mbps. In Scenario 3, at 11 Mbps, the constant throughput is about 1.2 Mbps. This is due to a higher efficiency of IEEE 802.11b compared to 802.11g. Although

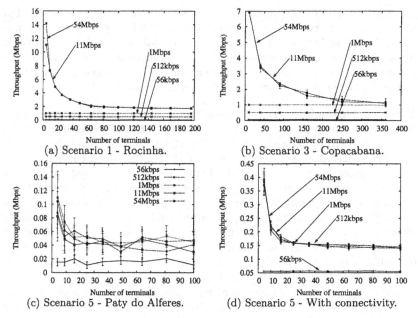

(a) Scenario 1 - Rocinha.   (b) Scenario 3 - Copacabana.

(c) Scenario 5 - Paty do Alferes.   (d) Scenario 5 - With connectivity.

Fig. 4. Forwarding chain throughput.

the data rates of 802.11g can reach up to 5 times the data rates of 802.11b, the control frames are transmitted in lower rates to maintain interoperability. This affects the 802.11g efficiency [10].

Scenario 5 is a rural environment. In this scenario, the nodes are randomly located and the distances, in average, are larger than in the other scenarios. According to Figure 3, it is necessary to use low transmission rates and antennas to achieve connectivity. Therefore, we use a transmission rate of 1 Mbps and antenna gain of 12 dBi. The gateway and the source are at the opposite vertices of the simulation square.

Figures 4(c) and 4(d) show the results obtained. In Figure 4(c), the error bars are big and thus the results are not conclusive. This is due to lack of connectivity between gateway and source terminal in some simulation runs. As the intermediate nodes are randomly located, non-connectivity events may happen forcing the throughput down to zero. The average throughput of the runs with and without connectivity results in points with a high variance. Eliminating the non-connectivity points (Figure 4(d)) we can observe a tendency of the throughput which is similar to the other scenarios. For a large number of nodes a throughput near to 150 kbps is achieved. Thus, the use of IEEE 802.11 is possible in rural environments but depends on antennas and the access terminals location.

IEEE 802.11 wireless ad hoc networks are suitable for urban scenarios, but not as suitable to rural environments. Besides, considering one-node transmissions, the throughput obtained can be up to 2 Mbps regardless the distance between gateway and source terminal. This throughput value must be lower if more than one node contends for the medium. The following simulation set focuses on the saturation throughput for multiple sources.

Network Throughput This simulation set verifies the maximum number of users before saturation and the performance of two routing protocols, the reactive AODV and the proactive OLSR. The AODV module is already available in the ns-2 distribution. On the other hand, to simulate OLSR it is necessary to add a patch to the simulator [11]. The nodes always send data at 56 kbps and the transmission rate of each scenario is the same used in Section 4.2.

The transmission rate of Scenario 1 is 54 Mbps. Figure 5(a) shows that independently of the routing protocols, the saturation is achieved for approximately 60 nodes. It is observed in both curves that after saturation, the throughput decreases until it gets stable. This behavior is typical of CSMA protocols without collision detection. In Figure 5(a) it is also observed that when every node is transmitting, unlike Figure 4(a), the maximum throughput is higher than 3 Mbps. This occurs due to spatial reuse, which allows simultaneous transmissions. The effect of spatial reuse starts after 36 nodes, when the diagonal of the grid is larger than the interference range of the source.

The difference in throughput between AODV and OLSR is due to the higher control overhead of OLSR. The OLSR protocol is proactive, flooding the network periodically to keep the routing tables updated.

The results of Scenarios 2 and 4 were omitted because they are similar to Scenario 1. In Scenario 3, IEEE 802.11b is used at 11 Mbps as in the forwarding chain analysis. Figure 5(b) shows that after saturation the aggregated throughput goes down and for a higher number of nodes it is supposed to become stable as in Figure 5(a). The performance of OLSR overcomes AODV because OLSR deploys special nodes called MPR (MultiPoint Relay). The MPR is a node chosen to send control packets. Each node chooses an MPR set per interface. This set comprises the minimum number of one-hop neighbors that can reach every two-hop neighbor. Thus, only the MPRs transmit packets to two-hop neighbors, limiting the flooding. In Scenario 3, the deployment of MPRs is more efficient than in Scenario 1 due to the number of nodes inside the same transmission range. In Scenario 1, the distance among nodes is 9.09 m and the transmission range is 12.6 m. Therefore, every node have only four neighbors and the MPRs produce no gains because all nodes are all MPRs. In Scenario 3, instead, the transmission range is 32 m and the distance among the nodes in the XY plane is 20 m. In this case, the number of neighbors is eight, plus the neighbors in the Z axis. Increasing the number of neighbors improves the performance of the MPRs because the flooding decreases.

In Scenario 5, the random position of the nodes and the low density affect the results. Using IEEE 802.11 at 1 Mbps and antennas as in Figure 3, it is not

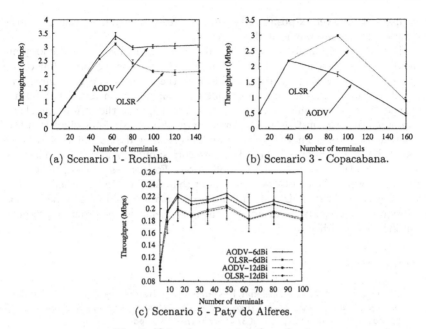

(a) Scenario 1 - Rocinha.   (b) Scenario 3 - Copacabana.

(c) Scenario 5 - Paty do Alferes.

Fig. 5. Network aggregated throughput.

possible to assure that the gateway is connected to the rest of the network in every simulation run. For the same reasons pointed out in the forwarding chain analysis, the variance is high as seen in Figure 5(c). AODV tends to present a better throughput than OLSR. Again, the low density hinders the MPRs gains. Also, note that even increasing with number of nodes, the saturation is not achieved. This happens because the number of nodes that transmit is limited to the nodes closer to the gateway.

5 Conclusions

The return channel of the digital TV can be used as a low-cost vehicle for digital inclusion of underserved communities. A viability analysis of the return channel must be considered to certify that the ad hoc technology is suitable.

In the connectivity analysis, we verified that in urban regions it is possible to achieve high connectivity with a reduced number of terminals turned on. Besides, in highly populated regions, 802.11 transmission rates up to 54 Mbps can be used. On the other hand, in rural regions, the deployment of antennas and the use of low transmission rates are mandatory to increase the transmission range and guarantee connectivity. Positioning the gateway at the center of the scenarios, 100% of connectivity is possible with a fewer number of nodes on compared to the vertex-positioned gateway. The average number of hops is also lower when the gateway is at the center.

In the capacity analysis, we considered different numbers of nodes keeping the density of residences constant. The results obtained by the forwarding chain showed that increasing the distance between the gateway and the source terminal, the user could obtain a reasonable throughput with an ad hoc return channel. For a large number of nodes, the throughput of the forwarding chain approximates to a constant which can be up to 2 Mbps. We also verified that the saturation occurs around 60 access terminals sending data at 56 kbps regardless of the routing protocol. This data rate corresponds to a dial-up connection and fits well the of the digital TV applications. For dense scenarios, the OLSR routing protocol shows a better throughput than AODV. On the other hand, in sparse scenarios, the AODV routing protocol is more suitable than OLSR. As a consequence, currently, we investigate the implementation of a routing protocol specific to the ad hoc return channel.

References

1. IBGE, "PNAD 2003 - National Research using Residences Sampling (In Portuguese)," 2004, http://www.ibge.gov.br/home/estatistica/populacao/trabalhoerendimento/pnad2003/sintesepnad2003.pdf.
2. J. Hsu, S. Bhatia, K. Tang, R. Bagrodia, and M. J. Acriche, "Performance of Mobile Ad Hoc Networking Routing Protocols in Large Scale Scenarios," in *MILCOM'04*, Oct. 2004, pp. 21–27.
3. J. Hsu, S. Bhatia, M. Takai, R. Bagrodia, and M. J. Acriche, "Performance of Mobile Ad Hoc Networking Routing Protocols in Realistic Scenarios," in *MILCOM'03*, Oct. 2003, pp. 1268–1273.
4. S. Armenia, L. Galluccio, A. Leonardi, and S. Palazzo, "Transmission of VoIP Traffic in Multihop Ad Hoc IEEE 802.11b Networks: Experimental Results," in *WICOM'05*, July 2005, pp. 148–155.
5. E. Borgia, "Experimental Evaluation of Ad Hoc Routing Protocols," in *PERCOMW'05*, Mar. 2005, pp. 232–236.
6. B. A. M. Villela and O. C. M. B. Duarte, "Maximum Throughput Analysis in Ad Hoc Networks," in *Networking'04*, May 2004, pp. 223–234.
7. IBGE, "Cidades@," 2005, http://www.ibge.gov.br/cidadesat/.
8. H. Bengtsson, E. Uhlemann, and P. Wiberg, "Protocol for wireless real-time systems," in *11th Euromicro Conference on Real-Time Systems*, June 1999.
9. S. Zvanovec, P. Pechac, and M. Klepal, "Wireless LAN Networks Design: Site Survey or Propagation Modeling?" *RADIOENGINEERING*, vol. 12, no. 4, pp. 42–49, Dec. 2003.
10. A. Amodei Jr., M. E. M. Campista, D. de O. Cunha, P. B. Velloso, L. H. M. K. Costa, M. G. Rubinstein, and O. C. M. B. Duarte, "Analysis of medium access control protocols for home networks," UFRJ - Brazil, Tech. Rep., Oct. 2005.
11. Francisco J. Ros, "OLSR-UM Documentation," Mar. 2005, http://masimum.dif.um.es/um-olsr/html/.

Understanding the Role of Mobile Ad hoc Networks in Non-traditional Contexts

Roberto G. Aldunate[1,2,] Gregg E. Larson[2], Miguel Nussbaum[3], Sergio F. Ochoa[4], Oriel A. Herrera[5]

1 Department of Civil and Environmental Engineering, University of Illinois at Urbana Champaign, Urbana, IL, USA
aldunate@uiuc.edu

2 Applied Research Associates, Inc., Champaign, IL, USA
glarson@ara.com

3 Department of Computer Science, Catholic University of Chile, Chile
mn@ing.puc.cl

4 Department of Computer Science, University of Chile, Chile
sochoa@dcc.uchile.cl

5 Informatics Engineering School, Universidad Católica de Temuco, Chile
oherrera@uct.cl

Abstract. With the rapid development of short-range wireless technology new venues to apply it in more sophisticated, complex, and dynamic environments have been opened. Nevertheless, the applicability of such technology in non-traditional settings like face-to-face encounters and disaster relief environments, remains unclear. This article describes a research effort aimed to narrow that gap by means of using two non-traditional settings as case studies; face-to-face encounters among unacquainted people and first responders in urban disaster relief environments. Among the results obtained are: a) interactions among unacquainted people may be promoted, though the level of interaction becomes easily constrained due to the current state of RF technology and the design of the experiments, and b) it is feasible to obtain a reliable communication platform for first responders operating in disaster relief missions. These results supports the idea that short-range wireless technology may play both a facilitator and a promoter role in face-to-face contexts, and at least a facilitator role in the case of users co-located in highly dynamic contexts.

1 Introduction: the role of MANETs in non-traditional settings is yet unclear

With the emergence of short-range wireless technology, researchers and engineers have been enabled with a tool to explore, investigate, evaluate, and understand the applicability of Mobile Ad hoc Networks (MANET) in non-traditional complex and

---

Please use the following format when citing this chapter:

Aldunate, R.G., Larson, G.E., Nussbaum, M., Ochoa, S.F., Herrera, O.A., 2006, in IFIP International Federation for Information Processing, Volume 211, ed. Pujolle, G., Mobile and Wireless Communication Networks, (Boston: Springer), pp. 199–215.

dynamic settings, like face-to-face spontaneous interaction or disaster relief environments, which have or may have high social and economic impact. MANETs have been envisioned by many authors as an attractive and feasible interaction means for mobile users in non-traditional contexts like the ones mentioned above.

The potential advantages of mobile ad hoc networking for areas without a suitable established infrastructure are well documented in research literature. For example, military environments are ideal for ad hoc networking and it has been recently noted that "today every advanced military is rolling out large-scale ad hoc networks to carry a variety of tactical communications traffic" [1]. Recently, much research is being conducted worldwide on using ad hoc networks in a variety of commercial applications, including emergency situations like fire-fighting and search and rescue operations where the probability of rescuing people trapped under rubble decreases as time passes after a disaster hit [2], inter-vehicle communications on roads, amusement parks, shopping centers, medical sensor monitoring, management at construction sites [3, 4], and many other sensor applications. Nevertheless, investigations on the MANET field have been mainly advocated to solve lower-level network problems, such as routing [5-11], following a technology-driven approach.

In spite of the high interest of the research community on MANETs, especially on lower-level network issues like routing and service discovery, the role that a MANET may play as facilitating and/or promoting interactions among mobile users in non-traditional settings remains unclear. The relevance of researching on non traditional and dynamic settings involving mobile co-located people is two-fold; at the same time that an increasing interaction or collaboration in these settings would facilitate the attainment of the goals of the people involved in such interactions, it would also help in understanding the boundaries for the applicability of infrastructure-less networks.

The rest of this article is structured as follows. Next section shows the research approach underlying this work. Section *WiFi for Face-to-Face Encounters* describes the investigation conducted to explore the facilitator and promoter role that this technology may play in such context. Section *WiFi for Chaotic and Dynamic Contexts* describes the work done on achieving a robust communication means for mobile first responders during disaster relief operations. The last two sections present a discussion regarding the research carried out and the conclusions and further work, respectively.

2   Research Approach: MANETs for two non-traditional settings

Current communication platforms or media used to support interaction between co-located mobile people in some non-traditional environments mismatch either satisfying highly demanding communication requirements or promoting the interaction among those people. Technologies such as sharing voice signal channels or semi-infrastructure solutions are adequate only for a reduced set of settings. In informal face-to-face interactions among unacquainted people the dependency on an infrastructure or a semi-infrastructure communication network is not natural because the interaction does not rely on information external to the actors, but on the information associated to and made available by each person. Face-to-face encounters among mobile users are considered in this research as an infrastructure-less peer-to-peer network where such network is created dynamically as people moves. Therefore, potential face-to-face encounters will continuously require searching and matching profiles (stored in the wireless enabled devices carried by the people) of people nearby other people. Forcing this model to fit into a semi-infrastructure communication network could generate an extra overhead on such network; managing a roaming service to provide information about the geographic neighbors of each user. On the other hand, in chaotic, complex and inhospitable environments where fixed infrastructure communication is unreliable, such as in battlefield or disaster relief operations, shared voice signal channels and semi-infrastructure solutions constraint the potential collaboration among people involved in such task-oriented environments. Although several initiatives are pursuing development of wearable computers adequate for non-traditional settings, usually those researches are centered on the person (usability, storage, communication capability), but not on the characteristics that the communication medium should exhibit in such contexts.

This research effort is aimed at understanding the applicability of mobile ad hoc networks as a useful communication platform for co-located mobile users in non traditional and dynamic settings with high socio-economical impact. The approach used to carry out this research was based on selecting two settings as test-beds. Such settings represent very exigent contexts where the role of the communication medium requires to be evaluated. The specific problems addressed in this research are: (a) how to facilitate face-to-face interaction among unacquainted people in social settings, and (b) how to provide a reliable communication infrastructure for first responders in disaster relief environments. The general significance of this research is on gaining knowledge on principles, characteristics, design goals, mechanisms and algorithms that make a short-range wireless enabled communication medium adequate enough to improve interactions of co-located mobile users.

The core of the research was undertaken through a formal cycle of knowledge acquisition, formalization, systematization, and testing/validation and refinement. Nevertheless, different strategies for testing/validation were used for each one of the settings. For the case of face-to-face encounters among unacquainted people in everyday situations the solution developed was tested through experimentation. For the case of mobile co-located people involved in task-oriented, chaotic, inhospitable, and highly dynamic environments, simulations and experimentation were combined, inasmuch as simulations provided insight to this research about the applicability of mechanisms, algorithms and concepts previous to test them with real experiments, when it was possible given the limitation in reproducing the setting studied.

3   WiFi for Face-to-Face Encounters: Facilitating & Promoting

The aim of this section is to describe how short-range wireless technology may facilitate face-to-face encounter among unacquainted people who are physically close and are (usually) moving in a given setting. In this way, people who do not know about each other's needs or knowledge could meet in a face-to-face scenario to establish a collaborative relation. The idea of Socialware is enhanced to a face-to-face Socialware. The communication/facilitator medium comprised 40 wireless interconnected Pocket PCs (IEEE 802.11b/g) under distributed agent architecture. The developed interaction model was evaluated with freshmen engineering students from the College of Engineering of the Catholic University of Chile in their social and academic life. The main idea here was to provide mechanisms for the users to break the social contact threshold and ignite a relationship among people. Hence, the WiFi enabled communication medium was not only providing a communication bridge, but also could promote interaction between unacquainted students. When new students arrive to campus, it takes a while for the students to build trust among themselves, to know each other, form groups, work and study together, etc. To enhance student relationships, it is desired to foster face to face contact with people that are close to each other. Pocket PCs using WiFi permit formation of an Ad Hoc network between students that are within the network range (within 50 meters). Each student participating of the experience had a mobile device, where a software agent on the machine supports the user on email, chat, and peer search functions. The details of this work can be found in [12].

A study involving 180 first year students of Engineering and Psychology to measure their preferences and the impact of short-range wireless technology as facilitator of interpersonal attraction was conducted. Two questionnaires of more than 100 questions each were given to each student at the beginning and at the end of their first semester. A factorial analysis was performed to identify the latent variables or subjacent constructs among the observed inter-correlations from the different measured variables. The results showed five factors of preference: 1 - Shopping and/or leisure activities, 2 - Sport activities, 3 - Intellectual related activities, 4 - Social activities, and 5 - Information activities. To identify patterns in the different profiles, a hierarchical accumulative cluster analysis was performed. This technique, based on the quadratic Euclidean difference as a measure of similitude, allows clusters to be identified that simultaneously present a high intra-group degree of similitude and a high inter-group degree of differentiation. Five clearly statistically significant ($p < 0,001$) differentiable clusters were found.

3.1 Results

Figure 1.a illustrates the total transactions performed by the students Pocket PCs, registered by the eight PCs that monitored the networked during the semester. (It is interesting to mention that week six was an exam week). To understand this data, at the end of the experience and exhaustive questionnaire was applied to the participating students. Each of the question had to be graded from 1 to 7 (7 the best), being this the standard Chilean grading system that they were used to. Students claimed that the reasons for the below average scores shown on Figure 1.b were regarding technological issues, as shown in Figure 2.

Battery life was a key issue for the poor system usage. In this experience Toshiba e740 Pocket Pc were used, which have an integrated WiFi. Batteries lasted up to two hours when kept on. When people are on campus more than 6 hours daily, having availability of the machine is important. Battery life explains the level of usage of the tools for supporting encounters; students' machine intersection time is rather short (less than two hours) decreasing the probability of encounters. Students also claimed that the network coverage was also a problem. There were only eight wireless Internet gateways available on campus, each with IEEE 802.11b/g limited distance coverage. This distance coverage restriction was also a problem for the peer to peer connection. It showed that outdoors, as on a university campus, an operating range of up to 50 meters should be expected.

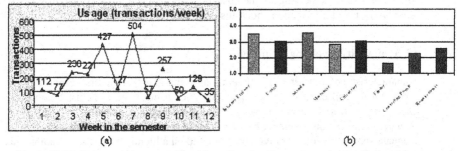

(a)   (b)

Fig. 1. (a) Students machine usage, (b) students functionality usage evaluation (1-7 scale)

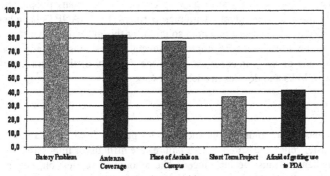

Fig. 2. Students problems usage evaluation

The first lesson learned through experimentation is that the high functionality provided to students played against their usability of the prototype. In addition, better battery technology is needed to improve the performance of the tools and improvements to the results of the study; the relatively scarce duration of the batteries in the experiments was the main obstacle in terms of communication. The results obtained in this work highlights that interactions were produced between people who were previously not familiar with each other, though the level of interactions was below the initial expectations of the undertaken research.

4 WiFi for Chaotic and Dynamic Contexts: Facilitating

To explore on the applicability of MANETs for chaotic and highly dynamic contexts, a disaster relief settings was chosen. For highly dynamic contexts like this, reliability is one of the key aspects to be addressed. To achieve a reliable MANET-based communication medium, the core of this work focused on achieving high availability and high connectivity in the MANET. Here, availability is understood as the capacity of the system to make its data, i.e., the data gathered and processes by the users of the MANET, fault tolerant despite the occurrence of varied types of failures. On the other hand, connectivity is understood as the capacity of the system to provide communication links among its members despite the occurrence of varied types of failures. (Detailed information about this issue can be found in [13, 14])

4.1 Availability: avoiding losing data

A characteristic of a disaster relief operations scenario is that the first response teams communicate and collaborate among themselves using radio systems, because the fixed communication infrastructure usually is collapsed, unreliable or overloaded. Nevertheless, the voice channel based collaboration medium is limited in providing adequate support to collaborative efforts. Based on a literature review and comments obtained through interviews with expert civil engineers as well as firefighters participating in disaster relief environments, it is highlighted that radio systems tend to collapse in the early phases of first response process, because many people share few channels (usually 2 or 3) to interact with their partners [15]. MANETs have been envisioned by many researches as a potential solution for this problem. Nevertheless, for a MANET to be useful in such contexts, several issues must be addressed, availability being one of the primary ones, given the mobility of the users and the potential failures of links and devices in such a network.

4.1.1 Redundancy

For a MANET-based communication medium to provide high availability in contexts like disaster relief operations where failures are difficult or impossible to be avoided, data replication must be introduced. The amount of replication, i.e., how many times data is replicated, as well as the manner in which data is handled, i.e., the size of data chunks and its replicas, will affect the availability of the system. The approach used in this research to analyze data replication is based on the illustration given in Figure 3. The approach used in this part of the work is quite simple. The whole data space available at a MANET is portioned in data chunks which are replicated among the nodes comprising the MANET. Figure 4 shows that if data chunks are reduced, the probability a system failure, i.e.; a piece of data is lost from the system, increases. Specifically, in Figure 4.a, if Machine A fails at time t1 and Machine C fails at time t2, the other members of the system, i.e.; Machines B and D, will still have the whole data set. On the other hand, Figure 3.b, if Machines A and C fail, A2 and C1 data chunks will be lost from the system generating a system failure. The objective of the research on this topic is to determine how to structure the shared space to that the impact of node or link failures are reduced as much as possible on data availability. To understand the impact of such parameters, a simulation model based on the strategy described above was developed (a detailed description can be found in Aldunate et al., 2006a).

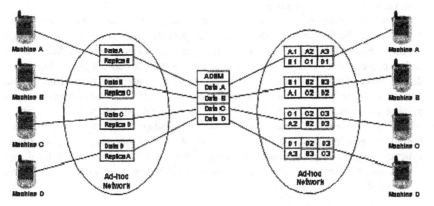

Fig. 3. Data replication example: (a) larger data chunks; (b) smaller data chunks

4.1.2 Results

During the first simulations (Figure 4.a), it was considered that 20 first responders including civil engineers would form a team (following FEMA, 1999 guidelines on the size of an Urban Search and Rescue Team [16]). In addition, the distance between two team members working in the disaster area (communication range) was initially set to be 50m, given our preliminary experimentation with IEEE 802.11b/g in semi-open environments, i.e., considering both inside buildings and outdoors. In order to assess availability for various disaster area scenarios and to identify the limits of the system, the size of the area was to change from $50x50m^2$ to $160x160m^2$. In addition, two sizes for the replicas were considered: Large Replica Units (LRU) where the size of each RU is defined as large as possible and Page Replica Unit (PRU) where the size of each RU is defined as a page, i.e.; 1-4 Kb. The simulation results demonstrated that the system's availability depends on the size of the replica; particularly, it decreases when the size of the replica unit decreases.

Moreover, high availability is obtained up to an area of about $130x130m^2$, if two or more large replicas are used. These results indicate that a team working alone using 2-LRU (2 Large Replica Unit) will be able to cover areas of $130x130$ m^2, maintaining the availability of the system in the range of 98%, when all the team members are inside the coverage area. Beyond that, extra support for communication will be required to avoid the isolation of some team members.

On the other hand, if the communication range is changed to 100m, high availability of 98% is obtained up to an area of about $250x250m^2$. It is clear that the larger the communication range, the larger the area will be that a first response team could cover while maintaining high availability of the system.

Additional simulations have shown that the availability of the system is also highly sensitive to the replication level introduced in the system and the number of team members. When a different number of replicas was used and each replica unit is defined as large as possible; Large Replica Units (LRU), it was noticed that the greater the replication level, the higher the availability. Finally, as expected, there is a positive correlation between availability and the replication level as well as the group size, as shown in Figure 4.b.

Once the platform was tested by computer simulations and the results demonstrated the feasibility of the system, the next step was to test it in a simulated disaster scenario. For that reason, a prototype was built to support a simulated search and rescue exercise. The evaluation of the system was carried out in parallel to the development of a normal search and rescue exercise conducted by the Illinois Fire Service Institute (IFSI) of the University of Illinois at Urbana-Champaign at its training facilities. The setting for this exercise included two office buildings and a pile of rubble, which simulate partial and total collapses, twenty-four apprentice firefighters and five people testing the system in situ collaborating with one remote structural expert. They assumed the roles of rescuers, team leader, and local and remote structural experts. The exercise was monitored by an expert in search and rescue operations.

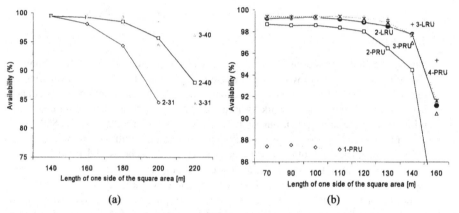

(a)   (b)

Figure 4 – System's availability depending on the size of the data chuck and the size of the operations area size for: (a) 20 team members and a communication range of 50m; and (b) a communication range of 50m and variable level of replication and number of members

The outdoors results outperformed the availability results of simulations runs, because of the difference between the empirical wireless communication range with the estimation made for simulations; 200m v/s 50-100m. In addition, although indoor communication range was highly variable depending on number and composition of walls, the system remained always available during the testing. Overall, it was observed that the difference between outdoors and indoor communication range is large, but the replication strategy reduced effectively the impact of this parameter on the system's availability. Another difference between the simulations and the experiment, which also explains the better availability results obtained during experimentation in comparison to simulations, is related to first responders' movement behavior. In the real scenario, the first responders moved in small groups using predefined paths, not randomly as was considered in simulations, decreasing the probability of network disconnections.

4.2 Connectivity: avoiding losing users

The next step towards determining the usefulness or applicability of MANETs for highly dynamic contexts is dealing with connectivity problems. The previous topic covered the issue of data availability in spite of users getting disconnected from the MANET. Nevertheless, in a real complex setting, like disaster relief operations or battlefield, it would be desirable to avoid as much as possible such disconnections. Maintaining connectivity within a MANET presents a challenge due to the fact that communication between short range wireless enabled communication devices can be interrupted by physical objects, environmental conditions affecting the radio frequency signal, hardware, software, and connection lost due to the mobility of users, among others. The connectivity problem due to the mobility of mobile users is considered by this research as the key factor for the development of the proactive nature of the mechanism. All the other causes of failure are considered as a whole in a parameter referred to as Link Failure Probability used in the analysis of the self-healing mechanism in the following sections.

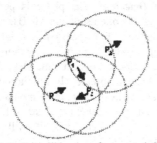

Figure 5 - MANET={P_1,P_2,P_3,P_4} will become fragmented, Set1={P_1, P_3, P_4} Set2={P_2}

The general connectivity problem generated by the mobility of mobile users is represented through the situation illustrated in Figure 5. In that figure P_1, P_2, P_3, and P_4 represent mobile users who communicate with each other using short-range wireless enabled devices, at a given time. Arrows represent the direction of movement for each mobile user. Thus, considering the direction of movement of each mobile user shown in Figure 5, P_2 will eventually leave the communication range of P_1, and vice-versa. In addition, P_3 and P_4 will remain within the communication range of each other, and also within the communication range of P_1. In general terms, this situation represents network fragmentation; i.e., subsets of the original MANET can not communicate each other. Depending on the movement behavior of the nodes comprising the MANET, network fragmentation can be either permanent, e.g., some fragments of the network do not enter into communication during the period of operation, or temporary; i.e., the fragments merge again at a further time during the period of operation.

4.2.1 Self-Healing Mechanism
To cope with the problem described above, unmanned vehicles enabled with communication devices similar to those used by the mobile users are introduced.

This idea is based on Darpa's Minefield Project [17], though the approaches are very different (see [14]). The unmanned vehicles, here referred to as Mobile Communication Bridges (MCB), should be able to detect "disconnection in progress" messages spread by P_2 and P_1 (Figure 5) and move accordingly toward the region between them, avoiding a disconnection or reducing the disconnection time as much as possible, in case it was not possible to reach the disconnection area on time. This approach is opposed to deploying static repeaters, which one can envision might be a straightforward solution for small areas, but it might not scale for very large areas.

An underlying problem to address under this topic is message delivery. The message delivery service in the designed system is based on ad hoc gossip multicast [11], because it offers a solution in between routing and flooding techniques. By using a probabilistic multicast technique, like gossip-based multicast, this research expected the healing mechanism achieves high reliability with moderate degradation of performance.

The self-healing mechanism relies on the following three-phase algorithm:

Potential Disconnection Detection: this phase is performed permanently by every node in the MANET; i.e., mobile users and MCBs. At every time step t, each node monitors its 1-hop neighbors. For each 1-hop neighbor that is located at a distance greater than a certain threshold, given as a parameter, the monitoring node records such distance at that moment. At next time step, the monitoring node will determine the new distance for each previously monitored 1-hop neighbor. If, for each 1-hop neighbor, the distance has increased, the monitoring node will try to find out if at least one of its other 1-hop neighbors is closer to the one under observation. If the monitoring node fails on such task, it will propagate a "potential disconnection" message through the MANET.

Correction: this phase is also implemented by both mobile users and MCBs. Once a node detected a potential disconnection, it will propagate a message through the network, using gossip-based multicast. Any MCB receiving that message will wait a given period of time for the counterpart message; i.e., the message sent by the other node involved in the potential disconnection. If the counterpart message is received by the MCB, it will ignore the situation because it means that there is at least one alternative route connecting both nodes. But, if the counterpart message is not received by the MCB, it assumes a disconnection is in progress and it will set itself toward that task; i.e., move toward the potential disconnection area.

Maintenance: this phase of the algorithm is applicable only to MCBs; i.e., not applicable to devices used by mobile users. Once the MCB is placed at the potential disconnection area, it tries to detect the presence of the requesting nodes. If the MCB does not find the requesting nodes after a given period of time, it will set itself back to Idle state. Nonetheless, if the MCB detects the requesting nodes, it sets its state to Supporting mode, adjusting its position dynamically based on the movement of the supported nodes. The MCB will remain in Supporting mode, until either the supported nodes are again in communication range or the supported nodes are apart and the disconnection is imminent. In such case, the MCB will play the potential disconnection phase.

The three-phase algorithm and the principles presented rely on two assumptions. On one hand, the set of MCBs is comprised of homogenous devices not only in terms of communication capability, but also in terms of mobility; i.e., they are able to move at similar speeds. On the other hand, it is assumed the environment is free of obstacles; i.e., the time for a MCB to reach a target location depends only on the distance to such area.

The correctness of the above presented algorithm; i.e., at least and at most one MCB will support a disconnection when there are one or more MCBs in Idle state, can be guaranteed only if the following special conditions are met: (a) the message delivery service is 100% reliable, and (2) the underlying location service is 100% reliable. If the former service is not completely reliable, it could be possible no MCB in Idle state hears about a potential disconnection call or that two or more MCBs "accept" one mission unaware of their concurrent movements. If the latter service is not completely reliable, the distance estimations a MCB makes while in Moving state could be decreasing no monotonically, and so, it could not be guaranteed the closest MCB is moving to the disconnection area where the disconnection call was generated. As the current state of development for both services; i.e., technology, can not guarantee fully reliable services, the three phase algorithm is not able to guarantee an optimal solution, e.g., two or more MCBs heading to a disconnection area could become aware of the race condition only when they are close to the target location (at that point, the Correction Phase solves this conflict), but a best effort solution.

During discrete-event simulation runs first responders are modeled as moving pseudo-randomly, with a probability for them to stay stationary for some time intervals, and failures like technology dependant network failures, failures of electronic components due to fatigue of material, battery consumption, software bugs, and death or accidents of first responders are modeled through a Link Failure Probability (LFP) factor. Also, MCBs are in one of three modes: (1) Idle, (2) Moving towards a specific area or (3) Supporting Communication. The Idle mode represents a stationary MCB waiting for messages indicating a potential disconnection is in progress. The Moving mode is straightforward up to the moment when it reaches the area near the requiring pair of nodes, then, it will check if any other node is acting as a bridge for those nodes. If this is the situation, it will set itself to Idle mode, otherwise will set to Supporting Communication mode. The Supporting Communication mode represents a MCB which has reached the pair of nodes requiring a communication bridge. In that situation, a MCB is considered to be able to determine the area between the nodes requiring connectivity by using some proximity or triangulation technique, like GPS. While in the Supporting Communication mode, the MCB will evaluate new positions of the pair of nodes for which it is providing connectivity. With that information, the MCB will reevaluate its area of operation; i.e., nearby the point at the middle of the line representing the Euclidean distance between the nodes supported.

4.2.2 Results

The results obtained highlight the relationship between the number of mobile users (excluding MCBs) and connectivity, as shown in Figure 6. It can be appreciated that connectivity positively correlates with the number of mobile users. It can also be appreciated that for a team of 30 mobile users operating in area of 400x400m², the number of disconnections are approximately 12; i.e., the MANET becomes highly fragmented. Nevertheless, the most important result shown in Figure 6 is that to achieve high connectivity in the MANET, al least 70 mobile users should operate in such area. A different way to understand the results shown in Figure 6 is that if high connectivity is required for a team of 30 mobile users in the defined area of operations, at least 40 MCBs without coordination and pseudo-random movement pattern should be deployed. Such strategy implies that MCBs are always active, reducing the chances for energy saving. Several other aspects of the dynamics of the self-healing system were observed (the reader can find them in [14]), nonetheless the most relevant is the relationship between Link Failure Probability (LFP) and the reliability of the self healing mechanism, as shown in Figure 7. For LFP < 0.7, the MCBs are mainly in Supporting mode, while for a LFP > 0.8 the MCBs mainly are in Idle mode. When 0.7 < LFP < 0.8, the system suddenly experiences a phase transition. In other words, the self-healing mechanism becomes useless for values of LFP >= 0.75. This dynamics is analyzed in the next section.

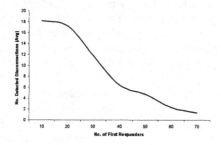

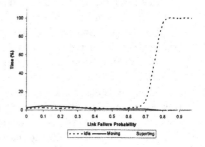

Figure 6. The number of disconnections decreases linearly as the number of first responders increase in an area of 400x400m², without participation of MCBs

Figure 7. MCBs exhibit high power consumption and low percentage idle up to a link failure probability of about 0.7. After that value, they become stationary

4.2.3 Mathematical Analysis

To better understand the dynamics shown in Figure 7, a mathematical analysis was conducted. Based on the diagram presented in Figure 8, and considering as transition probabilities p_{sx} = *Prob[(nodes supported by the MCB become able to communicate without the support of the MCB) OR (MCB does not receive answer from supported nodes to request messages generated by the MCB)]*; as $p_{xx} = \gamma(1 - LFP)^2 + LFP^2$, and p_{ss} = *Prob(MCB in Idle state receives potential disconnection messages & MCB is "chosen" to support potential disconnection informed)*; $p_{xs} = \lambda(1 - LFP)$, the plot shown in Figure 9 is obtained.

Although the main purpose of the analytical model developed in this section is to obtain a qualitative view of the dynamics of the system, in contrast to the quantitative and detailed view obtained through simulations. First, not surprisingly, for a MANET comprised of mobiles users which has a permanent demand for MCBs to provide connectivity, the self-healing mechanism will tend to collapse as the reliability of the communication decreases; i.e., a link probability failure greater than

0.7. Put in other way, the more reliable the message delivery used for the nodes of the MANET to communicate; i.e., mobile users as well as MCBs, the more efficient the utilization of MCBs. Also, the self-healing mechanism will require the MCBs spending more time in Supporting mode in settings where the probability of reencounter (communication range) between nodes communicated through MCBs; i.e., γ, is lower. Regarding vulnerability, for the self-healing mechanism to be less vulnerable to link failures, the proportion of MCBs in Idle (& Moving) state should be kept as close as possible to the demand for supporting disconnections; i.e., $\lambda \rightarrow 1$. Finally, a very interesting outcome is that the dynamics of the self-healing mechanism obtained through the analytical model which considers a large number of MCBs, and consequently a very large number of mobile users, is similar to the dynamics obtained from simulation runs considering small scale MANETs.

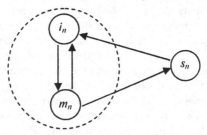

Figure 8. States diagram representing the proportion of MCBs in each state; i.e., i=Idle; m=Moving; and s=Supporting. States i and m comprise the state x, and p_{ij} represents the transition probability, per round, from state i to state j.

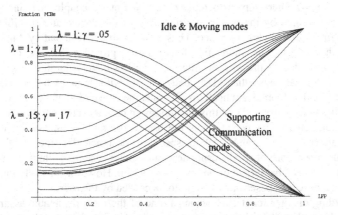

Figure 9. Impact of Link Failure Probability (LFP) on the attractors of the dynamics of the self-healing mechanism; a different pair of curves is obtained for different values of λ (the rate between the number of disconnections perceived by MCBs and the number of MCBs available to respond to disconnection calls). The lower the value of λ, the lower the LFP threshold on which the phase transition would occur. The LFP threshold for a phase transition to occur corresponds to the x value at the intersection of the pair of curves (decreasing curve represents Supporting mode, increasing curve represents Idle & Moving modes) for each λ.

5 Discussion

In addition to the encouraging results obtained, several issues arose regarding the applicability of MANTEs for the non-traditional contexts studied. For example, one design decision to experiment among unacquainted freshmen considered incorrect was the high degree of functionality provided to them. In opposition to initial expectations, high functionally limited the use of the system to interact with other unknown students. Another problem discovered during the experimentation in promoting face-to-face encounters was connectivity to the fixed infrastructure. Although the fixed infrastructure portion of networking was only used only for data gathering and monitoring, and not for connectivity between freshmen, the students claimed for the intermittent Internet service provided through the MANET. As only intermittent connectivity was possible between the peer-to-peer network and the fixed infrastructure; problems of reliability in monitoring and data collection processes were experienced due to the communication range of IEEE 802.11b/g. This problem relies basically on the decision of not introducing a routing mechanism, because multi-hop was against the idea of face-to-face interactions.

Another relevant issue related to the wireless technology used, IEEE802.1b/g, is the communication range, especially in indoor environments. During experiments the indoors communication range can dramatically be reduced depending on the nature of the objects interfering line of sight between the wireless enabled devices. These problems require that the design has to deal with the availability of the communication infrastructure, which could be addressed by adding replication or adequate communication mechanisms to maintain communication.

Also, battery duration was a key constraint for the experiments conducted; tasks where frequently interrumpted to replace batteries every couple of hours. Battery usage is determined by the energy consumption of the device and specifically the consumption of the wireless interface. Thus, a trade-off between battery duration and functionality arises. The more the functionality provided by the device and bandwidth provided by the wireless interface, the less battery duration, e.g., cellular phone batteries last longer than PDAs batteries, but with limited wireless bandwidth and consequently limited applications. It must be stressed that the short battery duration limits the current use of this technology in disaster relief environments. One possible solution for this constraint is the use of wearable computers which have strong battery duration and backup specially designed for the reliability of continuous operation of first responders and other users in infrastructure-less scenarios, such as a battlefield or on-site construction. However, this solution affects usability because it imposes more weight to be carried by the user.

Regarding disaster relief environments, one of the most disputable assumptions made could be the establishment of and scenario without obstacles. In real disaster relief environments the density, layout and structural status of the infrastructure will depend on the material as well as the construction processes utilized to build the physical infrastructure. Thus, a paramount effort would be required to be able to classify types of scenario from a detailed perspective. Nevertheless, this research effort did consider them; the impact of most of the factors which may generate communication failures was modeled as an general failure parameter introduced in both the availability and connectivity analises.

A second important assumption made related to the scenario of first responders is that they move pseudo-randomly in the field. Nevertheless, the movement of people in a real setting is not envisioned as random, but task oriented. Further research is required on this aspect to evaluate the impact of this factor.

Regarding the structure of the platform to supporting interaction among mobile users in chaotic and highly dynamic contexts, this research focused on achieving an autonomous communication platform. A open question is how to integrate this research with research efforts dealing with connectivity to infrastructure networks when they are available. MANET-based networks used in urban search and rescue contexts, could play the (analogous to a cognitive memory model) role of short term memory, inasmuch as long-term memory could rely on a fixed infrastructure communication platform. Specifically, one of the possible uses of this platform is to be engaged with a fixed infrastructure (or satellite) to provide communication between on-site users with remote users which would assist them in analyzing data, developing adequate problem analysis of ongoing situations, as well as making real-time solutions and decisions, among others.

In terms of usability one must face the question: to what extent would the devices really be used by the users? In the case of informal social encounters among unacquainted people, usability is not envisioned by us as a challenging problem in future due the growing popularity in the usage of handheld devices on the population, especially among young users. In opposition, in the case of first responders, usability is envisioned to be a challenging issue to solve, due to the imperious necessity of develop adequate interfaces to avoid that the medium becomes a cognitive or physical obstacle for the development of ongoing tasks. This article describes research focused on the technological feasibility of short-range wireless technology used to provide communication medium for first responders' collaboration in disaster relief environments, i.e.; focused on aspects are related to machine-machine communication and neither human-machine or human-human relationships.

Finally, the general approach taken by this research effort for the development of algorithms, methods and techniques was heuristic and distributed. Although in the academic environment it was possible to attach the MANET to an infrastructure network, which was mainly used to monitor interactions between people, but not to provide interaction between students, in the disaster relief environment case it was modeled completely in a distributed manner. Optimal analytical solutions would be more difficult, if not impractical at all, due to the mostly partial information handled by the users in chaotic and highly dynamic contexts [18]). Consequently, the solutions proposed for the availability and connectivity problems stated in this document are "best-effort" solutions.

6 Conclusions and Further Work

The research effort presented through this document was aimed to understand to what extent short-range wireless mobile networks are a useful medium able to support interactions among co-located mobile people in extreme interaction settings which have or may have a high social impact. The semantics of extreme setting in this document is defined as an interaction context where the level of exigency for the agent mediator of interactions, i.e., the communication medium, is far beyond the levels of exigency of settings such as formal face-to-face work meetings. In order to do this, two settings were chosen; face-to-face interactions among unacquainted people in everyday situations, and first responders communication in urban disaster relief environments. In the former setting, the medium was studied in terms of the role as facilitator/promoter of such face-to-face interactions. The communication between physically close people, e.g., a couple of dozens of meters, even if it is intermittent, is not an issue due the current available off-the-shelf short-range wireless technology. On the contrary, in the latter settings, the communication is the primary issue to deal with. Such priority is given by the need to provide the first responders with an autonomous, functionally adequate, and reliable communication medium for inhospitable, complex, chaotic and dynamic environments where fixed infrastructure computational networks are unreliable, or physically or logically collapsed.

The main conclusion of this research effort is that short-range wireless mobile networks can play key roles for extreme interaction settings involving co-located mobile people. The results obtained in this research effort, through experiments and simulations, show that: (a) a short-range wireless mobile network may promote face-to-face encounters among co-located unacquainted people in everyday situations, and (b) a short-range wireless mobile network may be established as a reliable communication medium to support interactions among first responders operating in complex, chaotic, and highly dynamic contexts.

Through the development of this research effort some of the leading original questions were answered, some of them only could be partially answered, and new ones rose. To what extent it is possible to generate long-term relations among unacquainted people by promoting their face-to-face initial contact through technology? What kind of interactions is more prone to be promoted by a technological promoter? How many different environments could exist in disaster relief operations considering the different nature of natural and man-made disasters? What are the most useful first responders movement models for each kind of disaster relief setting? Is it possible that technology plays adequately the role of promoter for stressing, hostile, chaotic, and dynamic disaster relief environments? How applicable are the concepts, principles, models, mechanisms, and algorithms developed through this research to other slow or business contexts? These and other questions will lead further research.

References

1. Elliot, C. (2003) "U.S. military pioneers ad hoc wireless networks in the battlefield." iApplianceWeb.com, http://www.iapplianceweb.com/story/OEG20030319S0054.
2. Yusuke, M. (2001) *Collaborative Environments for Disaster Relief.* Master's thesis, Department of Civil & Environmental Engineering, MIT, Cambridge, MA, June.
3. Amagar, S. and Hayashi, M. (2002) "Ad Hoc Networks: Applications and Merits." *ETSI Workshop on Broadband Wireless Ad-Hoc Networks and Services,* Sophia Antipolis, France, September.
4. Kirisci, P.T. (2002) "Context-Aware Environments for Ad Hoc Collaborative Business," *Technology Challenges Workshop,* Stuttgart, Germany, October.
5. Johnson, D., and Maltz, D.A. (1996), "Dynamic Source Routing in Ad Hoc Wireless Networks." *Mobile Computing,* Vol.353, T. Imielinsky and H. Korth, eds., Kluwer Academic Publishers, January 1996, Boston, MA, chapter 5, pp. 153-181.
6. Dube, R., Rais, C.D., Wang, K., and Tripathi, S. (1997) "Signal Stability based Adaptive Routing (SSA) for Ad-Hoc Mobile Networks." *IEEE Personal Communication,* Feb., pp. 36-45.
7. Broch, J., Maltz, D.A., Jonhson, D.B., Hu, Y.C., and Jetcheva, J. (1998), "A Performance Comparison of Multi-hop Wireless Ad Hoc Network Routing Protocols." Proc. *Fourth Annual ACM/IEEE International Conference on Mobile Computing and Networking,* October 25-30, 1998, Dallas, TX, ACM, New York, NY, pp. 85-97.
8. Perkins, C.E., and Royer, E.M. (1999) "Ad Hoc on Demand Distance Vector Routing." Proceedings 2nd *IEEE Workshop on Mobile Computing Systems and Applications,* February 25-26, 1999, New Orleans, LA, IEEE, Washington, DC, pp. 90-100.
9. Royer, E.M. and Toh, C.K. (1999) "A Review for Current Routing Protocols for Ad Hoc Mobile Wireless Networks." IEEE *Personal Communications,* April, pp. 46-55.
10. Nasipuri, A., Castañeda, R. and Das, S.M. (2001) "Performance of multipath routing for on-demand protocols in mobile ad hoc networks," *Mobile Networks and Applications,* Vol 6, pp.339-349, August.
11. Haas, Z., Halpern, J., and Li, L. (2002) "Gossip-Based Ad Hoc Routing." In Proceedings of *IEEE Infocom* 2002.
12. Nussbaum, M., Aldunate, R., Sfeir, F., Oyarce, S., and Gonzalez, R. (2004) "Ubiquitous Awareness in an Academic Environment." *Lecture Notes in Computer Science,* Springer-Verlag Heidelberg, Volume 2954 / 2004, pp. 244-255.
13. Aldunate, R., Ochoa, S.F., Pena-Mora, F., and Nussbaum, M. (2006a) "Robust Mobile Ad Hoc Space for Collaboration to Support Disaster Relief Efforts Involving Critical Physical Infrastructure." *Journal of Computing in Civil Engineering,* Vol. 20, Issue 1, pp. 13-27.
14. Aldunate, R., Pena-Mora, F., Gupta, I., Gasser, L., Nussbaum, M., and Ochoa, S. (2006b) "Self-healing Communication for Mobile Ad-hoc Networks in Inhospitable Context." Under review in *IEEE Transactions on Systems, Man and Cybernetics - Part C: Applications and Reviews.*
15. Jackson, B., Peterson, D., Bartis, J., LaTourrente, T., Brahmakulam, I., Houser, A., and Sollinge, J. (2001). "Protecting Emergency Responders: Lessons Learned from Terrorist Attacks." RAND, Science and Technology Policy Institute
16. Fema (1999) "Federal Response Plan." Federal Emergency Management Agency, 9130.1-PL. April
17. Altshuler T. (1999) "Opportunities in Land Mine Warfare Technologies. The Self-Healing Minefield." (Approved for Public Release, Distribution Limited) Defense Advanced Research Projects Agency (DARPA), Advanced Technology Office, Arlington, VA
18. Gasaway, R. Ready! Fire! Aim!. *Journal of Fire Engineering.* pp.16-17. August. 2003

A Time-based Admission Control Mechanism for IEEE 802.11 Ad Hoc Networks

Carlos Rodrigo Cerveira[1,2] and Luís Henrique M. K. Costa[2]*

[1] Diretoria de Telecomunicações da Marinha, Rio de Janeiro, Brasil.
[2] Grupo de Teleinformática e Automação PEE/COPPE - DEL/POLI,
Universidade Federal do Rio de Janeiro, Rio de Janeiro, Brasil.
{rodrigo,luish}@gta.ufrj.br

Summary. This paper presents a time-based admission control mechanism (TAC) for IEEE 802.11 ad hoc networks. The proposed mechanism was adapted to the QoS AODV routing protocol, which takes the quality of service requirements of the data flow into account in the route discovery process. TAC-AODV estimates the idle time of the physical medium based on the frames listened. The incoming traffic is admitted according to the offered load as well as the intra-flow interference, calculated based on the number of hops in the forwarding chain. TAC-AODV is compared to AAC-AODV, another admission control mechanism found in the literature, and the simulation results show that TAC-AODV is in average 12.5% better in terms of the packet delivery rate.

1 Introduction

The use of multimedia applications on MANETs is becoming more and more desired; however, most of the routing strategies used in MANETs only provide best effort service. To overcome this problem a number of QoS (Quality of Service) techniques have been proposed.

These techniques spread different layers of the protocol stack, such as multiple queues at the MAC layer, routing protocols which search for QoS routes, and through signaling mechanisms for reservation, admission control, and packet scheduling.

QoS at the MAC layer can be implemented through IEEE 802.11e, which establishes different medium access categories, in order to prioritize certain types of traffic [7].

The purpose of the QoS routing [5] is to find a way to satisfy the users request in terms of available bandwidth, end to end delay, or jitter. On the other hand, QoS signaling protocols allocating resources along the chosen route. Signaling and routing are very coupled.

Additionaly, Admission control should be used together with signaling and routing. Its purpose is to assist the routing protocol in choosing a path for

---

* Supported by DTM, CNPq, CAPES, FAPERJ, and FUJB.

Please use the following format when citing this chapter:

Cerveira, C.R., Costa, L.H.M.K., 2006, in IFIP International Federation for Information Processing, Volume 211, ed. Pujolle, G., Mobile and Wireless Communication Networks, (Boston: Springer), pp. 217–228.

the source node up to the destination node, with enough bandwidth for the transmission of flow and, without interfering with pre-existing traffic.

This paper proposes a new Time-based Admission Control Mechanism (TAC), which is based on a precise estimate of the available resources and on the intra-flow interference, taking into account the inherent characteristics of an ad hoc network. All nodes which take part in the route discovery process - from the source to the destination nodes - have their available resources checked and this new flow will be accepted, in case there is enough resources to fulfill the request and not to havoc the pre-existing flows.

This paper is organized as follows. Section 2 presents related work on AODV and QoS AODV. Sections 3 and 4 present the available resources and intra-flow interference estimations, respectively. Section 5 reviews AAC-AODV, an admission control mechanism proposed in [1]. Section 6 introduces the TAC-AODV protocol; Section 7 analyzes the performance of TAC-AODV through simulation and, finally, Section 8 concludes the paper.

2 Related Work

Ad hoc On demand Distance Vector (AODV) is a reactive routing protocol based on distance vectors [6]. AODV only triggers a route discovery procedure when there is a data transfer, using Route Request (RREQ) and Route Reply (RREP) messages. QoS AODV is an extension of AODV which takes QoS into account by adding extensions to the control messages and routing tables of AODV. The QoS AODV control messages carry the Maximum Delay and Minimum Bandwidth which are acceptable for the flow being started [3, 4, 5]. During route discovery, each intermediary node between the source and destination checks if the request can be fulfilled, otherwise, the route discovery is interrupted. QoS AODV finds a route that fulfills the QoS request, however, it does not take into account two factors: the impact on the ongoing traffic and the intra-flow interference. Two approaches are found in the literature which take these into account, Adaptive Admission Control (AAC) AODV [1] and Contention-Aware Admission Control Protocol (CACP) [9]. CACP supports only source routing protocols such as DSR, and does not propose any strategy to handle mobility and loss of QoS guarantees. AAC-AODV, on the other hand, is based on QoS AODV and introduces "lost QoS" messages to cope with changes in the QoS route. This work is based on AAC-AODV, which is described in more detail in Section 5.

3 Available Resources Estimate

In IEEE 802.11 networks, the medium is shared by the nodes located within the same carrier-sense region (CS nodes). The carrier sensing range is normally larger than the transmission range. Therefore, any transmission will have an impact which is beyond the transmission range. Assuming that two nodes are within the transmission area of each other, the bandwidth available at the "link" connecting these two nodes is considered as the smallest of all available bandwidths, belonging to their sensing range. For example, consider that in

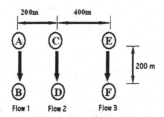

Fig. 1. Available resources estimate.

Figure 1 the flow AB is consuming 30% and the flow EF is taking 45% of the channel bandwidth. If we suppose a transmission range of 250 m and a carrier detection range of 550 m, the AB and EF flows do not interfere with each other. Now, suppose that node C wants to send traffic to D, and that the traffic load takes 40% of the channel bandwidth. Upon verification of the available resources, node C concludes that there is not enough bandwidth, as node C is within the interference area of both the AB and EF flows, which leave only 25% of the bandwidth available.

4 Intra-flow Interference

When a flow is transmitted using multiple hops, there will be interferences created by the traffic itself, because the carrier-sense range is larger than the transmission range. Suppose the scenario with five hops of Figure 2, where the full lines represent the transmission range area whereas the dotted lines represent the CS region. In that scenario, node 3 is in the interference range of five other nodes, which decreases its available bandwidth by five times. Therefore, another strategy is needed to accurately predict how much bandwidth is necessary in each node to accept a given traffic load. This phenomenon is called intra-flow interference. Now, suppose, a flow between node 1 and node 6 (destination) in Figure 2. Note that node 3 is in carrier-sense range of nodes 1 and 5. Therefore, node 3 not only suffers from the interference of nodes 2 and 4 transmissions, but also suffers from the interference of nodes 1 and 5, when they transmit. The intra-flow interference estimate is detailed in Section 5.2.

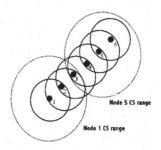

Fig. 2. Intra-flow interference.

5 Adaptive Admission Control (AAC) AODV

A straightforward way to guarantee that a flow is transmitted at the requested rate is to constantly calculate the available bandwidth and decide if a flow can be accepted based on an estimate of how much of the available bandwidth this flow will consume. The maximum available bandwidth can be computed from the IEEE 802.11 nominal transmission rate (11 Mbps for IEEE 802.11b), minus the overhead due to the time spent with the transmission of control bytes, i.e., the data frame preamble, RTS/CTS, and ACK frames, minus the time spent in the MAC operation, i.e., SIFS, DIFS, and backoff. The maximum available bandwidth depends on the packet size used by the application. Adaptive Admission Control (AAC) AODV [1] uses an approximation of this computation. AAC-AODV implements flow admission control based on two main mechanisms: Available Resources Estimate and Predictive Solution for Route Discovery.

5.1 Available Resources Estimate

To compute the maximum available bandwidth, AAC-AODV defines a "maximum bandwidth" of 5.1 Mbps experimentally obtained and considers a 40% reduction due to MAC overhead. That computation produces a maximum bandwidth of 3.6 Mbps for IEEE 802.11b [1]. The Bandwidth Estimate consumption at one node is the sum of the size of the packets sent, received, or detected during a predefined period of time. Assume that N is the number of packets sent, received, or detected by a node within a period of time T, and S is the packet size in bytes. Then, the average bandwidth used during T is:

$$BW(bps) = \frac{N*S*8}{T} .$$ (1)

5.2 Predictive Solution for Route Discovery

In [9], Kravets and Yang define the Contention Count (CC) at a node as the number of nodes on the multihop path that are located within carrier sensing range of a given node. In order to provide a good estimation of the expected intra-flow contention, AAC-AODV uses CC to estimate the number of nodes which contend with each other for the medium access. Each node forwarding traffic has to calculate a CC variable in order to provide a good intra-flow interference estimate.

The CC variable can be obtained from the Hop Count field of the RREQ and RREP messages of AODV. The RREQ messages stores the number of hops between the source and the node forwarding the RREQ, while the RREP stores the number of hops from the destination to the forwarding the reply.

To compute CC, the authors [1] consider that the carrier-sense range is more than twice the size of the transmission range. Therefore, every node on the path generally interferes with, at most, two upstream and downstream nodes.

Let h_{req} and h_{rep} be the number of hops obtained from the RREQ and RREP messages, respectively. According to [1], the Contention Count (CC) of one node is defined as:

$$\begin{cases} \text{if } h_{req} > 2 \rightarrow h_{req} = 2 \\ \text{if } h_{rep} > 3 \rightarrow h_{rep} = 3 \\ \quad CC = h_{req} + h_{rep} \end{cases} \tag{2}$$

The estimate can only be made after the RREP reception as both h_{req} and

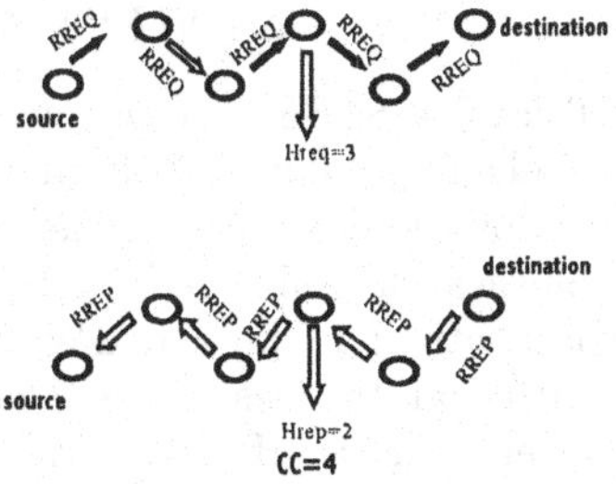

Fig. 3. Consider the nodes numbered from 1 to 6 beginning at the source node. By applying Equation 2 to the 4th node, we realize that the CC is equal to 4.

h_{rep} are needed. Thereafter, each node verifies if the bandwidth available is large enough to support a CC*Rate. If affirmative, the RREP is forwarded to the source.

6 Time-Based Admission Control (TAC)

The techniques presented in Section 5 are not sufficient to decide on the acceptance of a new traffic. It is still necessary to determine how much the new flow will take from the nominal bandwidth. Additionally, the intra-flow interference must be taken into account. AAC-AODV considers a maximum available throughput of 3.6 Mbps [1]. That value actually corresponds to the network saturation throughput using 1024-byte packets (see Table 1). Obviously, this approximation reduces the protocol efficiency for packets smaller than 1024 bytes. In order to avoid this shortcoming, we measure the channel idle time as an indication of the available bandwidth instead. In a saturated network, the channel is occupied at all times.

6.1 Available Resources Estimate

The estimate of available resources is based on a variable called Busy Time Estimate (T_b). A node can estimate the amount of time that the media is busy, T_b, by summing up the times that the media is busy with routing messages, RTS, CTS, ACK, and $DATA$ frames transmission, reception, and detection during an interval of time. The accuracy of the busy time estimate depends on the interval, t, between measurements. The larger t, the more accurate is the estimate. Nevertheless, t should be small enough to be transparent to the channel dynamics. Therefore, the choice of t is a tradeoff between accuracy and transparency [1]. The transmission of an IEEE 802.11 data frame takes the following amount of time, T:

$$
\begin{aligned}
T = DIFS + Backoff + RTS + SIFS+ \\
CTS + SIFS+ \\
Data + SIFS + ACK \ .
\end{aligned}
\tag{3}
$$

Consider that $DIFS$ is 50 μs, $3 \times SIFS$ is 30 μs, and that the backoff time is the product of a time slot and a random number from 0 to 31. Then, the average backoff is 15.5 μs, multiplied by the slot-time of 20 μs. The $RTS+CTS+ACK$ frames, including all the physical preambles have 120 bytes, or 960 bits, which are transmitted at the basic rate of 1 Mbps, taking 960 μs. The 192-bit data frame preamble is transmitted at the basic rate. $Data$ includes the payload received by the routing layer, and the IP and MAC headers, which sum up 48 bytes. Therefore, the average time packet, T_{med}, in μs can be calculated as follows:

$$
T_{med} = 50 + 30 + 310 + 960 + 192 + \frac{8*(psize+48)}{11} \ ,
\tag{4}
$$

where $psize$ is the payload received by routing layer. Then, the average throughput, V, can be computed as:

$$
V(Mbps) = \frac{psize*8}{1542+\frac{8*(psize+48)}{11}} \ .
\tag{5}
$$

The total busy time (T_T) during the period of 1 second can be computed as the fraction of the interval t where the medium is the busy, divided by the interval t:

$$
T_T = \frac{T_b+(DIFS+3*SIFS+Backoff)*NPD}{t} \ ,
\tag{6}
$$

where NPD is the number of data packets transmitted, received, or detected, T_b is the time during which the media is busy with the $RTS+CTS+ACK+Data$ frames and routing messages transmission.

A very important issue is the estimate of the backoff value when there are various stations contending for the medium. The stations will decrease their backoff simultaneously. When a station hears a transmission, the station will pause its backoff counter and re-start it when the media remains idle again for a DIFS period. Therefore, we can not use the average backoff value of Equation 4 for the calculation of the total packet transmission time. Bianchi [8] shows that the saturation throughput of an IEEE 802.11 network is defined by:

$$V(Mbps) = \frac{E[P]}{Ts + \tau \frac{1 - Ptr}{Ps Ptr} + Tc(\frac{1}{Ps} - 1)} , \qquad (7)$$

where $E[P]$ is the data payload, in bits and transmitted in a slot-time, Ts is the time spent, in μs, for the successful packet transmission, the second and the third terms of the denominator are the amount of idle slot-time and slot-times spent with collisions, both in μs, for the successful packet transmission.

With the RTS/CTS mechanism, Bianchi [8] demonstrate that if we have 5 or more stations contending for the medium and the initial size of the backoff window equal to 31, the saturation throughput does not depend on the number of stations. This is because the number of idle slot-times and slot-times spent with collisions for successful transmission of a packet are constant and small in relation to Ts.

By examining Equations 5 and 7 we obtain the values in Table 1, where the network saturation throughput is given for different frame sizes, considering only one node accessing the medium and with 5 or more nodes trying to access the medium. In order to calculate the saturation throughput by using the Bianchi [8]

Table 1. Packet size and Throughput

Packet(bytes)	V(Mbps) 1 node	V(Mbps) 5 or more nodes	Difference (%)
64	0.31	0.34	9.0%
256	1.16	1.25	7.5%
512	2.10	2.25	6.5%
1024	3.52	3.74	5.8%
2300	5.66	5.90	4.0%

model, the number of idle slot-times and slot-times spent on collisions was set to 8, in accordance to the graphs presented in [8]. In our simulations, in order to estimate the backoff of Equations 6 and 9, we used the 160 μs value (8* 20 μs slot-times), reducing by 150 μs the average time spent to transmit a packet.

To calculate the Available Free Time (T_F) of a node in 1 second, we only have to subtract T_T:

$$T_F = 1 - T_T . \qquad (8)$$

As described in Section 3, in order to precisely estimate the medium free time, the node needs to know the available free time of all of its neighbors. TAC-AODV uses the HELLO message to disseminate the available free time. The available free time extension of the HELLO message is the free time measured by the node that issued the HELLO message. Upon reception of a HELLO, a node stores the available free time of its neighbors in a cache table. The node's decision on whether to forward the RREQ and RREP messages is based on the minimum available free time locally measured and measured by one-hop neighbors.

6.2 Resource availability verification

When receiving the packet at the routing layer, the node checks the transmission rate used and the size of the packet. Therefore, it is possible to estimate the amount of time needed to transmit this packet. The transmission time (T_{tx}) using IEEE 802.11b, considering an average backoff of 160 μs is calculated as:

$$T_{tx} = \frac{num}{1000000} * (1392 + \frac{8*(psize+48)}{11.0}) , \tag{9}$$

where num is the number of packets generated by the application in 1 second, calculated by the ratio between the transmission rate of the application and the size of the packet.

Then, the node checks if its available free time is enough to fulfill the application request. The RREQ message will only be forwarded if the node can fulfill the request. TAC-AODV adds two new fields to the RREQ and RREP messages, which contain the traffic rate and the size of the packet generated by the application.

When the intermediary nodes receive the RREQ and RREP messages, they also check whether they can fulfill the request from the source node. The intermediary nodes use Equation 9 with the information on rate and packet size contained in the RREQ and RREP messages. Note that the node intra-flow interference (Section 5.2) is accounted for and multiplied by T_{tx}. The flow is accepted only if:

$$T_F - CC * T_{tx} > 0 \tag{10}$$

In case the node can not fulfill the request, it drops the RREQ or RREP message interrupting route discovery.

6.3 Node mobility

All nodes continuously check if the Quality of Service (QoS) is being met. Suppose that a node is forwarding a QoS flow and the node moves and begins to suffer from the interference of other nodes. The available free time of the node will be reduced and it might not manage to route the previously accepted flow at the requested rate. In that case, the node will send an ICMP QoS Lost message [5] in the direction of the source node, reporting that it might not fulfill the QoS request. Upon reception of the QoS Lost message, the source node will interrupt the traffic and will generate a new RREQ for this flow, in order to discover a new path to fulfill the request.

7 Performance Evaluation

The simulations were performed using the 2.27 version of ns-2 [10]. We used the IEEE 802.11b with RTS/CTS. The scenario used in the simulations consists of a network of 50 nodes randomly positioned in an area of 900x600 m, moving according to the random waypoint model with a speed of 5 m/s and 10 s pause time. Four CBR sources are used, with size 512-byte packets. The CBR transmission rate varies from 100 to 900 kbps. We performed 30 simulation runs for each rate.

7.1 Metrics

Since the admission control is performed at the routing layer, the application does not receive any information of the lower layer regarding an unreachable destination. This is the case of the ns-2 implementation. Obviously, in the real world it is possible to have cross-layer optimisation in order to pause the application if no destination route is found. In case there is no feasible route due to the admission control action, the data packets are dropped at the routing layer. Nevertheless, we did not implement any routing layer signaling in ns-2. Thus, we define a metric called the Packet Delivery Ratio (PDR) which counts only the transmitted packets, in bytes, delivered by the MAC layer of the source node. The received packets, in bytes, are the ones received at the application layer of the destination node.

The second metric, the Overhead is defined as a the ratio between the number of control bytes produced by the routing protocol and by the number of data bytes received at the destination node.

The third metric is the end-to-end delay. It is defined as the difference between the arrival time of a packet at the destination node's application layer and the time by which the packet was generated at the source node's application layer.

The fourth metric is the Flow Rejection. It is defined as the ratio between the number of packets dropped at the routing layer, due to the admission control action, and the number of packets generated at the application layer.

The fifth metric is called the Overflow. It is defined as the ratio between the number of packets dropped at the MAC layer, due to queue overflow, and the number of packets generated at the application layer.

7.2 Simulation Results

Figure 4(a), shows the packet delivery rate (PDR) as the source transmission rate is varied. The AODV, AAC-AODV, and TAC-AODV behaviors are the same for the 100 kbps rate. Up to this point, the network is not saturated. Figure 4(e) points out that, no packets are dropped at the MAC Layer. AAC-AODV and TAC-AODV admit all offered traffic, and no packets are dropped at the routing layer (Figure 4(d)). Nevertheless, as the load increases, TAC-AODV

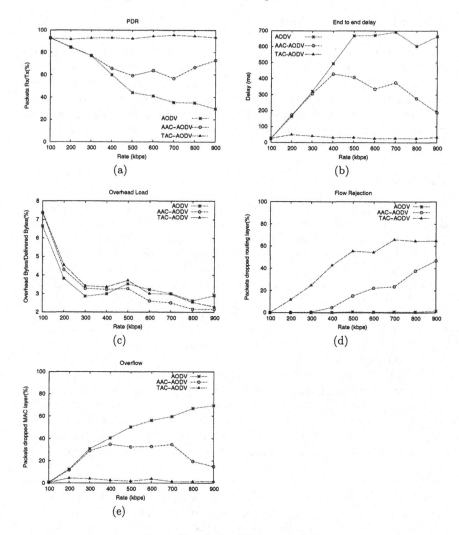

Fig. 4. Graphs for 512 byte packets.

rejects new traffic that would saturate the network, avoiding queue drops and sustaining the packet delivery rate above 90%. The delivery rate does not reach 100% because the mobility may cause route errors. With the increase of the network load the PDR of AAC-AODV starts to decrease. This happens because the network maximum throughput estimated by AAC-AODV for applications with 512-byte packets is not optimized and, therefore, the admission control accepts more traffic than the network could stand. AODV has the worst performance, as it has no admission control and accepts all of the traffic offered to the network.

Another important parameter is the packet average delay. Figure 4(b) shows that the TAC-AODV end-to-end delay remains below 50 ms, even with high rates causing the network to be saturated, which means that there is queuing in all nodes. AAC-AODV behaves similar to AODV for rates of up to 300 kbps. With higher rates, however, the admission control enters into action, since the traffic in the network reached the saturation value assumed by the protocol, reducing the delay, yet not reaching the delay obtained with TAC-AODV.

Figure 4(c) analyzes the protocol overhead. The AAC-AODV and TAC-AODV protocols employ HELLO, RREQ, and RREP messages which are longer than AODV. These messages carry additional fields used for admission control, as described in Section 6. The overhead of TAC-AODV is slightly larger than AAC-AODV due to the "packet size" field added in the RREQ and RREP messages. With increasing network load, AAC-AODV and TAC-AODV perform better than AODV. The admission control restricts the spread of RREQ and RREP messages, because they can be dropped if the available resources are not enough, reducing the number of routing control bytes. Figure 4(d) shows that only with a 400 kbps rate the AAC-AODV admission control is used, while TAC-AODV starts operating at the 200 kbps rates, restricting the admission of new flows. This means that, in the ns-2 simulator, packets are dropped at the routing layer. On the other hand, since AODV has no admission control, all packets are sent to the MAC layer. This causes an overflow in the MAC queue and, consequently, a high number of dropped packets (Figure 4(e)). Figure 4(e) shows the complementary behavior of Figure 4(d) and the efficiency of the TAC-AODV admission control, since TAC-AODV causes fewer packet drops at the MAC layer. AAC-AODV has a larger number of dropped packets due to an optimistic estimate of the available bandwidth, as previously mentioned. When

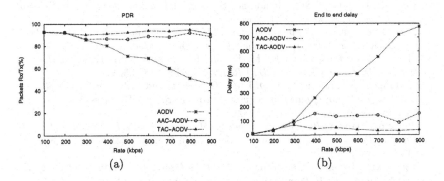

Fig. 5. PDR and end-to-end delay for 1024-byte packets.

the same experiments are repeated for 1024-byte packets, we note that the performance of AAC-AODV is closer to that of TAC-AODV. This is because with the 1024-byte packets the saturation throughput is closer to the maximum bandwidth value, which is used by the protocol AAC-AODV. Therefore, the optimal bandwidth estimate used for admission control depends on the packet size.

8 Conclusion

Admission control is a key component to guarantee QoS in IEEE 802.11 ad hoc networks. In this paper, we proposed an admission control mechanism and combined it with the AODV routing protocol. The basic idea of TAC-AODV is to use the channel idle time as an indication of the bandwidth currently used in the network. Moreover, TAC-AODV takes into account the intra-flow interference effect and the influence of the nodes which are in the same carrier-sense region to provide an accurate estimate of the available resources. We have demonstrated through simulation that TAC-AODV provides more efficient QoS guarantees than other admission control mechanisms found in the literature.

References

1. R. de Renesse, M. Ghassemian, V. Friderikos, A.H.Aghvami, *Adaptive Admission Control for Ad Hoc and Sensor Networks Providing Quality of Service*, Technical Report, Center for Telecommunications Research, King's College London, UK, May 2005.
2. T. Bheemarjuna Reddy, I. Karthigeyan, B.S. Manoj and C. Siva Ram Murthy, *Quality of Service provisioning in Ad Hoc wireless networks: a survey of issues and solutions*, Elsevier Ad Hoc Networks, 1999.
3. Stéphane Lohier, Sidi-Mohamed Senouci, Yacine Ghamri Doudane, Guy Pujolle, *QoS routing in ad hoc networks*, Med-Hoc-Net, Sardegna, Italy, September 2002.
4. Stéphane Lohier and Sidi-Mohammed Senouci, *A Reactive Qos Routing Protocol for Ad Hoc Networks*, EUSAI, November 2003.
5. Charles Perkins, *Quality of Service for Ad Hoc On-Demand Distance Vector Routing*. Available at http://people.nokia.net/charliep/txt/aodvid/qos.txt
6. Charles E. Perkins, Elizabeth M. Belding-Royer, and Samir Das, *Ad Hoc On Demand Distance Vector (AODV) Routing.*, IETF RFC 3561.
7. S. Mangols, S. Choi, P. May, O. Klein, G. Hiertz, and L. Stibor, *IEEE 802.11e Wireless LAN for Quality of Service* , Proc. European Wireless, vol. 1, pages 32-39, Florence, Italy, February 2002.
8. Giuseppe Bianchi, *Performance analisys of the IEEE 802.11 Distributed Coordination Function.* IEEE Journal on Selected in Communications, vol. 18 no. 3, 2000.
9. Robin Kravets and Yaling Yang, *Contention-Aware Admission Control for Ad Hoc Networks.* IEEE Transactions on mobile computing, vol. 4, no. 4, 2005.
10. K. Fall and K. Varadhan, *NS Notes and Documentation*, The VINT Project, UC Berkeley, LBL, USC/ISI, and Xerox PARC, 1997.
11. Villela, B. A. M. and Duarte, O. C. M. B. "Maximum Throughput Analysis in Ad Hoc Networks", Lecture Notes in Computer Science - Networking'2004, pp. 223-234, vol. 3042, Springer-Verlag, May 2004.

Evaluation and Improvement of Multicast Service in 802.11b

Christian Bravo[1] and Agustín González[2]

[1] Universidad Federico Santa María, Department of Electronics. Valparaíso, Chile
chbravo@elo.utfsm.cl
[2] Universidad Federico Santa María, Department of Electronics. Valparaíso, Chile
agustin.gonzalez@elo.utfsm.cl

Abstract. Wireless Technologies have allowed a fast growing of the Internet service in both public and private environments where wireless networks mostly consist of nodes interconnected with a fixed infrastructure; nevertheless, they do not offer a good performance in all the wide variety of services that are required for applications. Although the IEEE 802.11 MAC protocol is the standard for wireless LANs, this protocol shows a very poor performance and reliability compared with the multicast traffic transmitted in wired networks, this represents a significant challenge for existing 802.11 networks because it requires transmission over multiple unreliable channels to heterogeneous receivers with different connection bit rates and very limited feedback information to the sender. In this paper, we discuss the drawbacks of several protocols proposed in the literature that offer reliable multicast service. In addition, this work evaluates the performance of the wireless networks under multicast traffic and presents a proposal for actual IEEE802.11 networks to improve their efficiency. It uses a reliability control based on a polling service along with controlled retransmissions; this allows servicing nodes applications with a high efficiency without deteriorating fairness in the service. We present details of a prototype implementation and results that suggest that our protocol performs better than other proposed in terms of reliability as well as data throughput in our measurement scenarios.[3]

Key words: IEEE 802.11, Multicast, Wireless LAN, Reliability.

1 Introduction

The wireless technology has grown fast as a way to interconnect computers. Wireless networking applications continue to proliferate at an incredible pace as wireless features, functions, security, and throughput improve. IEEE802.11b [?] [?] is the standard on which wireless networking are based today, and products that employ the technology support a broad range of uses for enterprises

---

[3] We thank to the USM-23.04.26 Research Project of the Federico Santa María University for the support to develop this work.

Please use the following format when citing this chapter:

Bravo, C., González, A., 2006, in IFIP International Federation for Information Processing, Volume 211, ed. Pujolle, G., Mobile and Wireless Communication Networks, (Boston: Springer), pp. 229–242.

and home users.

An important difference between the wireless and the wired networks is the greater datagram loss rate of the first ones. These networks operate in a radio band that was originally reserved internationally for non-commercial use of RF electromagnetic fields and its power of transmission is limited. This condition, added to the interference of the radio frequency spectrum and the medium access protocol defined in 802.11b, causes a great number of datagram losses. Unlike most of the data-link layer protocols used in wired networks [?], 802.11 incorporates acknowledges (ACK's) to decrease the high rate of frames lost due to interferences, decay of signal, and collisions. In this way, it is attempted to reach reliability in unicast transmissions over wireless links. However, the ACK's and the retransmissions are omitted when the data destination is a multicast address, thus an implosion of ACK's or requests of retransmissions at the Access Point is avoided. Based on the same reason, the IEEE 802.11 standard does not include the optional extension RTS/CTS for multicast/broadcast transmissions [?] [?]. The multicast datagram loss rate causes that application programs such as radio broadcasting stations, television, distributed computing, chat and whiteboard applications and all type of Internet conferences show a very poor performance compared with them on wired networks [?]. This is explained because they are normally designed to operate with low error rates and because they interpret the datagram loss as congestion, reacting with complex mechanisms like changing of coders to decrease the transmission rate. Obviously, this does not solve the problem that has its origin in a high Block Error Rate (BER) at the physical level.

This paper goal is oriented to evaluate the problem that appears in a network with infrastructure, operating in the *Basic Service Set (BSS)* mode, where the stations are fixed in indoor and outdoor scenarios. Thus, we centered our interest on the multicast performance degradation of the wireless link that connects the AP with the wireless stations. In addition to this evaluation, we propose a protocol to improve the reliability of the multicast transmissions until achieve a performance close to the one observed in wireless unicast transmissions. The previously proposed solutions use Error Correction Codes [?] or suggest modifications to IEEE802.11 MAC protocol [?]- [?] which does not solve the problem of the networks that were already installed. We present related work in more detail in the next section.

2 Related Work

Several approaches have been proposed in the multicast communications area to reduce the effective packet loss rate and, at the same time, provide a reliable service. Some of them provide reliable multicast transmissions in the end-to-end sense assuming the existence of underlying routing protocols. Other solutions propose to analyze the subject of the losses recovery using errors correction techniques like FEC (Forward Error Correction) [?]. Several multicast protocols have been developed as an extension for MAC Layer described in the standard IEEE802.11. They try to improve the performance in the data transmission process between the nodes. Our proposal is in the same direction, looking for a mechanism based on the IEEE802.11 standard that improves the performance of the reliable multicast protocols proposed so far. Following, the proposals of our best knowledge to date are briefly described. The protocol proposed in [?] tries to extend the IEEE802.11 standard for multicast/broadcast transmissions using messages RTS/CTS (Request To Send/Clear To Send) in all network configurations. Obviously, this protocol presents the CTS's implosion problem in the source node. The protocol proposed in [?], known as Broadcast Support Multiple Access (BSMA), is an extension to the previous protocol [?]. Briefly, after the source node received the CTS of some neighbor, this one sends the data and waits for a determined time for a Negative Acknowledgment (NACK). A NACK is sent by the node that sent the CTS if the data does not arrive before a timeout occur. If the source node does not receive a NACK then it assumes that the transmission was completed. In the other case, it senses the channel to restart the RTS/CTS process. In this approach, the node that sent the CTS does not consider if the other clients received data successfully or not before sending an ACK or NACK which means that some clients could be losing data. Reference [?] describes another protocol known as Broadcast Medium Window (BMW). Where each multicast/broadcast message is treated like multiple unicast ones. In summary, the idea is to handle a list of the receivers and to make all the DCF (*Distributed Coordination Function*) contention, transmission and error recovery process for each one interested in receiving the message. Although it is an interesting option because it improves reliability, we considered that in this solution there is too much redundancy since retransmissions can be done using multicast frames. Thus, the error recovery process in a receiving node aids to the transmission of the same frame to others. Other proposals as [?] and [?] are focused on the IBSS (*Independent Basic Service Set*) network configurations also known as Ad-Hoc Networks [?], where it is assumed that all nodes are within the same transmission radio. The presented works have contributed to improve the performance of the IEEE 802.11 standard for multicast/broadcast transmissions; nevertheless, most of the proposals discussed previously are difficult to integrate to the already spread systems based in this standard. In our work a novel scheme is presented which does not require modifications to the MAC layer because it works in the application level and uses an interceptor between IP and MAC layer as it is described in section 4.

3 Measurement Scenarios

The first step in this investigation was the reproduction of the problem observed in the FDI-Corfo "IP Wireless Diffusion" project [?], where it was possible to detect serious performance problems on the applications when the physical medium was unable to reach a transmission rate similar to those observed in

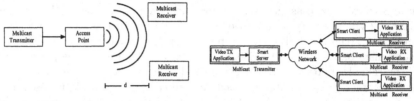

Fig. 1. Different Scenarios. Indoor scenario used d < 50 [m]. Outdoor scenario used d > 1 [Km]

Fig. 2. Proposed solution structure

wired networks using the RealNetworks technology. For that, two test scenarios were structured in which the problem had been observed. The first scenario is an Indoor environment (WLAN Network with a radio less than 50 [m]) and the second one is an Outdoor environment (WLAN Network with a radio over 1 [km]). The second scenario may need special hardware that allows elevating the power of the signal to obtain long distance transmissions (amplifying) or different antennas configurations. Figure 1 shows the previously described scenarios. A multicast server and client application were developed to transmit multicast traffic to multicast client applications. The server application transmits streams varying the transmission rate, the size of the datagrams and the time between each datagram (which emulates transmission of different codification rates videos). In the other side, the client application includes functions to measure the loss percentage of frames sent by the server. These functions were used to look for dependencies between the percentage of losses in receivers, the transmission rate and the size of frames. Besides, physical layer information provided by the driver of the WNIC was collected, for example, power level of the signals received or the Signal to Noise Ratio (SNR) to find the relation between wireless link quality and losses percentage in receivers.

4 Design of the proposed solution and Protocol Description

This section introduces the main idea of our solution and how our protocol works to improve the actual performance of multicast transmissions. The idea is to use efficient retransmissions methods by polling the clients, with the objective to improve the actual performance of multicast transmissions in wireless networks. As programming language, we chose Java because it allows our applications to be run on any arbitrary Java-capable device with an 802.11 interface without any further changes to the device itself. The JAVA platform that we developed consists of three main parts: The register of clients, the addresses mapping service and the retransmissions protocol.

4.1 The Register of Clients

In order for the Smart Server to be able to perform a retransmission protocol based on a polling system, a register of Smart Clients is needed. This register contains a list with information of all the clients connected to the multicast transmission. The information required includes the *IP address, Port* and *Life-Time* for each client. This allows us the regular maintenance of the state information and keep an updated database of the number of receivers in the group. For this, the Smart Server sends *Multicast Beacons* through a multicast control address. These beacons contain the Unicast IP Address and Port of the Smart Server. Smart Clients are also members of this multicast control group and, after receiving a beacon, they start a random backoff timer to reduce the collision probability of their responses. When this timer ends, each client sends a *Unicast Subscription Message* to the unicast address of the Smart Server. After that, each Smart Client will wait for another five beacons before start this timer again. Thus if this message is lost, the Smart Client will retry its subscription later. This *Unicast Subscription Message* format is *<IP address, Port>*. We added the application port because it will be used to receive unicast polls in our protocol. Once the Smart Server receives the Smart Client information, it adds a field of lifetime to each client pair. If the server already has the pair of the client, it will only update the lifetime field; else it adds the new client to the register. If no Subscription Message is received, the client is deleted from the list when its lifetime reaches zero. Thus, the Smart Server keeps an updated list of the active Smart Clients, and it allows to delete those that have left their multicast group.

4.2 The Addresses Mapping Service

This service consist in redirecting the multicast frames by changing the Multicast Address Destination, the Destination Port and the Time-To-Live (TTL) fields of the incoming frames. We installed a multicast traffic interceptor between the multicast transmitter and the wireless network, and other one intercepting the traffic between the wireless network and the multicast receivers, as the figure 2 shows. The technique we use is similar to that of Secure Shell (SSH) and others where it is possible to send the X-Windows traffic through the same SSH connection using a *tunnel* to obtain its encryption. Basically, the original source sends its traffic to a multicast address *A.A.A.A port XXXX with TTL=0*, which means that the stream will not leave the local host machine. Our Smart Server joins that multicast address and redirects the datagram with new parameters such as *B.B.B.B port YYYY with TTL=N* (where N depends of the network size). Therefore, the datagram leaves the local host with a multicast destination address known by the Smart Clients, they join to that address and perform the retransmission protocol. After that, they apply the mapping service again to deliver the stream to the final destination with parameters like this *A.A.A.A port XXXX with TTL=0*. This has to be the address to which

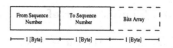

Fig. 3. Retransmission Protocol Header

Fig. 4. Poll and Poll Response Message Format. Poll Message does not include the bit array field

the final destinations joined in first place, and by setting the TTL in zero we limit the scope of the traffic to the specific machine which is running the Smart Client application.

4.3 The Retransmissions Protocol

The third and last module contains the retransmission protocol itself, that we named as *GroupPoll protocol (GP)*. The Smart Server map the multicast stream using the mapping service first and then is forwarded to the Smart Clients. Besides, when the multicast traffic arrives to the Smart Server it adds a header to each frame with information that includes a *sequence number, new-or-resent* and a *data-or-poll* field. The format of this header is shown in figure 3. The 1-Byte *new-or-resent* field can be used by clients to keep loss statistics of frames and the *data-or-poll* field to indicate when the multicast frame is data or a poll message. The *sequence number* field contains an identification number assigned by the Smart Server to be used in the retransmission algorithm. In our testbed, we assume that the sequence number is assigned to frames in the same order that they have left the original source, but this could be different if the protocol is implemented directly in the AP rather than in the same machine as the original source. Although we set 1-Byte for these fields for simplicity in the later performance analysis, we could have used less bits in both fields. Hence, once a small group of data frames has been forwarded, the Smart Server selects one of the clients included in its *Register of Clients* to be polled. The poll message is sent by the Smart Server to the unicast address formerly sent by the Smart Client and its format is shown in figure 4. The *From Sequence Number* and *To Sequence Number* fields indicate a window of datagrams being polled, and the *Bits Array*[1] associates one bit for each frame included in the window. For our measures, we set the group size in 8 to use just one byte, so each bit represents one of the 8 previously sent datagrams. As data frames arrive to Smart Clients, their sequence number is checked. While there are not missing frames, the retransmission protocol header is removed and the frame is passed to the client application. When a frame is lost, those frames with sequence number greater than the lost frame are held in a buffer until the packet is retransmitted and successfully received, or the buffer filled up at which point the lost packet

---

[1] This field is added only in the poll response message.

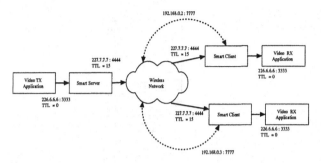

Fig. 5. GroupPoll (GP) Protocol Network Diagram. Solid Lines represent multicast transmissions and Dashed Lines the polling process.

is skipped and all waiting packets (up to the next lost packet in the buffer, if there is one) are sent to the client application. When the poll message arrives asking for the reception status of the last frames group, the Smart Client sets the *Bits Array* of the poll message depending if the frames arrived successfully or not. Once this poll response message is received by the Smart Server, it starts the process of resending the missing frames and advancing the sliding window depending of the message received. Thus, at any moment, the sender maintains a list of sequence numbers it is permitted to send. These are frames sent-but-no-ack and frames not-yet-sent. It is important to notice that due to the use of this sending window, the Smart Server can keep sending frames while is waiting for arrival of the poll response message without blocking immediately after send a group of frames. Once all frames in the sending window are sent-but-no-ack, the server enters in a blocking condition which could generate the loss of frames if they arrive during this condition. To avoid this situation, every time that a poll message is sent a timer is started. When a timeout occurs before receiving a reply from the chosen Smart Client, the whole last group of frames is resent and the lower edge of the window is advanced.

As our goal is not to achieve full reliability in all hosts but a reduction in frame loss for most of the hosts, we accept the loss of a packet if a retransmission limit is reached. Therefore, the retransmission limits have to be carefully set to decide how many times a frame should be resent before giving up. In our measures, we fix this limit to one retransmission, this parameter was chosen to achieve the delay/loss tradeoff required for video applications. A network diagram of the protocol is shown in figure 5. Figure 6 shows how the protocol works over the time. To compare our proposal performance, we also developed two other protocols that represent the worse and the best scenario in terms of reliability. The first one is called *Multicast-to-Multicast protocol (M2M)* and as its name says, it just works like a transparent tunnel for the multicast stream. Thus, this protocol represents the case of a multicast transmission over wireless links using the 802.11 standard. This can be seen as the worse scenario in terms

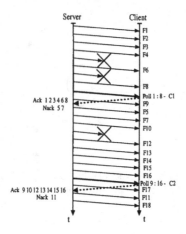

Fig. 6. GroupPoll (GP) Protocol over time Diagram. *Fx* is the Frame*x*, *Poll x:y - Cz* the Poll sent to Client *z* asking for frames in the range [*x-y*], and *Ack x y z Nack u v w* the Poll response message saying that frames *x, y and z* were successfully received and *u, v and w* were lost.

of reliability because of the high frame losses caused by the lack of any retransmission technique. The second protocol was called *Multicast-to-Unicast protocol (M2U)* and is a representation of the protocol proposed in [?]. In this protocol, the Smart Server treats each multicast/broadcast message like multiple unicast messages directed to each Smart Client. To do this, it uses the Register of Clients to get the client unicast addresses and then it uses the standard 802.11 unicast transmission for each one interested in receiving the message. As we said before, although it is an interesting option because it improves reliability and is the best scenario in terms of reliability, we considered that in this solution there is too much redundancy which harms throughput and delay. As a consequence of this redundancy, this protocol performance drops quickly as the number of clients or transmission rate grow even though the not-scalable behavior of this approach results incompatible with the multicast concept, we develop it to get upper bounds for reliability and delay. In figures 7 and 8, network diagrams are showed for these protocols. In addition, figures 9 and 10 show how both protocols behave over time.

5 Measurement Details and Results

This section presents the results that were obtained using the scenarios and protocols previously described in sections 3 and 4. In all our measures we used Java-capables machines in the same IP network and that were running Debian Linux with the kernel 2.4.22. Both clients used 802.11b Orinoco Silver Wireless Cards and the network interface of the server was connected through a

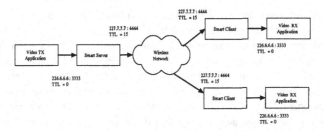

Fig. 7. Multicast-to-Multicast (M2M) Protocol Network Diagram. Solid Lines represent multicast transmissions.

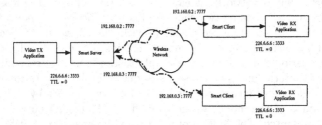

Fig. 8. Multicast-to-Unicast (M2U) Protocol Network Diagram. Solid Lines represent multicast transmissions and Dot-Dashed Lines represent unicast transmissions.

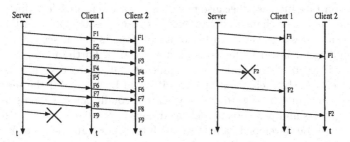

Fig. 9. Multicast-to-Multicast (M2M) Protocol over time Diagram   **Fig. 10.** Multicast-to-Unicast (M2U) Protocol over time Diagram

crossover cable with an AP-1000 Orinoco Access Point. To emulate the outdoor scenario we used an attenuator that covers the AP transmitting antenna. Thus, we were able to obtain the same values of SNR that those observed in the real outdoor scenario. It is important to notice that in the outdoor scenario is possible for nodes on opposite ends of the WLAN coverage area to be unable to hear each other. Under these conditions, the well known hidden and exposed terminal problems are quite likely to occur. To solve this, we forced to all wireless devices to use the RTS/CTS protocol when they transmit frames unicast without considering the size of the frames. To perform our measures, we generated multicast frames with a 972 [Bytes] size in the server application layer simulating a video transmission. The first 4 [Bytes] of each frame sent by the original source were used to add a sequence number and control information to automate the measures. Figures 11 (right) and 11 (left) show the percentage of packet loss calculated over a total of 10000 frames that were sent over the measurement time using a specific rate. We run this experiment several times varying the transmission rates and data were compiled until obtain averages values with an intervals of confidence of 5% for a confidence level of 95%. Also, it is important to notice that, like in the case of the measurements made with the RealNetworks technology, the same measurement was made using a Fast-Ethernet wired network instead of a wireless network, the losses remain close to 0% using the same two clients. This is an important point because it means that our protocol passed a sanity check that allows us to discard losses that could have exist because our implementation of the protocol. Besides, our network scenarios consider that the clients distance to the transmitter is one hop (without intermediate nodes) so losses due to buffers saturation during the intermedia routing of frames can be discarded. Let us start by examining the loss percentage of the indoor scenario. In figure 11 (right) curves of the two clients are presented. The M2U protocol losses remains below 0.05%, while the M2M protocol shows that all results are less than 0.2%. Our proposal measures appear in the upper curves, nevertheless it is possible to appreciate that the loss percentage do not exceed the 0.6%. All curves show a small growth as the transmission rate increases because more frames are sent in a less time, and in presence of fading or channel interference it causes greater losses. Although in our proposal losses are over the other protocols results in this scenario they are still negligible, for instance, in terms of video quality. Furthermore, one reason of this loss is the overhead added by the unicast polling process which could be useless when the channel is almost ideal. It could be avoided if the server had wireless channel information to decide when the conditions are good enough to stop this process and just directly deliver frames in standard multicast fashion. This issue will be developed as part of our future work. In the other hand, we have the outdoor scenario. Curves in figure 11 (left) shows that M2U has a poor performance because it has to perform independent transmissions for each client. In addition, when the wireless channel quality is poor, the M2U protocol have to perform several error recovery which makes it highly inefficient. The M2M protocol average losses is around 12% while our proposal average losses remains nearly the 6% which traduces in a much better video quality. Thus, our proposal reaches a better throughput as the channel conditions become worse.

6 Performance Analysis

In the following, we analyze the theoretical performance of our proposal. In figure 12, a transmission scheme for all protocols is shown. As our protocol

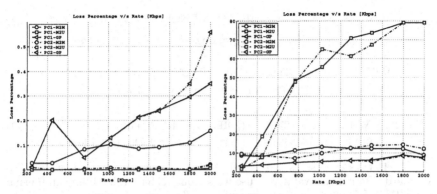

Fig. 11. Results obtained in the indoor (left) and outdoor (right) scenarios for the transmission protocols implemented using transmission rates between 250 and 2000 [kbps] with frames of 1000 [Bytes]

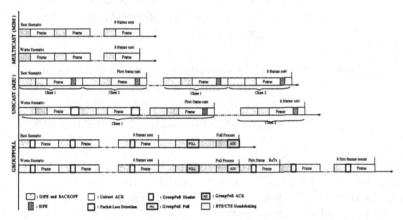

Fig. 12. Best and Worse Performance Scenarios for the M2M, M2U and GroupPoll protocols. Dot-Dashed Lines represents variable time where several transmissions took place.

works based on a group of eight multicast frames, we set this comparison over that ground. We omit some frame transmissions in the figure for space reasons, but they were considered in this analysis. Besides, we assume that there are only two clients present in the network. With the purpose of study these effects in detail, we point out differences in protocols considering both, the best and worse scenarios depending of the success of the transmission of frames. Hence, we assume that in the best scenario there is not frame loss while in the worse scenario, a successful transmission always takes place in the last attempt before the frame is dropped. Based in the figure 12 we define the time equations for all protocols. These equations are shown below.

$$\text{M2M Best Scenario Time}=(\text{DIFS}+\text{BACKOFF}+\text{FRAME})* \text{ 8 Frames} \qquad (1)$$

$$\text{M2M Worse Scenario Time}=(\text{DIFS}+\text{BACKOFF}+\text{FRAME})* \text{ 8 Frames} \qquad (2)$$

$$\text{M2U Best Scenario Time}=(((\text{DIFS}+\text{BACKOFF}+\text{RTS}+\text{SIFS}+\text{CTS} \qquad (3)$$
$$+\text{SIFS}+\text{FRAME}+\text{SIFS}+\text{ACK})* \text{ 2 Clients})* \text{ 8 Frames})$$

$$\text{M2U Worse Scenario Time}=((((\text{DIFS}+\text{BACKOFF}+\text{RTS}+\text{SIFS}+\text{CTS} \qquad (4)$$
$$+\text{SIFS}+\text{FRAME}+\text{SIFS}+\text{ACK})* \text{ 4 Retries})* \text{ 2 Clients})* \text{ 8 Frames})$$

In [4], Retries represents the LongRetryLimit constant of the IEEE802.11b standard. We use this value because we set our RTSThreshold limit in 0 using the RTS/CTS for all unicast transmission. Thus, every frame size is greater than this threshold which sets this limit in 4.

$$\text{GroupPoll Best Scenario Time}=((\text{DIFS}+\text{BACKOFF}+\text{GPFRAME}) \qquad (5)$$
$$*8 \text{ Frames})+(\text{DIFS}+\text{BACKOFF}+\text{RTS}+\text{SIFS}+\text{CTS}+\text{SIFS}$$
$$+\text{POLLFRAME}+\text{SIFS}+\text{ACK})+(\text{DIFS}+\text{BACKOFF}+\text{RTS}$$
$$+\text{SIFS}+\text{CTS}+\text{SIFS}+\text{POLLACK}+\text{SIFS}+\text{ACK})$$

$$\text{GroupPoll Worse Scenario Time}=((\text{DIFS}+\text{BACKOFF}+\text{GPFRAME}) \qquad (6)$$
$$*8 \text{ Frames})+(\text{DIFS}+\text{BACKOFF}+\text{RTS}+\text{SIFS}+\text{CTS}+\text{SIFS}$$
$$+\text{POLLFRAME}+\text{SIFS}+\text{ACK})+(\text{DIFS}+\text{BACKOFF}+\text{RTS}$$
$$+\text{SIFS}+\text{CTS}+\text{SIFS}+\text{POLLACK}+\text{SIFS}+\text{ACK})+((\text{DIFS}$$
$$+\text{BACKOFF}+\text{GPFRAME})* \text{ 8 Frames})$$

Here, in [5] and [6], GPFRAME represents a frame with a GroupPoll Header, POLLFRAME and POLLACK the Poll and Poll Response messages respectively. As transmission time for each frame depends on the transmission rate used, in figure 13 we present curves obtained from this equations for all data rates used in the IEEE802.11b standard. We also assume the values showed in table 1 for this analysis. These results allow us to examine the impact in latency added by our protocol and the tradeoff between reliability and delay when we compare our proposal with other protocols. In figure 13 can be appreciated that M2U protocols present a larger delay in both scenarios and this increases quickly as the number of clients grows. It is also clear that our protocol remains very close to the M2M delay in the best scenario (no retransmissions are needed), but when the channel quality gets worse it reaches almost the double (retransmissions are always needed). In consequence, our protocol leads us to achieve a better throughput over a wireless channel with poor quality when multicast traffic is sent. We also showed that in the worse scenario the latency of our protocol would be constrained to nearly the double of a normal multicast transmission but reducing almost by a half its losses. In this way, our tradeoff is better quality adding controlled latency to improve the overall efficiency in multicast transmission.

Table 1. Size and Time values used in the IEEE802.11b

Parameter Name	Size [Bytes]
RTS	20
CTS	14
ACK	14
MAC Header	34
IP Header	20
UDP Header	8
Application Layer Packet	972
GroupPoll Header	3
Poll Frame	2
Poll Response Frame	3

Parameter Name	Time [μs]
DIFS	50
SIFS	10
Average Backoff Time	310 *
PHY Preamble and Header Duration	192 **

Note*: see [?]; Note**: Long preamble, 24 [Bytes] sent with a 1 Mbps rate.

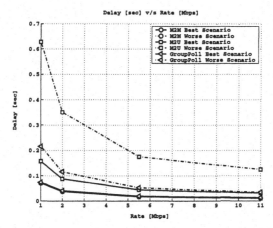

Fig. 13. Best and Worse Time Performance Scenarios for the M2M, M2U and Group-Poll protocols.

7 Conclusions and Future Work

In this paper, we presented a proposal for actual IEEE802.11 networks to improve their reliability for multicast data. A novel feature of this proposal is that its reliability control based on a polling service along with controlled retransmissions; besides, it does not require modifications to the 802.11 MAC layer because it works in the application level and use interceptors to forward the multicast stream. We recognize that the Smart Server could be seen as a single point of failure in our implementation, but our proposal considers the use of one Smart Server for each AP in the network. Thus, a commercial implementation could include the Smart Server protocol in the AP, inheriting in that case, the robustness of a network with infrastructure.

Our results show that our protocol performs better than other proposed in terms of reliability as well as data throughput in our measurement scenarios. Further work in this area will concentrate in improving our protocol adding features that will allow us to obtain delay and jitter measures.